MOTHERS
TALKING

Sharing the Secret

MOTHERS TALKING

Sharing the Secret

Frances Wells Burck

ST. MARTIN'S PRESS
NEW YORK

Note: In certain interviews, names have been changed to protect the privacy of the families involved.

Design by Claudia DePolo

Library of Congress Cataloging in Publication Data

Burck, Frances Wells.
    Mothers talking.

    1. Motherhood—United States. 2. Mothers—United
States—Interviews.   I. Title.
HQ759.B767   1986   306.8'743   86-3690
ISBN 0-312-54936-9

First Edition

10 9 8 7 6 5 4 3 2 1

To my mother,
Frances McCormack Wells,
with love and admiration

CONTENTS

CONTENTS

Acknowledgments

There are a few people who have been very special in the writing of this book. The first is my husband, Charlie, who has lovingly and patiently supported me as a wife, a mother, and a writer. Besides being a generous father to our daughters when I was less available as a mother than I might have been, he has contributed many skills and perceptions as an editor. I've learned so much from him about listening and clarifying, about cutting and shaping prose and appreciating the subtlety and nuance of language.

I must also thank my own mother, Frances McCormack Wells, and my daughters, Caitlin, Abigail, and Georgianna, for giving me my subject, for bearing with me and for telling me when I must finally stop.

David Outerbridge, my agent, has remained enthusiastic about this book from its inception. He has always been willing to listen. I wanted everyone to be in the book, and without David it would have been much more difficult to let go of any of the material. So I am particularly grateful to him for helping me to shape this book as a whole, and for offering his judgment and his objectivity about what makes a readable book.

It has meant a great deal to me that both Charlie and David have been moved by these stories. Without their involvement, I might have rather narrowly continued to perceive *Mothers Talking* solely as a women's book.

I would also like to thank my editor at St. Martin's Press, Barbara Anderson, for her patience, tact, sound judgment, and the attention to detail that she has lavished on this book as she shepherded it from manuscript to book form. Sue Dzamba typed the manuscript with great love and care and acted as my first "outside" reader, and Steve Schwartz at Riverrun Press cheerfully copied and collated reams of material.

I could not have written *Mothers Talking* without excellent child care. Mildred Burck has given above and beyond the call of a loving grandmother, and I don't know what I would have done without Nelly Davilla and Pearl Broaster, who have loved our family and taken care of all of us like their own. My aunt, Florence McCormack, has also pitched in. Suzanne Martinson, Jackie Jackson, Judy Lemmer, and Lisa Rightnour have been excellent babysitters and friends to my children. I am also most grateful to the women who have taught my daughters in their early years. They are Jenny Colbert at Jenny's Place, Pat Glynn and Alayne Johnson at The Children's Room Cooperative Nursery School, and Carol Schelin and Linda Fagan at the Community Playgroup.

I have relied heavily on the moral support and critical judgment of Rochelle Mayer, Jane Larkin Crain, and Anita Shreve, who know first hand about the stresses of combining writing with motherhood. I must also thank three other of my closest mother friends for just being there and helping me out in myriad ways. They are Bette Lacina, Judy Weber, and Lisa McMullin.

Finally, I would like to thank all of the other women who have collaborated on this book. Mothers talking is never a one-way process. Each of these women has done her share of listening to me. Each, during our exchange, has reaffirmed that motherhood is so rich and complex that it brings significance to us all.

They are: Kathy Alcorn, Cindy Anterton, Angela Apria, Rosalie Austin, Ann Banks, Virginia Barrett, June Barwick, Jenny Bealke, Kathy Bernard, Franny Breer, Mary Ann Burke, Susie Bussie, Cathy Carmany, Diane Churchill, Katie Claggett, Emily Collins, Barbara Cross, Anna Jo Dubow, Lynn Esmay, Maralyn Fischer, Sheila Fischer, Joan Foley, Murial Gale, Ellen Gellert, Betsey Grob, Vanessa Gruen, Edith Gwathmy, Cathy Haight, Judy Hardy, Harriette Heller, Arlene Herschberg, Jane Hirschmann, Jane Hopper, Vickie Houston, Pud Houstoun, Meredith Hughes, Carolyn Kent, Martha Krance, Emily Ann Kramer, Rochelle Kraut, Louise Kruger, Susan Lauffers, Cary Lee, E. J. Lee, Kathy Leonardi, Eleanor Magid, Pat Main, Betty McLaughlin, Hilda McNeil, Barbara Moment, Carol Morse, Eve Moser, Cathy Mutter, Mary Mulhern, Judy Myerson, Una Nilsson, Susan Oppenheim, Lilias Outerbridge, Pat Pilger, Hilary Porter, Elaine Rapp, Margaret Ray, Lynn Reineke, Mary Robertson, Karen Rochon, Jean Romano, Nancy Samalin, Lucia Saradoff, Ann Schaeffer, Rosemary Scharrenbroich,

Acknowledgments

Bonnie Shapiro, Cathy Prendergast Silverman, Patty Simpson, Karen Schlesinger, Janet Sonnenberg, Patty Stern, Ann Stith, Anya Taylor, Ingrid Taylor, Mooreen Terry, Bea Thibeault, Kathy Valyi, Kate Grimes Weingarten, Ann Werdel, Susan Wintjen, Sally Witte, and Margie Zeidner.

Introduction

My first child, Caitlin, is now almost eleven. When I think back to her birth, almost everything about becoming a mother was a surprise to me—from the mystery and sensuality of my pregnancy to the pride and terror of bringing home a six-and-a-half-pound person whose survival depended totally on me. I was stunned by the depth of my attachment to her; I felt that this person had swept in and taken over my life. Now I have two more daughters and I've finally gotten used to the fact that I'm a mother. Yet motherhood continues to surprise me.

The question that haunted me most from the beginning was whether my feelings—about almost everything connected with motherhood—were "normal." I was sure there was some secret about motherhood that I didn't know. Alone in the venture, because none of my friends had young children and my parents lived a thousand miles away, I searched in vain for child-care books to guide me through the anxieties. I couldn't find anything that was practical and supportive, sisterly and maternal—a substitute for the counsel of friends and relatives. So I began to talk to other mothers, and out of that came a book, called *Babysense,* which tried to convey on paper the grapevine information mothers used to get easily from one another in simpler times. Writing the book and getting to know those other mothers made me realize that my challenges and satisfactions were commonplace—and that the job was hard because the job *is* hard.

By the time *Babysense* was published, I had my second daughter, Abigail, and the nature of the surprises began to change. Taking care of Abigail was simple compared to dealing with Caitlin, who was as furious with me as she was with her new sibling. I had vowed never to be one of those frazzled, angry women I'd seen dragging their uncooperative children in a falcon grip down the supermarket aisles, but I was one of them. Was motherhood synonymous with being out of control? Perhaps not, but it wasn't getting any easier. And once again I wanted to know how other women did it. What was their secret?

I thought I would do a sequel to *Babysense.* This new book would be full of helpful suggestions gleaned from hundreds of women about dealing with the special concerns of preschool-age children: separation, toilet training, choosing a nursery school, etc. But the truth was, my heart wasn't it it. Motherhood was consuming my time and energy, my heart and my brain as nothing else had. It was touching all areas of my life and changing me as a woman, a wife, a daughter, a writer, and a member of the community. The secret, it seemed, was much more far-reaching than I had thought. I didn't want to know about the children. I wanted to know about their mothers.

A different sort of book took shape in my mind. I had read Studs Terkel's *Working* and remembered so vividly the people who were special for reasons beyond the interesting things they had to say about their jobs—because of their insights, their attitudes, their humanity, pride, love, and even their hatred and boredom. I imagined women talking about motherhood in the same way, each describing how the journey of motherhood had changed her. That was the book I wanted to read.

I wanted to hear one mother after another describe how she saw herself in her children, what she thought was hard as well as what was satisfying about mothering each child. I wanted to learn how she maintained her identity beyond motherhood, how becoming a mother—or grandmother—affected her sexuality, her relationships, her career or creativity. I wanted to know how she gave love to her children, and received it, and how she lived with the fears, disappointments, and anger.

I wanted to create such a book, but I wasn't sure I had had enough experience as a mother to do that. Women, more than men, can talk about themselves with one another, and I think mothers talk more intimately about motherhood than anything else, seeking and giving support and escaping the isolation that so often comes with the job. But did I know enough to talk to all the mothers I had in mind? How close could I get to a woman with children older than mine, or whose children had suffered more, or who herself had been through so much more experience and maybe hardship?

Introduction

Did I know enough to ask the right questions? How would I choose the right mothers to interview? I did not want to do a survey and, with three young children and a husband with a demanding job, I wouldn't be able to travel the country in search of an American cross-section. And then, assuming I somehow got mothers to talk in the first place, I didn't know how I would organize their stories.

But I felt compelled to do it, and so I began to listen (often with one or both of my children in tow)—on the street, in the park, in restaurants and supermarkets, on buses, at the pediatrician's office. I began to carry a tape recorder. With a dozen interviews in hand, I got a book contract three days before my third daughter, Georgianna, was born. Two years had passed since I conceived the book's idea.

Over the course of the next two years, the book began to take form. I found that I did not have to cross the continent; the mothers I was looking for were all around me. I was interviewing women from small towns and big cities, suburbs and rural areas. I interviewed women who came from other countries, and women who had not traveled beyond the communities in which they were born. Their voices and stories, I came to see, were at once individual and universal.

I had drawn up a list of questions; soon I abandoned it. A good interview, I learned, was when a mother talked about what was on her mind rather than what I wanted to know about. So I generally listened, prompting only in the silences. Some women were more articulate than others, but it didn't matter: Each in her way spoke eloquently about motherhood, and in every case offered a new insight into the secret.

No one turned me down for an interview, and it seemed that whenever I turned on a tape recorder and asked a woman to talk about her children, she was able to speak more intimately than I had thought possible—more intimately than she would have, I think, on any other subject. I found mothers eager to talk, for reasons as varied as the people themselves. Some, like Rosemary Scharrenbroich, were celebrating (though not without realism). Some, like Sheila Fischer, were confessing. And others, like Eliza Blake, were lamenting. Many were doing all of these things, and more.

With Carol Lauren, I heard an articulation of a reason I'd had all along for doing this book, but one I had avoided confronting

xv

squarely. "You know how people feel about motherhood," she said. "It's a second-rate occupation." That crystallized for me a major goal of my book: to honor the importance of motherhood. Mothers are cowed these days into not honoring what they do, feeling instead that they live in the shadow of the women out in the so-called real world who are "effecting change." But what, I finally allowed myself to ask, could be more important—more real—than giving birth, loving, caring for, and teaching another human being how to live in the world? And the full implication of that thought came clear when Eleanor Magid observed that "We have to take ourselves more seriously as mothers, because that experience of being a mother transfers itself to everything else we do." I was beginning to get a clearer picture of the secret.

But how would I organize these individual experiences? Fitting each woman into a neat category—divorced mother, working mother, mother with older child—proved impossible. Each woman's life was so rich and complex that I found I was creating a separate category for her. Broad themes such as love, patience, or separation were equally unworkable. To limit any person so severely was to cut out much of the truth, leaving disembodied bits of wisdom. I may have thought I would be accumulating a book of enlightening statements or little vignettes that would all add up to a giant mosaic of motherhood. Instead I discovered I was dealing with people, and that the women themselves were as important as what they were saying. Hoping to reduce the surprises of motherhood, I was finding that the experience was getting more complex, more contradictory—and more surprising.

Five years after I started, the book sorted itself into what now appears to have been the inevitable order: a simple chronology that reflects the passages in mothers' lives. Childbirth initiates women into the community of mothers; it is the first rite of passage. The others follow: nurturing a child through the preschool years; navigating a son or daughter through school and around the landmines of drugs, sex, and suicide; letting go at age eighteen or twenty-two, and seeing a child marry and have children; taking care of one's aging mother; and, finally, being taken care of by one's children. The journey is a familiar one, yet every trip is different.

In *Mothers Talking,* these passages begin with Judy Myerson's

Introduction

birth story and end with Augusta Jackson's pride in the way twelve children, fifty-four grandchildren, and twenty-seven great-grandchildren have brought her life full circle. In between are forty additional statements—forty little pieces of the truth of what motherhood is.

We have a hard time taking ourselves seriously in isolation. It is my hope that *Mothers Talking* will diminish that isolation for others as it has for me. These women have helped me understand my own strengths, weaknesses, and vulnerabilities as a mother. They have helped confirm the worth of what I do, justifying the hard work and the doubts.

I know in a deeper way that motherhood is an experience of love. Each child presents us with a unique opportunity to love, and that is the richness and reward as well as the challenge and the growth. I continue to learn from these women the obvious but hard lesson that what happens to you matters less than your attitude toward it, how you accept it and then deal with it.

In the end I did find the secret, and it was this: There is no one secret way to be a "good" mother. Each of us has to invent motherhood for herself and invent it over and over and over as we move forward through it. We can find the common threads of motherhood from talking to each other, but everyone is different. Each child is different, and we are different with each child, just as life is different for each child. No one can explain how to do it. Each of us must figure it out for ourselves.

It seems obvious to me now, and yet it's clearly not so obvious. Thousands of books are sold each year that promise to tell you the secret of how to be a good parent. I hate those books, because they cannot deliver on that promise. Being a good mother is doing what you are capable of doing under the circumstances that confront you, and those circumstances are yours alone.

One of those circumstances is the luck of the draw: Some children are simply easier and more pleasing to deal with than others. Another is how much physical stamina and patience a mother has, along with how much she knows about child development. In this area I think books can be helpful if a mother knows the limits of what she can do with the information. The kinds of mothers we are also depends a great deal on the influence of our own mothers—

xvii

what we learned and didn't learn from them—and on how much support we get from spouse, family, friends, employers, and the community and society in general.

For each reader I hope *Mothers Talking* will contain not forty-two statements but at least forty-three, for the reader has a statement to make, too, and can find his or her experience more accessible when viewed in the mirror of the experience of others. I hope that these women will help the reader explore her—or his—own role as mother, father, son, or daughter, and that these stories will lead to more talking and more stories. As a good friend said after reading the manuscript, "This is an unfinished book. What you have done is not definitive. It elucidates what must be continually elucidated: that motherhood must be attended to. The commonness of motherhood should not make it invisible."

In documenting mothers talking, I am celebrating the role of mothers, and it is a celebration of the ordinary. The women in this book are not famous, and they do not meet the criteria for a statistically selected sample group. Nevertheless, they reflect the complexity and contradictions of motherhood, and their stories—replete with humor, bewilderment, sorrow, and tragedy—weave a powerful web. *Mothers Talking* teaches us that the experience of motherhood is so rich that it brings significance to all of us who are mothers. We all have our stories. We are all worth listening to. We each own a piece of the secret.

MOTHERS
TALKING

Sharing the Secret

Sharing the Secret of Childbirth

JUDY MYERSON

Nothing has altered my life so dramatically as having a baby. Before, I used to hear women talking about their childbirth experiences at the checkout counter in the supermarket. I mean these women would tell anybody their stories, and I could never understand why. It seemed so personal, but at the same time so boring. But now I understand. It's a way of sharing. Until you have a child, you don't really know about childbirth. Men don't know about it, either. And I don't tell my story to men. I tell it to other women. They want to hear, and then they want to tell their stories. "Well, mine wasn't quite like that. I was in labor for twenty-seven hours." It's almost like communicating in code. Childbirth is how you join the community of mothers. It's something women have that women can share. It's a real secret, and it's a nice secret.

We waited a long time to have a baby. When I was thirty-five I was still saying it wasn't the right time. First it was school, then my career. And it was never the right time financially. But then a close friend got pregnant, and I asked her, "What are you doing for medical benefits?" Both of our husbands are self-employed. She said, "I don't know." I said, "Well, what are you doing for money? Your twenty-thousand-dollar salary isn't going to be there. And what will happen to your career?" She didn't know. I said, "I guess you don't have to know it all. Maybe we should just do it." That evening I said to Ed, "It's never going to be the right time. What do you think?" His answer was, "Let's give it a try."

Pregnancy brought a surprise. I had been superwoman. I could do anything. I was going to school at night and working full-time as a social worker, and though I planned to stop working when I had the baby, I would continue with school. But I found I was physically shot, nauseous from the day I got pregnant. I was also exhausted. I was having a December baby, and the thought of exams in January and then starting another semester with a newborn suddenly seemed crazy. So I took a year's leave.

During my pregnancy I was an emotional wreck. Ed said it was like being married to a yo-yo. We wanted the baby very much, but I was frightened. I was thinking that you can't have your life and a baby at the same time, because that's what happened to my mother. She was an artist and was very involved with what she did. Back then it wasn't accepted for women to have a profession, and she didn't have the support that is available today. I was also afraid Ed would be like my father. He worked all the time. Even when he was home, he'd often shut the door and go downstairs. Finally, though, I consciously examined these fears and started realizing that I wasn't my mother, and Ed certainly wasn't my father. It didn't have to be the way it was.

The first four months of my pregnancy were also colored by the amniocentesis. I didn't allow myself to feel pregnant. What if something was wrong with the baby? I'd have an abortion, of course, but suddenly that seemed horrible to me. I hate to say that as a feminist, and I still feel that should be every woman's choice, but I wasn't comfortable with the idea of aborting, at twenty-four weeks, something that had been moving around inside of me. I was also afraid of the amniocentesis procedure itself. I wasn't afraid of the pain—I knew it wouldn't hurt—but I was terrified that something might happen to the baby. I had been afraid to let the dog jump up on me, and there they were, putting a giant needle into where my baby was living, into that place I'd been so protective of.

Then I had to deal with the sex of the baby. I didn't want to know, and we had gone through a huge production not to find out. We actually had the doctor's receptionist whiting out all the references in the amniocentesis report so even the doctor wouldn't know. Why should he know if we didn't? But the receptionist forgot to white out the chromosomes. I was flipping through it, and I said, "Oh, my God! That's a Y. We're having a boy."

Ed didn't particularly care, but I had wanted a girl. I expected a girl. I was going to have a girl. I didn't think I knew how to be the mother of a boy: I'm not close to many men, and I've always been involved in women's issues. I asked my friend Mimi, who has two boys, "How can I have a boy? He's going to be a man!" Mimi said, "Look, you're not having a little boy. You're not having a man. You're having a baby, period, and you'll somehow figure out how to be the mother of that baby. We all do." Then she added, "Besides, it's wonderful to have boys. Mine love me. They don't have the conflicts with me I had with my mother; they have those with their father."

I still envisioned that Ed and this little boy were going to go off together, and I was going to be an outsider because that's the way I felt growing up. In my family, it was much better to be a boy. My two brothers shared a room; as the only girl, I was left out. It dawned on me finally that I wanted a little girl so I could align myself with her, just as my mother had with me: This would be my own little person. And I thought, hey, this isn't right. This is a different person. I don't want to do that to my child, whether it's a boy or a girl. That's when I realized it was crazy to think that Ed and this baby boy were going to be against me. In the end, I was actually glad I knew the sex of the baby, because it gave me a chance to figure all this out before Daniel was born.

I couldn't even think about childbirth until the very end of the pregnancy. I was reading about everything else in all the books I'd bought, then skipping the section on delivery. By the ninth month I was still thinking, "I'm not having this baby. I like him right where he is." We were friends. I talked to him. I patted him on what I was sure was his rear end. Many women say, "Get this baby out of me!" I was saying, "You can stay, you can stay."

I was scared by the prospect of the physical pain. I don't like pain. Who does? But I was also excited because some women say that birth is a wonderful experience. One friend had given birth after

3

a very difficult labor. When I visited her in the hospital, she had said, "Judy, don't do it. I've never been through anything so grueling in my life." But she survived. In fact she went ahead and had another baby. So how terrible could it have been? I knew I could get through it. An awful lot of women do, or we wouldn't all be here, right?

We had a false alarm about seven weeks before the due date. I had gotten very strong Braxton-Hicks contractions throughout the pregnancy, but never before with pain, so I thought I was in labor. The doctor said, "Go to the delivery floor and have them check you." Of course, I wasn't in labor. I felt like a jerk—how many people do that? But I didn't care. I would rather have done that than have something really be wrong. So we'd had our dry run to the hospital. We found we could pack a suitcase very quickly.

One evening when Ed was at a party, I was lying in bed talking to a friend. I'd been feeling uncomfortable all day with cramps—wraparound cramps that started in my back and came around to the front. I felt nauseous. She said, "You better call Ed."

By two in the morning the contractions were three to five minutes apart. I called the doctor, and he said, "When you're ready, come down to the hospital." I didn't know what he meant. In Lamaze class the instructor had said, "When you can't stand with a contraction, you might want to think about going to the hospital." I could stand, but sitting was much more comfortable. Ed was very nervous. In fact, I remember saying, "I'll drive."

Well, by the time we got to the hospital, the contractions had slowed down. When the nurse examined me, she said, "You're barely dilated, not even a centimeter. You shouldn't be here yet. This is hardly even early labor. If you were three or four centimeters, I'd say stay." I said, "Look, if this isn't even early labor, I don't want to know what active labor is, because this hurts like hell." She said, "Well, you can stay here if you want, but if I were you, I'd come back tomorrow or even the next day." I said, "Lady, you're out to lunch," and we went home. Once again, I felt like a jerk for being there, and she didn't help me to feel less like one.

By the time I got back home, I was in bad shape. The pains were so strong and deep I couldn't focus on the breathing. This made me feel panicky and out of control. The contractions were just taking me over. They were like waves of pain, except "wave" is much too gentle a word. Each one was a strong force that deepened and tightened and then subsided. There was nothing Ed could do to help, and I insisted that he get some sleep.

Actually, it was good to be by myself. I thought, "How am I going to deal with this?" I put on some familiar music. I used the beat of the songs to breathe to. In between the contractions I listened, which was relaxing and reassuring. I also found myself looking into my African violet. It was blooming at the time. I remember focusing on the deep yellow pollen in the center of the pink petals.

By the time the sun was up, the contractions were very strong and regular. My mother called and said, "Please, can't I come over?" I was happy to see her. Ed made the bed and straightened up the house while she timed the contractions. After each one ended, she would say, "Judy, you really have to go back to the hospital now. It's time." I said, "No, I'm not going back to be a jerk again. I'm not ready." Finally I agreed. As we got into the car, I looked over my shoulder. My mother was standing in the door, watching. That is such a distinct memory. The look on her face was very caring, concerned, and worried. "Mom, don't forget to feed the cat and the dog." Then we were gone.

In the car I thought I was going to go through the roof. It was a forty-minute drive, and the contractions were coming two minutes apart. I was gripping Ed's leg. I kept saying, "Hurry up! Get me there!"

When the doctor examined me, he said I was five centimeters dilated. I said, "Thank God!" I wasn't a jerk. I was having a baby. I wanted to go find that nurse and say, "See, I told you so."

I wanted a wheelchair, but the doctor said, "Why don't you walk to the labor room? It would be good for you." I thought he was crazy. The elevator was way, way down the hall. During each contraction, I had to stop and say, "Excuse me," as I crouched down on the floor. The doctor kept saying, "Good, good. That's very good for you." I couldn't even hold on to the wall. I had to be down on all fours. By the time I got up to labor and delivery, I was six centimeters dilated. I'd dilated a centimeter on the way up.

Then I didn't move for hours. Ed has a picture of me from that period. I was leaning on the tray table by the bed, collapsed. I would say, "Ed, I am sure I am going to die. I want to die." My eyes were closed, and I was moaning. Ed was wonderful. He'd lift my head in his hands, and turn it toward him saying, "Judy, look at me! Open your eyes and look at me!" He'd start huffing and puffing. "Breathe with me! Come on. Breathe! You're doing fine. You can do it." He gave me ice chips to suck on. "Fifteen more seconds." He put damp clothes on my back. I'd hit the peak of a contraction. "I'm going to die." "No you're not. You are *not* going to die! Now it's going to end." And the contraction would be over, though I'll tell you, I felt like there was no break between the pains.

I have few memories of the room or the people coming in and out to check on me. What I do remember are the voices from my music and Ed's voice, "Breathe with me." And then, "Look at me." I remember Ed looking right at me. "You're great, Judy. You're not going to die. This one is over." Occasionally the doctor would come in to take the heartbeat and examine me internally. Nothing was happening, and I didn't want to be touched any more. The worst thing was when I started having the urge to push. There is no way to describe the effort it takes not to go with that powerful urge, but just to pant for hours and hours on end.

At six o'clock the doctor said, "I have to leave. I'll be back by eight." Those two hours were the very, very worst. I kept waiting for it to be eight o'clock. Ed would say, "Only a little more. Another forty-five minutes." I said, "Ed, I can't do it. I can't possibly go another forty-five minutes." At one point I said, "I'm canceling this whole deal." I wasn't being funny, either. I made Ed call the nurse in. When he brought her in, I said, "I want out. I want a cesarean or an epidural, so get that fucking doctor back here. I want out right now." It was ludicrous. She said, "He really will be back soon. You're almost there."

I did a whole lot of cursing. "Where's the fucking doctor? I'm going to kill that fucking son of a bitch! Where is he? Get him here! Get that fucking son of a bitch here right now!" Then I'd apologize. "He's really not a fucking son of a bitch. I didn't mean to say that." I had lost heart. But Ed wouldn't let me give up. He kept saying, "Only a little longer." He kept getting me back by telling me to "Breathe! Open your eyes! You're not dying!" as he counted down the seconds. Finally, I was ten centimeters dilated, and the nurse told me to push.

As soon as I started pushing, the contractions slowed down. My uterus was just too tired. The doctor and nurses were conferring. They were watching the fetal heartbeat. It was going down. The doctor said very calmly, "The baby is in some distress, and we're going to have to get him out fast." He gave me a little pitocin to speed the contractions again. "I want you to really, really push," he said. They were taking the bed apart, getting it ready for the delivery. People started moving around and doing things quickly without explaining. But for some reason I was calm. I trusted the doctor.

When they slapped an oxygen mask on me, I felt a little panicky until the doctor explained, "This is for the baby." Both nurses began pressing on my abdomen. "Now push!" I pushed and pushed and pushed and pushed, three or four pushes to a contraction. I thought I was going to burst, but I'll tell you, it felt good. I had wanted to push for so long, and it was exciting. Our baby was going to be born. Ed was at my shoulder lifting me forward for each push. Everyone was rooting for me. "Come on, push, Judy. You can do it! The baby is coming!"

I looked up into the mirror. Everything was bulging. It looked like my rectum was going to turn inside out. The center of the bulge darkened. "The baby is crowning! The baby is crowning! One more push!" I felt some needle pricks as the doctor numbed me for the epidural. I didn't care. "Quick, push again. Your baby is going to be born now." I felt a tremendous pressure and a burning. It was as though my insides were going to pop right out, yet it didn't hurt.

"There's the head," the doctor said. "Look, there is a baby coming out of me," I cried. "Oh my God, look at him! This is a miracle. There is a baby coming out of me!" His eyes were open. He wasn't even out of me, and he was looking right at me. But he was so quiet. "Is he breathing?" I asked. "Is he going to be okay?" I looked at the cord, this pinkish, bluish cord literally wrapped around his neck and under each arm. The doctor said, "He's fine. I'm reaching around him now, and I'm taking the cord off." He said, "Look, it's like a little harness. I've got it off now." He said, "Now push once more."

I pushed and there was a sucking, slurpy feeling, and the baby slithered out so quickly. Then he was plopped on my abdomen like a little wet turtle. There he was on my belly. I remember saying, "He's so wrinkled." He had lizard legs and feet and lizard hands.

7

I looked at his nose and said, "Oh, he has my nose. He doesn't have your nose, Ed." Ed has the most beautiful nose.

Oh, it was quite lovely though, so lovely! They left us alone with him for quite a while. We held him. We looked at him. The nurses had put a little hat on him. He looked so fragile and so new. He was so tiny and delicate. His face had a wonder, an innocence to it. He was just there with this little face with nothing yet written on it. We talked to him. We said, "We're so glad you are here. We love you."

The lights were down. I looked at the wallpaper. It was soft and pink. And there was the African violet. I was so high. I loved Ed; he'd been so wonderful, and I kept telling him that. I had never seen him so present. He'd never had *reason* to be so "there." I remember feeling that this was the most important and best thing I had ever done in my whole life. And though that doesn't negate any of my other accomplishments, I still feel that way.

I jumped out of bed and took a picture of Ed holding the baby. Then I called my mother, and I called my best friend, Sandy. "We had the baby! We had the baby!" I gave them each a blow-by-blow description of the birth. I just had to tell the story. I think it's a cathartic thing. It's so intense. So much happens in such a short time that you have to talk about it to make it real. It's how you believe that this baby who has been in your womb, who has been a part of you, becomes a separate person in the world.

There are other reasons why you keep on talking about it. Even ninety-year-old women still talk about childbirth. I think you tell the story over and over again to keep from feeling the loss of that experience. To have participated so directly in the creation of life and to have held that life within you is so exciting. Then once you've given life, it's not yours to give again. That's the way it has to be, right? But you don't ever, ever want to lose that feeling of having given life. And every time you tell that story, you're trying to get back to that miracle.

The Miracle of Adoption

SUSAN LAUFFERS

Thirteen years ago we bought a bed. I always wanted to have a great big massive oak bed. We had this image of our kids, our cats, and our dogs coming in in the morning and jumping in. We'd all take a section of the paper and just snuggle up and be together. There was no room to set it up at the time, and we slept on a studio couch. We toted this bed from one apartment to another, waiting for the time when we would have a family.

Ten years went by. We said, "Gee, that was fast!" We'd both been so busy getting our graduate degrees. I was thirty, and years before had surgery to remove an ovarian tumor, so I thought it was a good idea to go to the doctor and be checked to see if everything was all right. I was always supposed to be able to have a child, but it just wasn't happening.

After years and years with the temperature charts and all that horrid, horrid stuff, we finally decided to get placed onto an adoption list. For my birthday I gave myself unlimited calls to agencies all over the country. Ironically, the one that offered the most encouragement was our local county agency. Once you sign up and begin the screening process, a kind of anxiety sets in: Are you the type of people "they" want to give a baby to? You cannot help but feel that you are being judged, and you are.

9

When you are adopting, you want "them" to want you to have a baby so badly. I remember when our social worker made a home visit. I even wanted my garden to look perfect. I spent hours and hours weeding it. Did my vegetables look good enough? Finally Danny and I sat down together. We said, "We're making ourselves absolutely crazy. We're going to just be ourselves. We're not going to hold anything back."

We didn't from then on. Part of the screening procedure was to participate in a discussion group with three other couples. First, we had to fill out a questionnaire. We had ten minutes to write about what our values are and what we wanted for our children. Everyone else in the group was finished. I was still sitting there pouring my heart out. I looked up, and Danny was watching me very anxiously. Later he asked, "What were you writing that took you so long?"

I'm very romantic. I had written on and on about how I'd like my child to be able to lie on the grass with me and look up at the blue sky through the green filter of leaves, and just love and appreciate everything that was around, and listen to the birds. I went on and on. It was so flowery and dramatic, but all true. It's very much the way I feel. What I want for our child is to love being alive, to enjoy what's there, to feel loved, and to be happy. And it all poured out.

I grew up in a very loving home. One of my nicest memories was our dinner time. There were no strict rules about it, but somehow my three brothers and I were always home for that meal. There was laughter at our table, and everybody participated in the conversation. It was a family house, and when Danny and I bought our own house, I wanted it to be like that.

When I imagine a family house I think of warm, rich colors and lovely aromas from the oven, of bread baking, and a pot of soup on top of the stove. I think of coming together at our kitchen table. We have a big, round table with sturdy lion-clawed feet. One child would be able to paint on one side while another did homework across the way. I could knead bread in the middle while Danny read the paper. It wouldn't matter what spilled on the table. It would be a place where you could be yourself, but at the same time come together. Sharing is a word that comes up a lot in terms of our whole life. We wanted to share our life with a child.

* * *

Not everyone is suited for adoption. What I mean is that there is a difference between wanting children and wanting to procreate yourself. We have friends who kept saying, "We want a child. We want a child so much." They have been saying that for as long as they've been married. They could have adopted one by now, but I think she especially wanted to experience pregnancy. And he felt that a child had to be of their flesh.

I cannot deny that there were many times when I was trying to become pregnant that I would dream of what our baby would be like. It was frustrating for me to look at the baby pictures of Danny and myself—blue-eyed creatures with very blond, curly hair. The two of us looked like cherubs. It was easy for us to imagine what our children would look like. Sometimes I would go past a maternity shop and it would make me feel very, very sad. Ultimately, however, I believed that pregnancy was simply a means to an end. It was the baby store with the cribs, the strollers, and the highchairs that drew me the most. I wanted a baby. And if you love kids, you don't care where they come from. You love children. Period. You want children.

When all of our records had been cleared, and the interviews and home visits had taken place, we received a letter from the agency saying, "You have been approved. You will hear from us when a baby becomes available."

When the first couple in our group got their baby, the wife called us up. She was crying on the phone. She was so excited. They had been given a girl. We were thrilled for them.

In our hearts we desperately wanted a girl, too. I don't know why. Maybe because I wanted to do all those things that I had done with my mother. We had had such a good time cooking together and shopping. Maybe I wanted a friend to go shopping with. I also wanted to dress her up in beautiful smocked dresses.

Then the next couple got a girl, and so did the third couple. We were the last couple in the group. The only thing that keeps you from almost not liking the others is that you are that much closer. We geared for a boy. What we wanted was a human being to love, and it didn't matter if it was a boy or a girl. I stopped looking at the pink clothes. "His name is going to be Jonathan."

We knew it had to be soon. The last couple had gotten their baby

11

in May. Well, I spent June, July, and August sitting on our front porch within one ring of the phone. I did not walk the twenty-five yards to our mailbox without first turning on the phone machine. I even changed my work schedule so that I would be home on Wednesdays. That's when the agency usually called. They tell you the background of the family and the child, and about the delivery, and, if possible, the circumstances for the biological mother giving up the baby. Then you go and see the baby. You have another day to think about it. Normally, you then take the baby home on a Friday, so that you are able to have a whole weekend home together as a family.

The only thing that would distract me was trash novels. The house never, ever has been so clean. Then, one Thursday I came home from work. I started playing back the phone machine tape. Oh God, there were so many messages. I had an excruciating headache. I decided not to listen to them then. But the third one was from our social worker. "Please call me as soon as you can." The blood drained. My hands were numb. The next one was from Danny! "Honey, please call me. It's very important." I called the social worker, but she was gone for the day. I called Danny. I got his secretary, who said he was doing rounds up in the wards.

Finally, he called me back. His voice was so soft. His tone was so reverent. He said, "Congratulations, Mommy, we have a little girl." All I could say was, "It couldn't be. It couldn't be. It just couldn't be!"

People talk about the miracle of birth. It must be a tremendous experience to see a child being born, your child. Maybe I have no basis for comparison, but the miracle of adoption is an equal miracle. It must be a powerfully exhilarating thing for someone to be able to hand you a living human being. It is the most extraordinary gift you can ever give. There's nothing to match it. You could hand me a bushel basket of the rarest, most precious stones and do you think I wouldn't kick them out of my way to go to the baby? There's nothing, *nothing* like it. And you appreciate having that child so much. That child truly, truly becomes yours. You put your heart on the line for your child. And you don't want your child to experience any of the pain in the world.

Entering a New Era of Our Lives

MEREDITH HUGHES

Tom was late coming to pick me up at the hospital. It turned out he was wrestling with the infant car seat. He arrived huffing and puffing in my room, which had already been stripped of the blankets and sheets. Gulliver, who was still wearing his hospital knit cap, was curled up in his little carrying case. We were surrounded by a sea of shopping bags, flowers, and suitcases.

Tom came in dressed up for the occasion. He had on his favorite tie with red trees on it. He had on his English hacking jacket, which is a beautiful green plaid, and a pale green sweater his mother had knitted him. He looked lovely. He said, "Well, I wanted to look proper to bring home my baby."

We rang for a wheelchair. You're supposed to have a wheelchair to take you out. We waited, and we waited, and we waited. Finally, I just grabbed a nurse in the hallway, and I said, "Hey, I want to get out of here!" The elevators weren't working, and she walked us down the stairs, through the surgical wing of the hospital, down back alleys. We finally came out blinking into the daylight. There I was with this tiny baby, wrapped in a yellow blanket that his grandmother, Emily, had knitted for him.

We put him in his car seat, and he slumped way down and closed his eyes. I got in the back next to him. I was feeling really giddy and light-headed because I was out for the first time and on my feet. I'd been lying on my side for several weeks before his birth.

Tom deliberately drove us all the way up Pennsylvania Avenue, pointing out the sights. "On our right is the White House, and there is the Old Post Office." He was going on and on. "And over there is the FBI, Gulliver." I kept saying from the back seat, "Gulliver is *asleep*!"

We parked near our house and got out of the car. As we walked past Hayden's Liquor Store, the manager *ran* out with our first month's supply of diapers, which had been delivered there. He said, "Hey, you're going to need these!" A guy was walking along the sidewalk in front of our gate. He must have noticed this teeny weeny thing and the fact that I was still wearing my plastic identification bracelet. He asked, "Are you just coming home from the hospital?" We said, "Why yes, we are!" He said, "Well, congratulations and the best of luck to you!" Then Betsey from next door below the stairs opened her window and yelled out, "Congratulations!" We introduced Gulliver, and she said, "So, he has started on his travels."

It was threeish when we walked into the house. The last of the leaves had just fallen, allowing a beautiful light to stream in our bay window. It was sort of a golden light. Everything looked so peaceful and orderly. We had been reading all these baby-care books that said you *must* have the house clean when you come home. Tom had vacuumed, dusted, and straightened until the house was as neat as a pin.

I immediately sat down on the little green settee in the bay window with Gully. Tom sat in the pink chair. We folded his blanket down, and we just looked at him. Then he looked all around the room—at the bookshelves flanking the fireplace, at the brass samovar, the oil painting of a Belgian cafe. We said, "This is your house. This is where you are going to live." We talked again about his birth, and we kept saying to each other, "We're a family. We are a family."

We must have sat there just talking quietly for about forty-five minutes. Then Tom said, "You must go out! You must go out!" He wanted me to get out and go smell the coffee and the spices at the store and say hello to Howard at the cheese shop. I didn't really feel up to it, but I went because it was important to Tom.

I went out and shuffled along our path to the gate. I felt like an eggshell, and, of course, my insides felt like they were going to fall out. As I was crossing the street, I suddenly realized that I was no longer a pregnant lady, and that no one would stop for me, and that I had better be more attentive at crossing because I didn't have any belly to protect me anymore.

I did run into Howard, our cheese man. He looked at me and said, "Did you have your baby?" I said, "Well yes, Howard. We had it, a boy, two days ago." He said, "Well, that's wonderful, just wonderful! But what is that?" pointing at my stomach. I had never known that once you have a baby, you would continue to have a rather large belly. I discovered it when I went to the baby-care classes at the hospital. There were all these women in their bathrobes with these fat little bellies, all of us. We sort of looked at one another and said, "Oh, yes, you have one, too."

I must have been out about fifteen minutes, and then I came rushing right back. I said, "Well, that was very nice." Tom said, "It was wonderful looking out the window and seeing you cross the street and knowing you were back on your feet again." He was very moved.

Other than that little flurry of activity, we sat in that corner wrapped in the beautiful light. Tom brought tea on our big round tray. He put a very pretty towel on it and little napkins and cake and sliced lemons. It was lovely. We just sat. For a long while, we didn't talk at all. We just looked at this baby, this perfect creature, this perfect miracle. Then Tom started holding him, and I took a photograph. Those were the first photographs we took.

We must have sat in that spot on the settee in the bay window for three hours. I held Gulliver and nursed him. He slept. It was very peaceful. Part of the pleasure for us of that pause was being back in our own home after two years abroad, being rooted. Everything we owned had been packed away. I enjoyed the sunlight on our pink Persian rug. I could see that beautiful fuchsia my mother had given me. The light was on that plant, and a cherrywood box of ivory dominoes from my great-grandmother. I looked down the hall and into the dining room and at the bust of a fine-nosed young girl, Rita, on the mantelpiece. We bought her in a junk shop in Belgium.

But the embrace of all these things was not felt as much as a true sense of love in the house. A new person was entering our lives, a new person was making us three instead of two. We wanted him to feel at home. We wanted him to feel that he was surrounded by love. We wanted him to feel comfortable and harmonious. We didn't want to be tense and running around and worried.

We were entering a new era of our lives, and we wanted to start out on the right foot. Tom said later, "I'm so glad we did that, so glad we just sat there and enjoyed him and looked at him and were calm, because if we'd come in and immediately started organizing the stuff from the hospital and getting the diapers out, I don't think that would have been the right thing to do."

After three hours in that corner, in that lovely light, it began to get dark. We turned on a lamp, a favorite lamp with a rose-colored shade we had bought long ago. Then we carried him upstairs. That was it. After that moment of quiet and calm, we started the business of being parents.

A Baby Is a Completely Humbling Experience

JOYCE SEILER

Before Lucy B. came into our lives, I worked. For eleven years I was at IBM, and then I moved on to McKinsey and Company, a management consulting firm. It was a very serious professional commitment, and for many years I liked it. A typical work day began about seven-thirty and ended at ten at night. Sometimes I worked straight through for two days including the night in between.

There was the immediate ego satisfaction of doing a good job, but it was not a job that I wanted to be defined by. It was a job that if you did not want the official rewards, there was not another carrot to keep doing it. Improving the profit margins or strategic position of a *Fortune 500* company is not something I have any true and lasting personal interest in. I felt I was sufficiently strong as an individual not to be compelled to keep working and have to be successful because I was a woman making it in a man's world. I think in a broad sense that means you're liberated. I quit.

We had wanted to have a family for quite some time. We were ready. I wouldn't have believed, though, that it could be so hard. Having a baby is a completely humbling experience. I'd had no experience with children, no brothers or sisters, no training. I have never been so tired! Some of that might have had to do with age. I'm thirty-eight. The last experiences that were truly new to me were work-related, when I was in my early twenties. Dealing with the baby is not only physically and emotionally demanding—I've had those experiences before in other contexts—but it is also brand new. I wasn't used to being a novice, and that added tension.

Also, the skills I had were problem-solving skills. I remember page numbers, points of view. I was accustomed to being successful in novel situations by applying analytical and organizational skills. However, bringing your intellect to bear with a baby doesn't always help.

I had read somewhere in a book that over time you will notice differences in the way a baby cries. Well, I consider myself reasonably observant, but I couldn't hear any differences in the sound. I couldn't tell if she was or wasn't hungry. When you fail the quiz because you can't figure it out, then you are frustrated and that takes even more energy. You become tired and you start thinking maybe this baby doesn't like me, maybe I'm inadequate. And here I was, supposed to be so smart. I've been advising company presidents.

I used to be very athletic, and I know the stages of physical exhaustion from physical exertion. I've been exhausted from mental activity and tension. This baby produced in me a gruesome combination of both, with an underlying solid base of fear that I was going to do something terribly wrong. A baby is a small thing. I was afraid I was going to kill her, inadvertently commit manslaughter.

The first day the baby came home from the hospital was the worst. She hadn't been a big eater, and prior to that morning, she had eaten only an ounce or so at each feeding. Her appetite had started to pick up, and at nine that morning she'd had two ounces. The nurse said she'd probably be hungry by one. After we brought her home, she looked around for a while and conked out—comatose sleep. There was a lot of checking on our part. Is she still breathing? One o'clock rolled around, and the baby didn't wake up. In the books, they say that little babies wake up and cry, and that's how you know they are hungry. She didn't wake up, so I woke her up. The books say new babies should eat three ounces for every pound, so I figured she had to log twenty-one ounces somehow that day. The baby had three sips and *clearly* was not going to eat any more. She fell asleep again, a couple of hours went by, and I tried again.

I remembered reading in a book that you can't let a newborn baby sleep ten hours through the night because it's far too long for a baby to go without water, no less milk. You have to wake them up. I tried again. No luck. I was getting a little nervous, so I tried to call the doctor. I couldn't get through to his office. It was constantly busy. It got to be four o'clock, and finally I got scared. I called the nurses in the newborn nursery at the hospital: "I'm really sorry to bother you, but I wondered if there is some trick, or if something could be the matter. The baby refuses to eat."

The nurse said, "Do you mean to tell me that the baby hasn't eaten since nine o'clock this morning?" In other words, she was saying, "Are you trying to kill that kid?" That's what she's saying to me, right? So I said, "Well, I just don't know what to do. I can't get through to the doctor." The nurse said, "Wake her up. Play with her feet to make sure she's awake. Get her to eat, just a couple of ounces." She was trying to be helpful. Her first reaction, though, was the instinctive one, to question me. But can you imagine what that made me feel like? Inadvertent manslaughter, it's what I was up to!

My sister-in-law was there that day to help out. We had those little premade bottles of formula. You take the cap off and replace it with a nipple. Before she left that night she prepared the next bottle, but she left it on the counter, so by two or three in the morning, maybe it had gotten a little spoiled. I don't know if that was the reason, but the baby was violently ill from about three to six A.M. My second attempt at manslaughter in a twelve-hour period. I couldn't believe it. If you're so damn smart, the high-powered token lady executive making it in a man's world . . . I mean it's a *completely* humbling experience. I had two attempted murders on my record, and I was in a state of high panic.

The baby's first trip out of the house was also a nightmare. I felt uncomfortable about it in the first place. Brookes said, "You're being neurotic. All the books say babies will sleep anywhere." The friends who invited us have a theory: Either you adapt to the baby's life, or the baby adapts to your life. They said, "You go out a lot, so come up here on Easter." We were supposed to leave at five. I thought, that's good, Lucy will be tired. Sure enough, the motion and the rumbling of the car knocked her out. When we arrived, we settled her in their bassinet in the end bedroom. She seemed fine. I thought, she'll sleep, and we went into the living room to have a drink. Quite a bit later, by some instinct, I went back to check on her. I opened the door, and there is outrageous crying, major wailing.

I couldn't calm her down. I think she was scared about being in a new place, especially when nobody responded after her first cry, which was very unusual in her life. Who knew how long she had been crying? I felt guilty that I had caused such unhappiness. I thought I'd feed her a little to try to settle her, even though she couldn't be hungry. It worked. She fell back asleep out of exhaustion, *screaming*. We didn't go out again for two weeks.

My mother arrived when Lucy was about two and a half weeks old. I slept for twelve hours straight. After she left, the baby went into a period where she'd eat two ounces, then stay awake in an agitated state all day. I would feel compelled to talk to her when I wasn't feeding her. I was so afraid not to feed her when she appeared hungry because I wanted her to develop an appetite. When I wasn't feeding her, I was washing her clothes by hand because our washing machine hadn't arrived yet, or I was cooking her damned bottles.

I finally called the pediatrician and said, "The baby is fundamentally unhappy all day. She's cranky, she's not getting enough sleep. I don't want her to go through life thinking to be awake is to be unhappy." We were going to switch to the formula without iron because he thought the iron was causing her gas. So I went out and bought a whole new batch of formula. The next day I had to use up a couple of bottles of the old stuff, even though I had new cans. She was fine. Geselle and Ilg, the child development experts, have a theory that babies go through a period of disequilibrium while they're changing stages. I'm not sure I know what a stage is, but that's the only way I can explain that behavior.

It's extremely frustrating, though, to deal with somebody who's being a pain in the neck for no reason other than the fact that she is somewhat uncomfortable. It's annoying. If you've changed her clothes three times, and she's vomited on you and urinated on you, and nothing you can do will cheer her up, it's very frustrating and not pleasant. There are times when I can understand child abuse. I can really see it. I joke with her. I say, "Listen here, stop this. You're going out the window." There are times when I've yelled —me, who is opposed to violence. My response to anger is to yell. As many as six times in the last month I may have said, "Listen, you *have* to stop this. This is truly offensive!" And I can see that if I were prone to violence . . . It's not in my nature to hurt anybody, however, so I don't.

The interesting thing to me, though, is no matter how mad I am, once she takes the nap and wakes up and smiles, I forget *completely* that four-hour stretch that preceded it. It's evaporated. Normally, if you have a fight with your husband, and even if you yell and get it out of your system, you can remember it the next morning. With these little babies, the anger just disappears. My sense of well-being is tied up with the baby. I'm so intimately involved with her that if she's happy, I'm happy.

Lately, I'm finding it completely enjoyable to deal with her. I can't quite understand why. I mean I was *never* interested in babies before. I understand being committed to relationships that are peer relationships, or a relationship where the other person is, in some sense, more advanced than you. I've had no experiences where I was the strong half. As a matter of fact, I've tended to shy away from those relationships because I didn't want to be somebody's "mother." This is my first experience where I'm the stronger half. But it seems legitimate and it is very rewarding.

My mother told me, "You should talk to the baby all the time. I used to talk to you all the time, and you spoke in complete sentences by the time you were nine months old." Now, as a responsible adult, I feel that one of the most important things in life is to be able to articulate your ideas. Therefore, it behooves me to try out my mother's theory on the off chance she is right. In the beginning, it didn't come naturally to speak to an infant. It was like being here during the day and having extensive conversations with the cats. It's a little bonkers. I had to practice. After a while, though, it became very easy because it was clear the baby was responding, and it's really fun to talk to her, fun to try and figure out what, within reason, both of us can talk about, that is, not baby talk and not computers. It's like playing again—having the excuse and the self-confidence to have a good time playing, doing things that aren't even legitimate enough to be called avocations or hobbies, but are just sort of fun. The only thing that a lot of adults know how to do that is in that category is to get drunk.

I can't talk any more right now. I have to go make up a batch of bottles. By the way, the subject of sterilization is mysticism. The minute baby-care books get to anything that has to do with sterilization, they fall apart in logic. Are you ready for this? When can you stop sterilizing the formula? Page 177 in Dr. Spock: "As long as you're making twenty-four-hour formula that contains water, you have to sterilize the formula in the bottles. Period." Right in the very next paragraph he says, "In the case where you are using prepared concentrated formula . . . there is no need to sterilize." What kind of a person who is speaking normal English says you have to do something *period* and then one paragraph later says you don't, without even referring to it as an exception?

I called Dr. Richards. He said, "Now that the baby's two months old, stop sterilizing." I said, "Spock doesn't say that." He said, "Well, Spock is wrong." My solution was to read everything, and then I asked a friend. I don't quite believe the pediatrician about stopping altogether. Neurosis reigns. I'm doing it in stages. I've decided the equipment is where milk bacteria might breed, so I'll keep doing the bottles. I don't sterilize the water. I've decided to do it my way.

It's a Gentle Life, Sometimes

KATE GRIMES WEINGARTEN

When I was about to go on maternity leave, the company wouldn't negotiate about it at all. They didn't want to talk about my taking four months, or five months, or six months. They have very little experience in the matter of women managers going out on maternity leave, and their rigid policy was three months maximum.

I called up the personnel man in September, and I told him I couldn't come back the first of October, but that I would like to come in and talk about it. I had been with the company for eight years, and was also due for a promotion. There are only three times in the year when raises and promotions are given. One of them was last month. The personnel manager called me up the next day and said, "Your promotion has been withdrawn, and we will accept your resignation!" I could not believe that I had invested so much of my life in such people.

I said, "I've tried to deal with you as decently as I can about my time to have a baby, and I wanted to talk to you about the possibilities of coming back in the future, but you are just so small of mind, and so ungenerous of spirit." He was a fairly decent guy. The

23

official reason, he said, was that they don't give promotions to people who are on leave. What really happened was they thought I was going to play by their October first rules, but I couldn't, so goodbye.

I was one of the four major investment people in an eight-billion-dollar pension fund, and now I'm just another boob! There was this article in the *Wall Street Journal* recently about pregnant professional women. As I recall, the only people they talked to were those who went right back to work. The implication is if you want to be a professional-type businesswoman, then you're going to have to surrender the fact that you are a mother to the corporate structure.

They give you an office as if you are one of the boys. They try to forget you are a woman and treat you as an equal. Then you get pregnant, and don't come back when the baby is only twelve weeks old, and it is betrayal. One way you get to be one of the boys is not to be perceived as a woman. They don't want someone who could be like one of their wives. The women who are coming up the ladder and getting MBA's are being forced to be a cookie-cutter image of the men they work with. Look at the three-piece suits they wear!

There was a soft-spoken, very demure woman at the company, and they were confused about how to deal with her. She was the kind of person who, when she was on a business trip with the men and the luggage carousel came around, they felt like picking up her suitcase. That is intimidating because on some level these men realized she was like their wives. They wouldn't want their own wives to leave a twelve-week-old baby. They also understand that a woman with a twelve-week-old baby is still recovering from childbirth and is exhausted from getting up all the time, and is tired from nursing the baby, and probably isn't going to be the most productive worker in the world. At some level they understand that. But the other aspect is obviously much stronger. They expect you to play their game by their rules. When I didn't want to do that, they just said, "Screw you."

It would have been nice if they'd said, "You were a valued worker. We would like to talk to you about working it out." Instead, they told me they had overpaid my Social Security, and now that I was quitting I would be getting a bill from them. I felt like saying, "You can shove your Social Security bill where the sun don't shine."

I will eventually go back to work, just as I will eventually wean Danny from my breast—when it seems right for him or for both of us. I want to be with him: not twenty-four hours a day every day, but I don't want to be without him two or three days a week. I just love being with him. It's very hard to realize that caretaking begets love unless you've done it. I never thought—of course who knows what it's like to have a baby until you have one—that I would.

There are some things I find hard. I have no particular structure to my life except what he imposes. I sat at home yesterday. It was so quiet, so very quiet in my house. All the kids were in school. Danny was taking one of his rare daytime naps. I realized that in front of me stretches the fall, the winter, the spring, and finally summer. You know, I wanted this child. I waited a long time to have this child, but there was something about the isolation I felt yesterday that truly scares me. I have to build a whole new life.

On the other hand, there's a gentleness to this life that is unlike anything I've ever experienced. There is a rhythm to it. I love the early morning feeding. It's not quite light. He sucks on me in his sleep. Occasionally I'll hear the geese fly over. It's lovely. And then I'll bring him back into our bed next to Seymour.

Just to have the time to sit in a rocking chair and love this baby, or to spend fifteen minutes playing peekaboo with this baby, or to make pumpkin bread at ten o'clock in the morning . . . I've never had the time. No, that's not true; I've never had the inclination to do anything like that. It's just so totally pleasurable to watch this little guy, to have this little guy. I don't know what, just to be with him, to have him love me, have him need me, to watch him change and laugh.

It's also nice to be able to care for other women with whom I have this in common. I had almost lost touch with my friends who had children. Now I know them in a new and different way. That's part of the gentleness, too, to love other peoples' babies and children.

Even though we were married, Seymour and I have lived our lives separately, in a sense.

25

We've lived all these years calling one another saying, "I'm having dinner with such and such a client," or "I'll have to stay late today, and I'll meet you on the eight-forty." Now we are becoming a family. I asked Seymour, "Would you go pick up the cat at the vet's?" He said, "Fine, I'll get the cat." I've never had that before. It shows he cares for me. I didn't realize how nice it would be to have someone take care of me. It's a whole new life, really.

A couple of weeks ago I said to Seymour, "I want to talk to you about my decision not to go back to work." He said, "It's your decision." I thought about that for a day or two, and I said, "Not only is he your kid, too, but we now have a life together as a family unit. I expect you to tell me what your perspective of it is as the father of the kid, the husband, the breadwinner. It's not just my decision anymore." It's the first time we had thought of anything in that way before.

Not that it has been perfect. We took a plane from California, and I've never been so mad at any human being in my life! The baby and I sat in a series of seats, and Seymour said he didn't want to be with us. He went and sat somewhere else. I mean, I've never been so . . . I mean, I was absolutely . . . I mean . . . the row was six seats abreast. There was a woman and her husband and me and Danny, while Seymour sat somewhere else.

The woman said, "You know, we could move if you'd like to have your husband sit here!" I was very cool. I said, "Oh no, no! That's all right. He has work to do." Then Seymour and I ran into each other when he was going to the john, and I was walking up and down the aisles with the screaming baby. I've never hated him before. I *hated* him! So we came home and had one of those divorce-type fights.

There definitely is a common experience among most mothers. I can see it in the way that other women looked at my pregnant shape. I used to believe they were thinking, "Oh, I wish that were me," and more recently I was sure they thought, "Am I glad that isn't me!"

It's both.

Having a Baby
Is Like Falling in Love

CHRISTINA DAY

Before I had a baby, all I could think about was the drudgery of it. I had read these horrendous accounts of how overwhelming the work was. What I couldn't imagine was the joy.

Then while I was pregnant, we met a couple with a baby. The husband said, "Oh, I knew I would love my child, but I didn't know it would be like having a crush. When you're away from them, you can't get them out of your mind." I thought, how odd, how peculiar.

For the longest time I would wake up and go in to get her every morning. I'd stop at the threshold of her room and just look at her, at her skin, her hair, her eyes. I'd smile at her, and I'd wait for her to smile back, and it didn't matter how tired I was. I felt like I had won the lottery. It's like having a dream that something wonderful has happened to you. You wake up, and it hasn't, but this was like waking up and finding that something wonderful really has happened, and it keeps on happening.

The satisfaction is partly physical. Taking care of a baby means constant touching. In our culture you're almost never allowed to touch someone except in a sexual context. This is the one time when you can get enough of what you can never get enough of in the whole rest of life—the holding, the kissing, the nuzzling, and the stroking. Not only that, you can get it in public. It's completely sanctioned.

The love is utterly uncomplicated. There are no strings attached. You can't give too much. You don't have to think about whether it is appropriate behavior. It's what you should be doing. Your complete mandate in the world is to hold this soft, cuddly, sweet little baby, and it just feels so good, the weight of a baby on your shoulder, or the way she fits against your body when you're nursing her. You get the feeling of union you long for your whole life. A baby is someone you can let your boundaries down to.

My friend Elizabeth is trying to get pregnant with her second child. She said she held a baby in the park, and she experienced a sensual satisfaction that was almost overwhelming. I said to her, "Well, I felt that for almost six months."

It is like those feelings you have when you're young, and you have some sort of premonition of your sexuality. Those diffuse erotic feelings aren't complicated by the tension of sex itself. I felt I was glowing all the time.

When I think about it, these feelings are almost like falling in love—except they last much longer. You're obsessed with this person, and there's a physical attraction, a strong desire to be in their presence. Every new revelation is fascinating. Each new gesture is a surprise. What interests her or makes her laugh is a delight for both of you.

I had no hesitation about nursing her in public. It was almost as if no one could see us. We were secluded. We were almost out of time. The baby and you are a closed circle, a refuge from whatever might be going on around you. The baby transforms everything, every kind of mundane experience, into something magic. When you are first in love, you can be waiting for seven hours at customs crossing the border, and you're still having a wonderful time.

Yet, while you're remote, you're accessible in other ways. It's almost as if you are part of a charmed circle when you are a new mother. Other women, complete strangers, may stop you on the street. "What a lovely baby!" and "How are you doing? Is it going well?" That is just wonderful. Though I hesitate to use the word, it is almost like being in a sorority. It's a new world you become part of, and maybe always will be a part of.

Yesterday I was looking at the other babies in the park. I could imagine their mothers had the same passion for them that I had for Katie, but to me they just looked like babies. In fact, one of them seemed rather homely. I asked myself, would I love my baby as much if she weren't so beautiful? And I thought, "Yes, I would." If it's your baby, it looks wonderful to you. Katie looks so much like herself, and I never could have imagined who she was going to be before she was born.

Anyway, the difference in how I respond to her and how I respond to other babies, no matter how cute they may be, is like traveling across the Grand Canyon. You may have a lover who has a twin brother. One of them you love, and the other you don't. This is *my* feeling for *my* baby.

I think I now understand why some women just go on having these babies. It's to replace the one who leaves, to maintain that simple union. Other women whose children are older would come up to me. "Oh, a baby, a baby! Can I hold your baby? I remember. It's so short before they run away." They *longed* for what I had, and that made me appreciate it even more.

It *is* a short time. Elizabeth was telling me about her two-and-a-half-year-old son. He had climbed onto her lap and put his arms around her and said, "Mommy, I love you." They were snuggling together on the couch, and she put her feet on his little footstool to get more comfortable. He said, "Get your feet off my stool right now!" It was such a double message. "I love you. I need you, but get your feet off my stool!" How hard it was, she said, to allow the child to decide alternatively that he wants you and doesn't want you. She longed for the simplicity of a baby.

It sounds so trite, but it's so amazing that this little baby is something that is created that never was; and now, sixteen months later, she can hold a banana and eat it. She doesn't even want me to peel it for her anymore. What I find the most difficult is the pain of separation. I say, "Can I have a kiss?" and she says, "No, don't want it!"

My Back Is Up Against the Wall

LINDA STEIN

My husband, Ken, wanted a big family. He's one of four and liked it. He wanted a child every two years. After the first kid you'd think he would have learned.

It took us a long, long time to have our first. We were under the impression it would take a long time for the second, so we started trying a little bit earlier than we would have normally, and, of course, the first shot out . . . I was just enraged. I was furious. I was sick with the whole thing—physically sick. I had thought it was a safe time; I was just doing it to get him off my back.

I wasn't going to have an abortion just because this baby was inconvenient, so I've gone ahead. But I feel like somebody has put a bag over my head after I've just started to climb out of the first bag. An extra six months would have made a big difference. Peter would have been toilet trained, and he might have been a little bit less dependent on me.

I'm in my ninth month now, and I still look down sometimes and think, "You're pregnant?" I don't imagine any of the nice things. I really don't ever see myself playing with two children. I know I should be happier about having this baby, but I just see two children crawling into my bed on Saturday morning and jumping on my head. I feel like I've had that already. It's not cute anymore, and it's not what I want. I don't want any more children!

Peter was born early. He was in the hospital for six weeks. They weren't sure how well he was because he was so little. It had been my nightmare: My baby would be born, and it would take them a long time to say he was okay. It was like a prophecy. I didn't even want to know him. I didn't want to touch him. I didn't want to be involved. Ken kept saying, "Well, we have to go and visit the baby. We have to do it."

Every day I would go to the hospital to see him in his little box. Always something new, some new crisis. His head was small. "Can you remember offhand if your husband has a small head?" the doctor wanted to know. I didn't know. The doctor said, "Well, does he wear hats?" I said "No," and so the doctor said, "Maybe it's because he can't find a hat to fit him." I made Ken leave work in the middle of the day. I was frantic to have some jerk measure his head. It turned out he had a large head, which made it worse, because then Peter's head wasn't hereditary.

I was so ashamed that I couldn't love this . . . I mean a chicken is bigger than he was. I didn't want to hold him. I didn't want to touch him. I didn't even want to give him a name. Not that he would not live, but because this was not the way it was supposed to be.

This pregnancy is different: It has been normal. But I'm worried that I don't have any place to hide these negative feelings. I don't have any place to put the fact that I don't want to breast-feed. With Peter I'd say, "Oh, I couldn't do it because he was in the hospital." But it's not my style. I'm not the nurturing type, I guess.

People give you a hard time if you aren't nursing. They say, "Why not? It's much healthier, and what about the bonding? You're not giving your child the love it needs, you know." Peter was also very colicky. They said, "If you breast-feed, no colic." When he got too old for colic, and would still scream from six in the morning until ten at night, we discovered he had a milk allergy. Then, of course, it was, "Breast-fed babies don't have allergies," and "You're telegraphing these negative messages."

* * *

You want to be the best at whatever you do. You're not working, so motherhood is like your career, and you'd better be good. Other mothers weren't any help. They made me feel like I had to be supermom. Somehow, everybody else's child either slept through the night or started to roll over or weighed twenty-three pounds before mine did. If I had a problem and asked, "What do you do for it?" and got an answer, I'd go home and try it, and it didn't work. I'd make myself crazy. There's only so much you can do to make a child the way you want. If they get a good kid, these women really are stupid enough to believe it has to do with them!

Now Peter bites. He's a real two-year-old boy, a real motor kid. At our playschool, one of the mothers was complaining, "Today he tried and tried to get the other kids to play train with him." "Well," I said, "why didn't you let them? He wasn't asking them to vandalize the neighborhood! He wanted to play train!" She said, "Because it was arts and crafts time." I said, "You can't expect all two-year-olds to sit still for an hour and do that. You just can't." Someday, the fact that he's active and alive and imaginative might be the thing that is most precious about him.

I have to stick up for my kid, but then I have doubts. Doubt is also where other mothers come into play. "Maybe you ought to do this. Maybe you should try that." Even my own mother sows doubt. We'd take Peter to their house, and he'd get the crazies and beat up on his cousin. She'd call the next day. "Having trouble with Peter? It could be the sugar in his diet. Do you give him much sugar?" "Sure, Mom. Every morning I say, 'Open your mouth,' and I pour it down his throat." Doubt. She tinkles on the piano of doubt. And you know, in this business of motherhood, that doubt is your worst enemy. If you're positive and you're wrong, at least you can forge ahead, but if you're feeling "I'm not sure," you're in trouble.

In the beginning, though, nobody admits their deepest, darkest dreams to another mother. I'd been up all day with a screaming kid. I wanted to put him in an oven like a duck. But nobody else would admit to that anger. I've got to connect with these women. But they don't sympathize with me. You're not friendly for any other reason except that you're a mother, so what else do you talk about but your kids?

Their babies ate, slept for four hours, woke up and ate again. Mine didn't. I felt like a baby-sitter watching a stranger's child, because I couldn't believe this horrendous baby was mine. I used to sit with this baby and think, 'When is his mother coming to relieve me?'

My mother said, "What's your problem, Linda? Why are you letting it make you so crazy? We'll find somebody to take care of the kid. If you're not happy, and the kid is giving you the business, go someplace. Go shopping. Be better to yourself. A happy mother is a good mother." I couldn't do that. Then she would say, "Somebody else can't be with him and change his diaper?"

Finally, we got the formula straight, and he started eating real food. He wasn't unhappy anymore. I found I *wanted* to go into his room at night to make sure he was okay. That was wonderful. Then I would stand for a long time and look at him sleeping and smile all over.

Will that happen with this baby? Where does the time for this baby come in? It seems as if I'm constantly in motion now. I've already let so much go. How can I get any looser? I don't read anymore. We don't see friends. I used to make regular dinners, even though when Peter was tiny, five o'clock was his zaniest hour. I was compulsive about trying to get this meal on the table. There was no pressure from Ken. He'd say, "We'll eat at ten o'clock. Don't worry about it." But I would think, I've got to do this. It's not fair to him. What kind of wife would I be if I served the vegetables out of a pot?

Now, after we've finally eaten and Peter has gone to sleep, I go into the bedroom and flop down like a zombie. Ken sits in the living room, and he's a zombie. I said to him the other night, "Do you think it's bad that we don't talk at all?" He said "I need quiet." I said, "I need quiet, too." "Then it's okay, Linda," he said. But that quiet time is probably going to be when this new baby is up and wanting to boogie!

Peter is crying in the middle of the night. He only wants me. I'm angry because I don't want to get up. But then I realize the kid's not stupid. He knows what's going on. I feel badly for him that he's upset now. Once this baby is born, he's *really* going to feel it.

My parents have a bunch of old home movies. My brother was

only twenty-six months older than I. In these movies he's constantly banging me on the head with spoons or sticks or trucks. Being special for a little while longer would have been nice for both of us.

The weather starts getting bad, and I think, "This is a December baby. I'm going to be in all winter in this tiny place with two children."

I suppose I'll get it together some day, and it will be all right. But tell me, where is the time, the energy, the psychic energy going to come from to take care and love and nurture another person? It must come from somewhere. I just can't imagine where unless love is like a muscle. The more you exercise it, the more you have to give. *Please,* tell me.

Two Babies Are Easy Compared to Two Sick Babies

LUCIA RAFFETTO

After the twins were born, they sewed me up. They gave me something, but I would feel the pinches of the needle going in and out. For some reason I didn't say anything until I finally couldn't stop myself from saying, "Ouch! Ouch!" Then they knocked me out.

I tell you, I felt like everything was just pouring out of my body. I felt like every bit of blood had been drained from me. I felt like I was bleeding to death.

In a way, it's a relief when you have a baby. You feel bottled up, but when the baby's born, you just flow. Well, when they were born, it was like I was flowing too much. I felt completely weakened. Not with my first child, but with the girls. I was completely weakened.

I lay on the table. I could feel myself all opened up. I said, "Never again! I feel like I'm dead." It was horrible. I felt vulnerable—like I was opened up on an operating table.

The doctor kept sewing. He kept saying, "I want to get you right!

I want to get you right! I want to get you back together!" When I finally looked, the scar went all the way up my behind. I could feel it inside, too.

I was happy to have two girls alive, but I was afraid Jane was going to be retarded. The doctor cut Jane's cord, thinking it was Christine's, while Jane was still unborn inside of me.

The first one, Christine, got bigger, I think, because she had jaundice and they fed her a bottle with a giant hole in the nipple. She drank and drank and gulped it down. The second one had lost blood, probably by having her cord cut. She was very pale. For a year she didn't get the same color as the first one. She was always paler and always thinner. Her head is shaped differently. She has a longer face and a thinner head. Others wouldn't see the difference in photos, but as their mother, I can.

They gave Jane to me right away. I put her to my breast, and she sucked immediately. She was so strong! She was grabbing me. She was so aggressive in a nursing way. I knew then she was strong.

I said to the girl in the bed next to me, "What should I name her, Jane or Christine?" She said, "Name her Jane because she's tough like Tarzan's wife." But it turned out that she's not the tough one. She's the gentle one, but she is more wiry.

Chris is fatter and into her food. Don't take her food away! Jane cares about her toys. She's never caught up with Chris's weight, even though it's only ounces. She also seems to be more sensitive. She was more into nursing for a long time. Chris wanted to gulp. She'd drink fast. Jane was a little slower. Nurse! Nurse! She could never get enough. I didn't have time to let her go on and on the way I did my first child.

I came home after four days. My son was a stranger to me, after being left for four days. The girls came home together after six days. They were very, very small, and were nursing every half hour. What was it like? It was hell! I read a book, *Twice the Trouble, Twice the Fun*. The author was really organized, and it was still hell for her. I'm not a good housekeeper. I can't sterilize bottles or anything.

At the hospital I had them on a schedule. One would have a bottle. The other would nurse. Then I'd switch them. When I got home, even though I knew who was who, I would forget which I had nursed last, because they're so much alike. What's the difference? They're still little babies sucking on you.

It was crazy! There was not one minute's peace! I almost had a nervous breakdown. It was really hard. I was going crazy with the nursing and the bottles. My husband was pressuring me for the bottles, to make them sleep longer. I started to give in.

We were really broke at the time. I'd stopped working. Money was bad. We'd just gotten a bigger apartment, which we couldn't afford. I ran out of money for the formula. I was giving them the soy formula, which is really expensive. I would run out, or the store would run out. So then I would buy whatever was on the shelf. I found they wouldn't take the bottle as well as they nursed. I always felt guilty about the bottles.

My husband would give them bottles of just milk and water or plain milk to try to make them sleep a long time. "You can't give that to a little baby!" I would tell him. "Boil it." But he took over in the beginning.

I'd almost stopped nursing because it was so confusing. Without nursing, I lost that settled feeling. The hormones change. You lose those mothering hormones, and I felt completely detached from the two babies. I felt like a servant, not a mother. Anybody could do what I was doing. They just arrived and took over my life. I didn't even know who they were. It was a horrible feeling.

Eventually, after a month, they got sick from those bottles. My son, who had an ear infection, was always taking their bottles, and the girls caught the ear infection, and became deathly sick. Two babies were easy compared to two sick babies. It was hell!

They started getting runny noses, and then they started coughing. They couldn't pull up the phlegm. They would cough and cough and cough. The coughing would get slower, then they would turn blue in the face.

They would turn completely blue. I was so scared, I would breathe in their mouths. I don't know if it was a good thing to do, but it would push the phlegm back, and they would gasp, and at least take a breath. When that happened, I took one to the doctor in the area.

I went to a private doctor. I never paid the guy. I took the worst one, which was Jane. As they both had the same thing, I figured he could just look at her. He said, "She's too sick to be out. I think it's whooping cough. Take them to Coney Island Hospital." However, I had already had bad experiences with them in the hospital, and asked if he would be there. He said, "No, I work at Maimonides." He gave me some medicine and the name of a doctor who accepts Medicaid.

I was too scared to take them to the hospital. I was afraid they would die there, and I would be told they died of congestion. Maybe it was my paranoia, but what could they do? I was sleeping with them at night and every time they woke up, I woke up. My husband was sleeping with one. I had the other one. But, of course, we could not go against the doctor's orders, so I got on the bus with them and went to the Medicaid doctor.

It was a woman doctor and she was very good. She was at a clinic for poor people in a bad section of Coney Island. It was far away and a crazy trip on the bus, with them in front packs, one strapped over each breast.

She said that it was not whooping cough. She put them on an antibiotic, cough medicine, and a decongestant, something with salt in it, and baking soda drops for their noses, and she said I could keep them at home. I told her I thought my family was allergic to milk. I thought they'd do better on the breast milk than on a formula. So she gave me the go-ahead to nurse them, and she said not to breathe in their mouths. They would come out of it by themselves.

So I would turn them upside down and rub their backs, or I'd lay them down on my knees when they coughed. My husband slept with one, right in his arms on the couch. I slept in bed with the other one, then eventually slept in my bed with both. It made my back sore!

I threw all the bottles out. I said, "This is it. I'm doing it my own way!" I went back to nursing them. When they were sick, I nursed them as much as they wanted. I gave them water with a dropper, so that they wouldn't be dehydrated. I was nervous that I didn't have enough milk. I was constantly tired. I gave them both an herb tea that is super-bitter. It's horrible, but it cleans out your sinuses. I also fed them honey and lemon.

They had fevers, but they were low. Thank God they were only very sick one at a time. I would take the sickest one. She looked like a little bird with no life in her body. I've seen animals die on me like that. It was frightening. I was thinking that one might die right in my arms. She looked dehydrated, so I kept giving her water. I knew she needed liquids more than food, water more than milk.

As long as they were nursing, I wasn't worried. But at one point Jane got too tired to eat. I stayed awake watching her all night. I could feel . . . I could feel she was teetering between life and death.

The crisis wasn't that long. I think it went on for a week. Then slowly they came back, but when I saw that they both could die, I realized I really wanted them both. I got very close to them when they were sick. I got to know them, holding them, sleeping with them, nursing them again. In a way, it was a good thing because before I had been so detached from them.

My son was insane by then, and rebelling. He had gone from having had all the attention in the world to having none. He would shit in the toilet, and then throw it around the room. He wanted me to hold him constantly. I tried to let him help me with them, so he would like them. I tried to turn it into a game. It's *hard* to get close to two babies. I tried to include him. "And now we'll get the babies up! These crazy girls," I'd say. "When I put them back to bed, we're going to get some rest together. They're driving us crazy!"

The insanity went on for at least six months. My husband brought Valium home, and that helped me to get to sleep, but then in the morning, I was very cranky. It doesn't keep helping. I finally started drinking a little to relax at night. I'd never drunk before.

I still don't get out with them a great deal. It's just too hard. I wish I had a backyard, so they could get the sunshine in their eyes. I used to put them in the two front packs. Then I had a double carriage. Now I have the umbrella strollers hooked together. But they never learned to be outside babies like my son, who I took everywhere. They just want to be fed and go to sleep.

They were so good, I started worrying they were retarded, because they didn't demand anything of me. I didn't talk to them. I had nothing to say. My son talks a mile a minute. He talks me out! I had nothing to say to them. I only felt physically close to them. I called them two old ladies—Arsenic and Old Lace, I called them.

Finally, I started taking them out one at a time to get to know them. It took at least a year before I really started understanding them as people, yet I felt I understood my son the day he was born. I had always nursed them at the same time, instead of separately, the way you're supposed to. I figured they didn't know, anyway. I figured they were lucky just to be nursing.

When they were babies, I had so much milk, especially after they got sick, and I nursed them all the time. I felt like I could feed the world of babies. I would see babies with bottles in their mouths, and I would have fantasies of just nursing them. Now sometimes I look at little babies, and I think how cute they are, and how big mine have grown, but I don't have that feeling anymore of wanting to nurture a newborn. I don't think I'll have any more of my own kids, but perhaps I would adopt one. I have always wondered what it would be like to adopt a child. So, maybe when I'm thirty or forty I will. It's not that far. I'm twenty-five. Five years goes fast with kids.

The Doctor Said, "This Baby's Probably Not Going to Make It"

MARILYN HELLER-GREEN

I took the kids to the mall to see Santa Claus and I came home remarking to myself how wonderfully it had gone. I felt really fine considering I was six months pregnant and had been on my feet most of the day. That evening we went to my sister's for dinner. My mother was there. They all told me how healthy I looked.

Back home I was sitting in a chair reading the paper, and I felt this bizarre cramp. I thought, "That's a strange thing." It lasted for maybe twenty seconds. Then it went away. I had really forgotten what contractions are. It had been so long since Amy was born. My mental image of a contraction was something that was pulling inward, not how this felt.

Twenty minutes later I was still reading the paper, and I had another cramp. I got into bed and I fell asleep, and about twenty minutes later I woke up and got another one of those pains. Then Fred came to bed and went to sleep, and all of a sudden I started getting a lot of these pains. I had no idea what was going on. I was walking around thinking, "I've got such bad gas." After an hour, though, I couldn't let it go any longer. I called up the doctor's service. I was going to an obstetrician who had two partners. One was going to deliver me. I'd only been to him a few times because that's how far along I was. I was wondering whether I should call him directly at home, but decided it was probably nothing.

I called the service and I got the other partner, who is a disgrace to his profession. I said, "I'm getting these terrible pains. They're five minutes apart. They're really intense." He said, "That's totally normal." I said, "Are you sure this could be normal?" He said, "With a second pregnancy, the uterus contracts. It just feels like contractions, but they aren't." I said, "But it's been going on for an hour. They're very, very regular, and they are very, very intense." He said, "Just take an aspirin, and get yourself into bed, and don't worry about it." I said, "When should I become alarmed? What if they go on all night?" He said, "That's fine. They can go on all during the rest of your pregnancy." I said, "Well, thank you very much."

I said to myself, "Whew, am I glad this is normal!" But none of my friends told me this happens in a second pregnancy. Maybe they don't tell you that this happens in your sixth month, or you wouldn't want to get pregnant. So I took my aspirin, and got into bed, and of course it did nothing at all. Soon the pains were three minutes apart. Then I got my books out, hoping that I could find out a reason for this phenomenon, when I started bleeding. I was too discombobulated to do anything more than call up the service and get the idiot O.B. again. I said, "I'm bleeding." He said, "Well, maybe you better go to the hospital."

They brought me upstairs and a resident, who was of course on her first day of the job, examined me and said, "I can't see anything! There's so much blood pouring out of you I can't see a thing!"

Finally they got the chief resident, who said, "You're nine centimeters dilated. We're going to deliver the baby." Fred was in the other room where they always shove the husbands. He didn't know what was happening, and still thought I had gas! As they rushed me into the delivery room, they passed by him and said, "Your wife is going to deliver," and he said, "Not my wife. She's only six months pregnant!" They said, "She's now fully dilated. She's going to give birth momentarily." He said, "I want to be with her. I never had a chance . . ." They said, "Sorry, you have to stay by yourself."

44

I felt myself surrounded by all sorts of doctors and nurses. Pretty soon, as I huffed and puffed and blew and all that, they delivered the baby. I just sort of assumed this was going to be like a miscarriage. I did not ever think that a sixth-month baby could live. The resident said to me, "Do you want to see her?" and I said, "No!"

Meanwhile, they had this team of neonatologists standing by. I was saying, "I don't want this baby put on supports if there's massive things wrong with it." I was terrified that the baby would have a zillion things wrong with it, and might be an institutional case for the rest of its life. One of the neonatologists said, "The baby did cry and is pink, and those are good signs."

Then the idiot showed up just as the resident put in the last stitch. He said, "Oh, you stitched her up. I hope I don't rip them out when I examine her." I thought, you jerk. He nearly killed me by punching my stomach. Then he had to feel the uterus internally to make sure it hadn't ruptured from the cesarean I had with Amy. I had no anesthetic. That was agony.

I repeated to him that I didn't want the baby put on life supports if there were massive things wrong. "Well," he said, "that baby's probably not going to make it anyhow because it hasn't opened its eyes." Those were his words of consolation.

So then they took the baby away, and they wheeled me into the recovery room where Fred was. I had lots of I.V.s in me, so they shot Valium and Demerol into me through them and I went out. Ten minutes later I woke up. Fred and I had to talk about the situation. We had to make some decisions. The pediatrician came in and said, "This baby is a viable baby. She is pink. She cried. But she's very, very tiny. Her chances of surviving are somewhat slim." I can't remember exactly how he put it, but he also said, "We can't tell if there's damage. The baby might live anyhow without support systems, and she'll be in a lot worse shape."

What could we say? He was spelling out the blindness from the oxygen, and the horrible things that might happen, so we would be prepared, I guess. Here I was all zonked out from the drugs. Fred was just in a state from the whole event, and we had to make this very major decision. On the other hand it was almost made for us when the doctor said, "The baby may survive anyhow." We felt very, very discouraged. Nobody was coming in and saying, "Hey, this could work out."

I called my mother: "Something *terrible* has happened to me." She said, "Who is this?" She didn't know who it was. I said, "I had the baby!" She said, "What are you *talking* about? You couldn't have had the baby." I said, "I did, and it's still alive," and my mother said, "I have to hang up, and I will call you right back." She was in a state of shock, but I felt better when I could tell Mom.

Then she called back and said, "Don't worry about anything. I'm coming right in. We'll get the strength to go through this. We'll see all the doctors." I thought, "Oh, thank God I have a mother who will take care of me." I had never felt that so strongly before.

She came to the hospital, and my sister came with her, and the good obstetrician I was supposed to have had came, too. He said, "Why didn't you call me? I feel so terrible! I've seen the baby, and I think she's going to be all right." I said, "From everything they've said, I'm discouraged." He said, "I can't give you any guarantees, but I think it's only a matter of time that she'll be a healthy baby."

Then he said, "Why don't you go up to the nursery and see her." He tried to prepare me for what the baby was going to look like. He said, "She's going to have a lot of tubes. She's not going to look like what you're used to a newborn looking like. You may feel depressed and sad and anxious and rejecting when you see her. But remember this is your first view, and after a while she will seem much more normal."

When I saw her, I was shocked. I thought, "Oh, God! There is nothing I can relate to as a baby." She had tubes in her nose. She had I.V.s and all kinds of tubes in the umbilical cord, and there were monitors all over her tiny body. She was thirteen inches long. Imagine, she weighed two pounds. But at least I'd had a few words of encouragement, and I didn't feel quite so horrible.

The chief neonatologist came over to talk to me. He said, "The baby has a fifty-fifty chance of surviving. There is no gross organic damage that we can see. But we can't give you any guarantees. We don't know what the future will be for her."

I think I saw her one more time, while I was there. Fred and I agreed we were going to have to figure out how to deal with this. We decided that in the beginning we wouldn't visit often, and we wouldn't give her a name so we wouldn't feel as badly if things went wrong.

I woke up at six the next morning. There was nothing for me to do in the hospital. There was nothing to look forward to. I was away from anything that could have distracted me or have made me feel better. I waited until eight, and called Fred. "When can you come and get me?" He just jumped in the car and came and picked me up. I was so happy. I then realized I was depressed. I was going home. I had no baby. I didn't know what was happening.

After a few days the doctor called me up. "Why haven't you been coming here?" he asked. "You haven't called me." I said, "I've been sick." It was true, and since Fred didn't seem that anxious to go, I didn't want to push him. The doctor said, "Sometimes men feel more distanced from the situation and find it harder to come to the hospital," which I think was true. Women can usually respond more quickly.

I felt the doctor's call was helpful because they noticed that we weren't coming, which showed they knew who we were, and they were taking an interest. I was just glad they cared. He wasn't saying the baby was doing great, but that she was doing well for this stage of her life. They had turned the respirator down to a low setting. The oxygen was down. They were all good signs. She hadn't undergone any major setbacks. They stress this because organs can fail and other terrible things can begin to happen.

Fred and I decided to see a psychotherapist. We told him the whole story. He said, "Listen, you have to name this baby. You have to start visiting her because after talking to you, I know you are already very attached to this baby. If you don't go to visit, and don't name the baby, you are denying what is there. It's not going to be protective to you even if the baby dies. Denying is not going to help. In fact, it will make you feel worse."

He also said, "It's not going to be good for your older child to see you not naming this baby or visiting her. Amy will feel: What if it were me? If I get sick is this the way my parents are going to treat me?"

I remembered that when we came home from the hospital Amy said, "What's the baby's name?" We told her we hadn't given her a name yet. Amy asked, "Is that because she's so small?" I said, "That's part of the reason." She said, "Well, maybe we can give her a very tiny name. Then when she gets bigger, we'll give her a big name."

We wanted to name her after my father, who died before she was born. His name was Harry, but there's no decent name that starts with an H. I was toying with Hilary. But when I saw this baby, I said, "She's not a Hilary." Hilary is a big name. This child was so tiny. My sister suggested that we name her Hope, but I didn't want to remember for my whole life that there was a problem in the beginning. Fred said, "We should give her a name that means something strong." He looked in a name book, and he picked Katherine, which means strength. I thought Katherine was a beautiful name.

I started visiting. By my second visit Katherine was already off the respirator, but she was under bright lights. That was depressing. They put big gauze bandages over her eyes. Her face was the size of a lemon, and she couldn't see at all, and the tubes were coming out of her body. I kept thinking, how could this be good psychologically? Everybody said, "This is nothing. As part of the treatment, this is the most minor thing she will have. Don't worry."

Then they got rid of the lights and took the bandages off her eyes. They put her in what they call a head box, a little Lucite box with an opening for the neck, so they could feed her oxygen. They also put her in an isolette, which is like an incubator. She still had an I.V. and monitors, and her chest was sunken because she had to struggle so much to breathe. But she started looking a lot better to me then. She had grown a bit.

I was waiting for them to take the head box off because I had heard that too much oxygen could damage the eyes. After a week it came off—but then there was a setback, and they had to put it back on. She was being fed through a tube in her nose down to her stomach, and they must have given her too much formula too fast because she had an episode where she turned blue. They stopped feeding her, put the head box back, and turned it up much higher than it had been. Then they started all over again.

I visited almost every day. It was horrendous, because it took me so long to get to the hospital. I tried to go when Amy was in nursery school. I'd rush up to the hospital. I used to look in the box, and feel inept because I wasn't doing anything. But I wanted to know what was happening. One time I saw that her face was dirty. I said to the nurse, "Could you please wipe her face?" I realized then I could serve a function. That was my child. I could look and notice things. Then I was allowed to put my hands in the holes. I could put my hands under her head and change her diapers. I could participate.

One day they gave her a bath while I was there. They stuck her right in a little bowl, soaped her up, washed her hair, and wrapped her in a towel afterwards. She was very alert after the bath. It was the first time I had seen her wide awake. She looked right at me with big eyes. That was nice. She still weighed only two pounds and five ounces. She was not that much bigger than my hand. I felt like Paul Bunyan. My hand looked so strange next to her.

The hospital will have to keep her at least two more months before she can come home. My main goal before she was born, when I expected her to be a normal child, was to get a mother's helper right away. Now I don't want help. I don't want a strange woman taking care of her until she's been with me for a long time. A friend said, "After all this, she better not give you another worry for the rest of her life." But you can't count on that.

Send Aaron Back to the Sky

SHEILA FISCHER

All during my second pregnancy I worried about Max. I kept thinking, "I love him so much. He isn't such a terrible two-year-old. We have everything worked out. We have such a special relationship. It's so much fun." I was really worried that I was doing some irreparable damage to Max. And I was. There's no doubt about it. He'll never forget his brother's birth. It will always be an issue for him. But then I would tell myself that a sibling is a fact of life. As an adult, I love seeing my two sisters. I'd think, "I just hope that the good parts balance out the bad," but I still worried whether I could possibly love another baby the way I loved Max.

When Aaron was born, Max came to the hospital. I'll never forget it. On some level I had a secret wish that my child would instantly fall in love with his baby brother and that we'd have no competition whatsoever, no jealousy, only love. Well, we marched down to the nursery window to show Max the baby. He had *absolutely* no interest in looking at Aaron. He said, "Let's go back to the room, Mommy. Let's make the bed go up and down." It didn't bother me. Actually, I thought it was kind of funny.

51

When we got home, it wasn't funny anymore. Ron was holding the baby when we came in, and I had all the baby's stuff. I sat down on the couch. Before I had my coat off, Max was pulling on my sleeve. "Read me a book. Read me a book!" I wanted to undress the baby and show him to Max. It was January, and Aaron was all wrapped up. "Read me a book *now*, Mommy, right now!" I said, "You'll just have to wait a minute, or Daddy can read you the book." "No, now!" Max stated, and he started to cry. The baby started to cry, too.

From that moment on, the question was: Do I do what Max wants me to do, or what the baby wants me to do? And what about the fact that I'm tired? What I really wanted to do was to go to bed, lie down and do nothing. I couldn't decide whether I should read Max the book to make him happy, or undress the baby to make him comfortable. I couldn't figure out how you do it. I still can't. There should be some manual on how to do it. How do you be the mother of two children who both need you at the same time?

Pretty soon Max was obnoxious most of the time. He wanted me available whenever he wanted me. The baby would cry, and I would pick him up to nurse. Max would try to elbow Aaron off my lap and climb on. Or he'd go and take the phone off the hook just as I'd settled down, or he'd dump all the pillows on the floor, or accidentally hit me with his ball or run a toy truck over my toes. Or he wouldn't cooperate when I wanted to change his diaper. I'd be running around the apartment with the baby in one arm, a diaper under my chin, trying to catch Max and get him down flat on the floor. Or the baby would be howling with the nighttime crankies, which he had decided to get after being the perfect baby for the first two weeks, just as Max would announce he wanted his dinner. I'd be jouncing the baby on one shoulder as I tried to break an egg with my free hand.

I felt pulled in eighteen different directions. I could hardly make toast, and then when I finally did manage to put dinner in front of Max, he'd throw his scrambled egg on the floor anyway, and go over and pinch Aaron on the leg or push him on the stomach real hard. "I know you're angry, Max, but you can't hurt the baby," I'd snarl through gritted teeth.

Very quickly he learned how to imitate me. "Oh, baby! Pretty little baby! Pretty little sweetie," in a high, singsong voice. I could hear my own voice in his, and it was so fake. Oh God, it was so saccharine, but that was better than having him hit the baby.

I'd finally get the baby settled down in his crib, so I could spend a few minutes reading to Max. I'd say, "This is our special time together," but it was never enough. If I read three books, he wanted four. No matter what I did, it was never right. He was a bottomless pit of need.

I don't think Ron understood how hard it was. He'd say, "Sheila, you can handle it. I know you can handle it. It's not that bad." I remember saying to him, "No. This time I've bitten off more than I can chew. Whatever made me think I was capable of doing this? I've got to have been crazy. Things were just settling down with one child. We had a life together. We could get a baby-sitter. I could get my house clean and cook dinner. Now I can't do anything. I can't even make toast. I can't get out the front door in less than two hours. This is a mistake I cannot undo."

I was feeling loving emotions for the baby. I was quite adoring of him. But I still felt his birth was definitely a mistake, and there was nothing I could do about it. I'd have to live with it. Forever. For fucking ever! It's more forever than getting married. Ron would say, "It's not that bad, it's not that bad." But you know, six months ago I could not imagine how it would get any better.

My friends would call up and say, "You're doing so well." I'd say, "Are you kidding me? I am going out of my mind." They'd say, "But you seem so calm." And I'd say, "But I'm not calm." I remember telling one friend, "The headline of the day is: Social worker abandons two children." That was right after my old friend, Ellen, came over to see the baby. I'd really been looking forward to the visit. Ellen and I have been friends since we were eighteen. We shared our first babies, and now she was five months pregnant with her second. She was bringing David, her little boy. I thought, great, he will occupy Max, so that I can really talk to Ellen.

I soon realized, though, that this was not going to be the visit I had planned on. David was very curious about the baby, and Max was furious at any attention David paid to Aaron. Max wouldn't let David touch a single toy. They fought over every truck, every block, every book. Max pushed David down a couple of times, but the final straw was when he threw a metal car and hit David right over the eye. I'd had it! I started screaming at Max: "You've got

53

to behave yourself! This is bad behavior! You may not hurt another child! What is the matter with you?'' I turned to Ellen, ''Where did I get this angry, angry child?''

Ellen had this very judgmental look on her face. ''Now take it easy, Sheila, take it easy,'' she kept saying. ''He's only a two-year-old.'' I could see she was wondering how I could treat him like that, this poor child who needed my sympathy and support. I was furious. I was screaming, ''Max, if you don't stop hurting other children!'' And Ellen kept saying over and over, ''Take it easy, Sheila. Yelling at him doesn't help.'' I felt totally embarrassed. I wished she wasn't even there. Every time she said, ''Take it easy, Sheila,'' I felt like screaming at her, ''Who do you think you are? Wait until you have to go through this! Wait until you see what it's like. You know something, Ellen, this is no bowl of cherries!''

But instead of saying that, I just sat down and started to cry. I sat there and cried and cried. I had totally lost it. I felt: ''I just can't do it right. I don't know how to do it.''

Normally, Ellen is a very physical person and a very caring person. I would have thought that she would comfort me, but instead she left me by myself and went to take care of the kids. I think somewhere the whole scene was making her think, ''Oh-oh, I'm going to have to go through this.'' She still had all those fantasies that I had had back when I was pregnant. She was worried about what was going to happen to David when her new baby arrived. In fact, she wasn't particularly interested in Aaron.

It's not hard to be judgmental. I'm telling you, you don't know what it's like until you go through it. There was nothing to prepare me for the intensity of Max's jealousy, or for my own rage. I also felt I wasn't giving enough to the baby. I'd think: ''This *poor* baby. Look at all the time I gave to Max, all the time I talked to him, read to him, held him, and this baby hardly gets any of that. He's lucky if I can nurse him for more than five minutes at a stretch.''

I suddenly became very admiring of my mother, who had my two sisters and me each eighteen months apart. I called her up and I said, ''Mom, how did you ever do it?'' She said, ''I went crazy.'' I felt better the more I heard that everyone else went crazy.

Sometimes the situation would get really out of control. It would usually start because Max wouldn't listen to me when I told him to do something. I used to be able to cajole him—make a joke about getting his shoes on. But I couldn't do that anymore. I was too strung out to make jokes. Instead, I would overreact and yell at him. Then he'd be worse because I had no patience. It just built up. All I could do was put him in his crib, and by that point I couldn't decide who was the two-year-old, him or me. We looked the same. My face was red and I was screaming at him, "I could kill you. You're so obnoxious! Why don't you do what I tell you to do?" My fists would be up and clenched. He'd be screaming back at me with his fists up. "You're a bad mommy! You can't do that to me! It's bad behavior! You're bad, bad, bad!" I'd scream back at him, "You'd better stop that! You better stop being so obnoxious!" Very quickly the baby learned to cry whenever Max cried. So if Max got really hysterical, Aaron would rev right up, too. Then I'd feel like I just wanted to walk away. And, of course, you can't walk away, not very far at least.

I would feel totally depressed, because I never used to be like this. I never lost my temper before. I was always one of the most patient people. I started thinking about my clients, women who have more than one child and who have limited emotional and financial resources. And then I began to understand the roots of child abuse much more clearly than I ever did before.

I wasn't always angry with Max. I would alternate between wanting to slug him and feeling sorry for him. And as time passed, he could actually say, "Put Aaron down and hold me," or "Leave Aaron at home and take me out," instead of hitting Aaron. That's so clear, and it's a healthy, nonviolent way of dealing with his anger. The most poignant thing he said was, "Send Aaron back to the sky." I said, "The sky?" and he said, "Aaron came from the sky." I said, "Where did you come from?" He said, "I came from the sky. You came from the sky. Send Aaron back to the sky." I put the baby down, and I took Max onto my lap and just held him for a long time.

It got to the point where I had to have a bottle of red wine in the house, so that at five o'clock, when everyone started going nuts, I could have a glass—then two glasses—in order to make it through the night. I would be completely worn out by the time Ron came home. I would say, "Let me tell you what my day was like," and I'd recount everything awful that had happened—how Max had done this and Aaron had done that, and I had done this much laundry and cleaned the refrigerator, and washed the floor.

I really didn't mean to criticize Ron for not doing enough. What I wanted was sympathy. I wanted him to say, "Oh, it sounds awful. You poor thing." Instead he'd say, "Well, what do you think I did all day? I've been working hard, and then I come home, and Max is on top of me. He wants me to play airplane, and I don't have two seconds to sit down. You want me to hold the baby while you cook dinner and then watch both of them so you can take a shower, and then I've got to bathe Max and put him to bed, and you'd really like it if I'd also be a good guy and wash the dishes, so who's done more?" Then I'd say, "I didn't ask for a competition here," and we'd be off and running.

Every couple of weeks I'd say to him, "Do you think we're going to make it? Do you think we're going to end up getting a divorce? All I seem to do is yell at you. I criticize everything you do and tell you how you're not helping me enough." But he's such a nice guy, he'd say, "It's not that bad. It's not that bad." I kept arguing, "This marriage is in big trouble."

There was hardly a moment when we could be together. We would think we had finally gotten both of them to sleep when Max would get out of bed for the fourteenth time, or the baby would wake up. Ron would say, "Let's make love." I'd feel I didn't want to touch anyone. I'd been holding children all day long, and I didn't want to hold him. He'd be annoyed. I'd say, "Don't you understand I don't want *anybody* to touch me? All I want to do is veg out in front of the TV. I don't even know if I can concentrate on a movie."

When Max started to be disturbed about going to nursery school, it really got bad. It's only two hours, three times a week, and he'd always loved it before. Suddenly, I couldn't leave him. He threw such tantrums—right out of the books—on the floor, kicking, screaming at the top of his lungs, my lovely child. I tried to walk out, thinking once I'd left he'd stop, but it was so bad the teacher called me back. So then I didn't even have the two hours during nursery school alone with the baby.

I tried sending him off with his old baby-sitter, Narrada, whom he used to love. I walked them to the park, and when I started to leave, Max got hysterical. "Narrada will take you on the bus!" I said. "You'll love the bus. Narrada will buy you an ice cream!" I was bribing him up and down. When I came back, Narrada said,

"It wasn't just for effect. He really did cry off and on for the entire two hours." Every time he saw another child with its mommy, or even if he heard the word "Mommy," he started crying.

I felt so terrible. I guess I felt mad, too, because I thought, "I can't go anywhere." I felt everything was out of control, and I didn't know what to do about it. So I went back to my old therapist. The first thing I asked was, "Am I doing something wrong that Max is going through this?" I needed to hear what I already knew, that Max was having a hard time and that he needed me to be there as much as I could to help, and that he would get through it. The therapist also said, "Be as patient as you can be. You can't be any more patient than that. You stay with him when you can stay with him, and you leave him when you have to leave him."

I went back to work, seeing my private patients six hours per week. I felt very guilty. I thought, "Oh, Aaron's only a baby. I shouldn't be doing this." I imagined I'd be thinking about him all the time. I couldn't fit into any of my clothes, and I felt lousy. I finally got myself together to go out. Max lay down in front of the elevator and grabbed my skirt as I tried to get past, wailing, "Mommy, don't leave me! You can't leave me! Mommy, please don't leave me." But this time, though I felt bad, I really had to go, and Ron was there. I said to Max, "No matter what you do, I'm leaving. No matter how much you cry, I have to go. That's the way it is. I know it makes you sad, but Daddy is here with you, and I will be back." I could hear his screams all the way down the elevator shaft.

Well, I got out that door, and I'm telling you, I couldn't believe it. I felt lighter—literally lighter, almost weightless. I loved it! As I walked down that street, not pushing a stroller or carrying a backpack, or having a child hanging on me, I loved it! I loved it! I loved it! When I got to my office, I was so involved in my work, it was like I was paying someone to let me go to work. I felt terrific! I was so sure I was going to feel nervous and guilty. Well, I didn't even think about the kids until it was time to go home. Then I suddenly felt anxious to feed the baby and to see Max.

My mother called the next day to see how it had gone. Ron answered the phone. I heard him tell her, "It's the *hardest* job in the entire world. It really is," and I said, *"Good!"*

57

Guilt Is the Main Emotion I Feel

CAROL LAUREN

Things are really unbearable now. The job is all-consuming. My own child hardly ever sees me and is acting impossible. Isaac and I are fighting. He's fed up with being almost completely in charge of Zachary and the house. Allison, the baby-sitter, nearly quit. And I feel cheated of any time for my family, not to mention myself. I also feel guilty. Guilt is the main emotion I feel for spending so little time with Zachary.

It's awful. The job is horrible. I've had very little flexibility as far as being able to leave at an appropriate time at the end of the day. I work eleven-hour days. Some mornings I have to be in by seven-thirty. I have to go in on weekends, too. I've also been traveling for periods of five and six days. I leave Sunday night and get back late Friday after Zachary's asleep. That's six nights away from him. Can you believe this morning they called me at 4:45 to tell me the computer had broken down? Isaac was furious, and I don't blame him.

I'm going through guilt in both directions. Guilty when I leave work too early because I haven't finished what I have to do, but also guilty because I'm not home. I haven't seen Zachary. One more time, Isaac has had to bail me out because his schedule is more flexible than mine. Today I had to call my sister in tears and ask her to please come rescue Zachary because Allison had to leave and Isaac could not get home in time to relieve her.

The saving grace through all this stress has been—knock on wood, I keep knocking on wood!—that Allison has been so ultra-reliable. She is there. I never have a question in my mind. She hasn't missed a single day in a year. She had a bad cold, but she came in. There are a few things about her I don't think are perfect, but that's because I'm a supercritical person. She's not the warmest person in the world, she's somewhat rigid, and she gives him too many sweets. But her values are very decent, and Zachary seems happy with her. She's very patient with him. She taught him how to blow his nose. If it were me, I'd be blowing his nose forever. The other day I bought him a new pair of shoes, and he said, "Boy, is Allison going to be surprised to see me in these." She's now a big part of his life. He told me he needed different shoelaces, though, because these laces give Allison a hard time. They won't stay tied.

Allison almost quit last week because of something stupid I did, an implied criticism. She didn't take him out. I said, "You weren't out on this beautiful day?" She said, "You just have to trust me. I had so much housework to do that I couldn't get out." I should have let it pass, but I didn't. How many days did I stay inside when I was at home? Plenty. Fortunately we smoothed it over. I went into a complete panic thinking she was going to quit!

Thank God the business trips are over for now. I got out of the last one. I said to myself, "I can't do this anymore." I arranged it so that other people could do it for me. But in the meantime Zachary entered a period of acting impossible. He refused to coop-erate or listen to me in any way.

In the store last week, I lost control. He was outrageous. He kept running away. I would chase him in a circle, and I couldn't catch him. He kept turning around backward and staring at me mania-cally and laughing. I'd yell, "Zachary, will you stop that immedi-ately!" He'd yell back, "Zachary, will you stop that immediately!" Finally, I grabbed him by the arm. I dragged him into the ladies' room. I beat him up! That is the only way I can describe it! I beat him up! My hand hurt! I did it twice in one day! I just lost control totally.

We talked about the incident, about what's wrong and why he's acting this way. I can understand what he's angry and upset about. He's very verbal and said, "I don't know what's wrong with me, Mommy. It seems that the only thing that stops me is a spanking. I just can't control myself. There has to be a control button, and it's just not there."

I feel so guilty, plus so sad that the time I do have with him is often horrible when I'm trying to make it nice. There's so much pressure to make it nice. Often he clings to me. He even wants to eat sitting in my lap. Some of it I allow. To some of it I say, "I don't think this is really necessary." The message is pretty clear that he misses me.

I rarely get to take him to school anymore, but the other day I did. He wanted me to come up to the classroom instead of dropping him at the door. I was in a rush, but I went up anyway. He wanted to show me a lot of the things he had done in his classroom, his artwork, the science project, and the toys that he likes to play with. I felt really sad. He wants so to share this, and I want so to know about it. It's not only for him, but for me, too. I'm losing out by not being involved.

My latest guilt is that he's not getting invited to other kids' birthday parties because I don't know the mothers. I've also been very remiss in making arrangements for him to have other kids come over to play. A few days ago he said, "I feel so sad, Mommy, that I didn't get invited to Sara's party." I felt like crying myself. You know how it felt when you were left out as a kid?

My days are jam-packed. I suppose I could force myself to call some of the other mothers if I could summon the energy after eight o'clock at night. The problem with school—and it makes me angry —is that it's not really geared toward working mothers.

My problem at work has been that I felt I had to be strong and not complain. I was not prepared for what was involved in starting a new department from scratch, but I thought asking for additional help was an indication of failing on my part. I had to prove to them that even after being at home for three and a half years with a child, I could do the job singlehandedly. I went overboard in never saying I had to leave early because of my child. If I have to take Zachary to the dentist, I'll say I have to go to the dentist myself. My friend who also works says, "Why isn't it legitimate for you to have to take him to the dentist? If a man came in and said he had to take his child to the dentist, that would be acceptable. Everyone would be touched! 'Isn't he an involved father,' they would say. 'Isn't he a nice guy?' "

I don't feel comfortable about doing this because I think they would say, "See! She can't do this job. She has a child!" Maybe I am a little paranoid, but I'm also partially right. Being a mother is not a position that many people view as valid or valuable. It is considered a second-rate occupation by a lot of people. It's sad, isn't it? When I took this job, some people in the company indicated to me that I should act as if I did not have a child because the management doesn't have much confidence in a woman being able to do a hard job of this sort, much less a woman with the responsibility of a child.

As a result, I have bent over backward not to leave early. It's okay if a guy says, "My wife is going to be angry if I get home late," but I don't think it's okay to say, "My husband's going to be angry if I get home late," or more to the point, "My child is going to be angry."

Professionally, I have gained this tremendous confidence that I can do a difficult job and do it well. It's funny, my coworker, a guy, and I used to get along really well. He wanted my boss to hire me in the first place. But since I've been back at work, we've had our differences. I realize the person he thought I was is not the person I am. I was much more malleable, much less confident a year ago. I was so tentative. Once I got my teeth into this and started demanding what was due me, he and I have had some serious disputes.

Isaac feels cheated, totally abused, and that he has nothing for himself. He feels everything revolves around me and Zachary—and it's true. He feels he's keeping me and Zachary afloat, and that nobody's worried about him. He understands my situation, but he has to reschedule a million things so that he can be available. He can only do this because he teaches. He tries to be supportive, but it is difficult. When the company woke us up about the computer, he said, "If there's another week like this, either you quit that job, or I'm leaving." I would go crazy if his job called him at that hour, too.

There has been a role reversal, and he feels like he's a failure. When I stayed home with Zachary and was a full-time mother, Isaac was more successful because he felt better about himself. Isn't it possible for two people to feel good about themselves at the same time in this kind of situation?

Isaac and I hardly have time to talk to each other. We used to have dinner together after Zachary went to bed, but now we all eat together. We think Zachary needs to be with me and have some sense of a family group. By the time dinner is over and Zachary is in bed, I'm exhausted. I have to go out of my way to try to be congenial with Isaac when I don't feel it. I feel like this relationship has to be put on hold. That's not fair, I know, but it's not fair to me either. Sometimes, though, when I'm not really feeling up to it, Isaac and I will go out anyway because he feels a desperate need to get away from the house and have some kind of a relationship with me.

I have no time. My mother called up and asked, "Have you done anything for Chanukah?" I had to say no. I didn't have time to find the menorah and take out the candles, or buy presents for Zachary. He knows that he's Jewish. They have discussed it in school. He pointed to every menorah in every window as well as in our building lobby and said, "Mommy, don't we have a menorah?" I finally dragged it out on the fifth night.

When I think of all the freedom I had! I think, did I ever have that as my life? Some days I wish, oh, if only I could go back to staying home. But then I think, well, that's ridiculous. Of course I would like to, but financially it's totally impossible. Our savings are gone from my staying home for three years. I have to work. I feel very trapped.

Zachary is getting bigger. Some nights I take him to the bathroom in the middle of the night before we go to sleep. Then I carry him back to bed. I hold him in my arms and I think, he's not a baby, and I'm never going to have another baby to hold again.

My friend Margie has really been sympathetic. I didn't know if we would continue to be such good friends when I went back to work, because I wasn't sure what the real basis of our friendship was. Our major point in common was our children, but I find we still are close.

I got home late one Friday night and was exhausted. I knew Margie was going away the next day, and I called to say goodbye. When her mother came in to take care of Annie, Margie left a list of parents to call and set up play dates with. The year before, when I wasn't working, I'd helped her mother out a lot with Annie. Margie's mother asked, "What about Carol? She's not on the list." Margie said, "She has a full-time job now and really can't help out at all. There's no one who has filled her shoes, though, in terms of friendship." That made me feel really good, not only that she told her mother this, but that she told me as well.

I find I'm desperately looking for other working mothers to talk to about how they handle their lives. I need to talk to someone other than Isaac, who's fed up with the whole subject. I saw Gloria Steinem on the street a few days ago, and I had this urge to run up to her, grab her, and say, "Could I meet you for lunch sometime?" Not that she's in my situation, but maybe she could help me. I do feel angry. There is a stigma on the working mother. It's not quite the right thing to do, or else why wouldn't there be better arrangements?

Basically, I think Zachary will make it. When I went to Chicago a few weeks ago, I called home and asked, "Do you miss me?" He said, "Yes, Mommy, but I know you're coming back." Last week he was playing "Mommy," planning his trip to L.A., and he packed his suitcase and his briefcase to get on the plane. I heard him say, "I'll be back late Friday night. You will be asleep when I get in, but I'll sneak in and give you a big hug, and I'll say, 'I'm home, and I really missed you, but I'm so happy to see you. You know, I really love you.'"

In a Bizarre Way, My Children Are Everything

JANE SILVERMAN

Being home with my kids was the first occupation in my life that I found absolutely compelling. But at the same time it was driving me crazy. Why did everything my children did, whether it was misbehaving or having temper tantrums or having problems in school, why did it overwhelm me to the point where I was paralyzed?

It came out in therapy again and again that I was not seeing them as being separate from me. If Edward was having a temper tantrum in public, *I* was the one who was losing control. There was no way that I could help him. I was *panic-* stricken about the whole thing, *sick* with fear.

I don't know how therapy works, but gradually—it will never be totally done—I was able to put some distance between me and these kids. It was not just to write them off or say, "Well, fuck them! Let them sink or swim!" But that they're one thing, and I'm another. I'm the mommy, and they're the children, and when they freak out, I don't have to go ahead and do it right alongside of them.

For most of the women I know, their children are far and away the most important things in their lives. They basically live for their children, not in a sick, self-denying way, but if you asked any of us, "What is the most important thing in your life?" the answer would be, "My children," whatever form it takes.

But you have to live, too. And the fact is, as my doctor said, "Most children are a pain in the ass most of the time." Even with the best will in the world, they will drive you nuts. You feel you have to beat them away, and then the guilt starts. You start thinking, "I don't love them enough. I don't snuggle with them enough." I fell asleep last night bludgeoning myself because I don't read aloud to them anymore. So tonight I'm going to drag out *Robinson Crusoe*.

There is a woman my age, Sue. She was married to somebody years ago when her children were in nursery school. She divorced her husband. Her mother took care of her children during the day when she went to work. She started out as an hourly worker at a major candy company. Now she is director of operations. She did it all herself. She went to classes at night.

Sue is a fabulous mother. She has great kids. They are teenagers now, and they're not in any trouble. She lavishes a lot of attention and structure on them about their school and their homework. Yet all she can do is flagellate herself morning, noon, and night because she doesn't spend enough time with them, because she's not sitting at home with them like I am.

I had a long talk with her. I said, "It's the Mother's Legacy, the guilt. No matter what you're doing, you think that there's an entirely different way to do it, to give your children what they need. And you'll never be equal to the task. You'll never love them enough. You'll never give them enough. We've got this *I Remember Mama* fantasy of what a perfect mother should be. And it's just got to be a fantasy. I mean, looking realistically at the women we know, who does it perfectly?"

What your children do to you and how they make you feel are the kinds of things that a lot of people don't talk about. These are the kinds of things that you keep to yourself. If in fact some of the women I know felt that they were out of control as mothers at any time, it would be the last thing they would discuss. Oh, Ann might say, "Allen is having a problem at school. What am I going to do

66

about it?" But it never would go to the next level of, "I have caused this in some way," or "This is terrifying me."

There are many people who will not engage in intimate conversations, who will not discuss intimate things. And what your kids do to you is the *most* intimate subject. Because what it brings up, and I know it sounds banal, but it's that little child inside yourself. And what is more private than that entity?

What I think I have in common with every mother on the face of the earth is the primacy of one's children in one's life—that they're everything in some bizarre way. You get to the point that they are what you're working for in your marriage. You're thinking about providing for them all the time. You're planning for them. And, "Thank God we finally bought a house, so that in ten years we can get a second mortgage on it to pay for their tuition." You're thinking about the values you're trying to teach them, and the fact that you want so desperately for them to be happy and successful, but at the same time you don't want to try to make them have the successes that you never had as a child.

And, oh God! I wish I could deny them all pain. My therapist kept telling me that I can't protect them forever. But I think of that wonderful moment in *To the Lighthouse* when Mrs. Ramsey is looking at her children. She thinks if only they could stay this way forever, precisely to be protected from all the pain in adult life.

Perhaps I am unusual. I've met a lot of people who don't feel they had an awful childhood like the one I recall. I think that's why it's harder for me to see my kids go through things: It reminds me of something so agonizing. Many people don't have agony in their background. They've got problems and pains, and they go through it, and they come out at the other end. My husband, Jack, doesn't remember anguish, but I do. So it's important for me to be constantly reassured that my children aren't vulnerable to that.

Poor little Edward is the one I identify with. I was almost passionate about not identifying with my daughter, Jessica, when I first started seeing this therapist. "Jessica is exactly like her father! There's *nothing* like me in her!" Even when people would say that we looked alike, I'd always say, "No, she looks like Jack." Panic would wash over me. "Oh no, no, no! We are nothing alike! She will never be fat. She will never be miserable! She will go to the

senior prom! We are not at all alike. She will never fail chemistry!''
And then I think . . .

But then I have to get to the point where I say, "You're not that
bad, Jane. It's not like a death sentence if either one of them has
some of your qualities because there are a lot of good things there
as well.''

Any Mother's Greatest Fear

JUDY WEBER

Allan and I were sitting on the beach talking. Josh had gone up to the top of the sand dune. It's very, very steep—about a hundred feet high—and is a place where kids love to play. There is a foundation of an old house they use as a fort, and a clay pit they dig in. It's a safe place to play. The kids love to run straight down the dune because it's so steep. If they fall, it's only sand. I've done it myself. It's fun to run so fast and with such a sense of abandon.

I looked up to make sure Josh was there. I saw his red bathing suit. He had his back to me and was bent over. It looked like he was digging away very happily. There were other kids coming and going. In fact, his little friend Karen, who is five, was standing right next to him.

Then I just started to feel something wasn't right. I yelled to Josh. He didn't answer. But that wasn't at all unusual. He loves to playact and fool people. Sometimes he'll even pretend that things have happened to him that haven't. He loves the drama of being saved. I have told him the story about the little boy who cried wolf countless times, but it is still a joke to him. He has scared us a lot, and for that reason I hesitated and turned my attention back to Allan.

69

Then I knew something was very dangerous.

I yelled to Josh again. Karen was still standing there and gave me a little shrug. I started running as fast as I could. I was running and running without even thinking, just running up the dune feeling the sand fall away beneath my feet, slowing me down as I ran straight up. Allan was yelling to me, "I see him. He's all right!" But I knew he wasn't. I couldn't stop. I just kept climbing as fast as I could. "He's all right!" but I was saying to myself, "Fuck it! I have to *know* he is all right." I had the most powerful feeling, it was almost physical, right in the center of my body, that he was in trouble.

I got to the top of the cliff. Two boys were there. They were laughing. "Oh, he got buried in the sand!" All I could see were Josh's legs and feet. There was no movement. I screamed. He had dug himself into a tunnel, which had collapsed. I grabbed him by one leg, and I just yanked as hard as I could. I pulled him free and turned him over. I could see his lips were blue, and his eyes were closed. His face was ashen, and he was not breathing.

The first thing I tried to do was get his mouth open in order to do mouth-to-mouth, but I couldn't. It was totally shut, clenched. I couldn't move it. I checked his nose. It looked clear. He was absolutely still.

I thought he was dead, which is any mother's greatest fear. It's a fear I feel I've walked around with ever since I've had children. I shook him. I patted his face. I rubbed him. I kept screaming, "Please, Josh, breathe, breathe! Please just breathe!" But he was limp and lifeless. I'd sensed danger, and I'd hesitated, and now it was too late.

I experienced an overwhelming helplessness. I have always felt I could overcome anything. I ran up that cliff in record time, and had pulled him out of the sand, but now everything within me was exhausted. I felt that I was at the mercy of God. I had a flash: He needed this experience to understand that he was cared for. I hadn't paid enough attention.

A crowd of people had gathered around us. I felt Allan beside me. I felt his support, and I felt his horror. Then I saw Josh's eyes move under the lids, a little flutter, and I could feel him start to breathe. And then he started to wail. It wasn't a cry. It was a very deep, low noise, a sound of the pain and terror he had been

70

through. It was his fear starting to come up from deep within his body. Someone said to him, "Oh, don't cry! Don't cry!" and Allan yelled, "Let him cry! Go ahead and cry!" and then I started to cry.

Later, when we were home, I said, "Oh, Joshey, you were so scared, weren't you?" and he said, "Yes." I said, "And you were screaming. You were calling, weren't you? Inside you were screaming and calling." And he said, "Yes, Mommy." He said, "Did you save me?" I didn't answer. Allan didn't answer, either. He said it again. "Who got me out?" and I said, "I did." He said, "You really care about me, don't you, Mommy?" I said, "Of course I care about you." He said, "Well, sometimes when you're angry at me I'm not sure." I said, "No, I always care about you." He said, "Is that how you heard me?" I said, "I don't know. I felt I heard you."

Should I Tell Them I'm Adopted?

CAROLYN KENT

We always told Amanda that she was adopted. We made it into a lovely story. "There were a man and woman who loved each other, and they worked hard, and they had a lovely house, and everything was all ready, and they wanted a baby and couldn't have one. . . ." We told her the story of her: How the man and the woman went to the city and after being asked a lot of questions, they got her. Amanda has seen the adoption agency from the time she was small.

We always said that her birth mother must be a wonderful person and very smart, because when she couldn't take care of her child, she chose adoption, which is the hardest thing for any mother to do. We tell her that we have fond feelings for her natural mother because she gave us the greatest gift that anybody has ever given us.

And if you ask her, Amanda says she's lucky that she's got two mommies. One day I guess I was a little annoyed, and I said, "Well, you know, you have two daddies, too." She looked at me. I shouldn't have said that. To her, Dennis is her daddy, but in her mind there are two mothers.

She was convinced that she was loved more because she had been adopted—which meant we really, really wanted her. She felt totally comfortable with this idea and thought adopted was a good thing to be. Also, it wasn't something unusual for her. She had two good friends who were adopted.

But then when she entered kindergarten, they had "family time." I think they did it every couple of days. Each child would have his turn to bring in pictures of his family and tell the class about them, their pets, etc.

Amanda went through the albums and picked out the pictures she was going to show of the three of us together and her cats, and her grandparents. But she was upset. For weeks she kept asking me and Dennis, "Should I tell them that I'm adopted?" I said, "Well, it's part of you, but it's up to you whether you tell people or not." I tell her that still. At first I used to tell people, and then I realized it was not fair of me, so now I let her make that choice. She also went to Dennis, and he wouldn't advise her what to do either. Five-year-olds do not have an easy time making decisions, and she agonized over it. One day she was going to tell them, and the next, she wasn't.

When she came home after her "family time," I asked her, "Did you tell them?" She said, "Yes," but she didn't want to talk about it too much. Then the teacher called me. She explained that Amanda had told about her family and told the children she was adopted, and that most of the children in the class didn't know what it meant. Amanda explained it meant that when she was born, she had another mother and that mother gave her away to her current mother and father.

After that came a lot of questions that she had no idea how to answer and which were difficult for her. "Why did your mommy give you away? Didn't she love you?" "Is she alive?" "Where is she?" A lot of it Amanda hadn't thought about, and it upset her. Some of the children questioned it in a negative way: "Were you naughty? Is that why you were given away?" Most of the children thought after hearing this that parents could give children away, so this was a shocker.

The teacher was trying to field all this, and at the same time let Amanda have her say. She did interrupt and say, "No, parents can't give away their children like that," to try to make the other children feel comfortable. But for Amanda it was traumatic because she realized all of a sudden that something she had very positive thoughts about, other people saw in a negative light.

I explained to Amanda why the other children would feel frightened. It's not a fear she has, because she didn't have the feeling she was given away. We always told her that her mother loved her, and was suffering because she had to give her up. But when these children started asking what reasons could there be for a parent to give away a child, Amanda said, "Well, maybe they were very poor, or didn't have jobs." But that wasn't a good enough reason. Then the children worried: "What if Daddy loses his job? Will he give me away?"

After that experience, she became less open about being adopted. Only recently has she started talking about it again. I think the Cabbage Patch dolls have triggered that, but it has taken three years for her to come around to discussing it openly again with other children. Recently, I overheard her tell the story of her natural mother to a friend. "My mother has long brown hair, and she's very beautiful." I said, "Well, she could have. You have long brown hair, so it could be that she does too."

We've said, "When you're older, if you really want to meet your natural mother, we will help you to find her." If I were adopted, I would like to know where I came from, too. I don't feel threatened by that. I'm convinced that we've built a loving relationship, and that Amanda loves us.

Mother is the person who mothers you, who cares for you. If Amanda ends up feeling that I'm not her mother, and that the other woman is, it's because of something *I* did, not anything her birth mother does. There are a lot of people we love in this world. There is room in life for more than one mother.

I Am out of
the Baby Stage

LOUISE PARKER BIGGS

As I talk with women, I've found so many who have been in my situation, women I never would have guessed about. It's not something you go around wearing a sign about, a sign that says, "I had one. I had an abortion." I remember years ago the tales about the knitting needles and the coat hangers, the pain and the completely unsanitary, life-threatening situations. When I was in high school, there was a newspaper story about a woman who had hemorrhaged to death in an isolated farmhouse as a result of a botched abortion. I can still remember the photograph of a bare lightbulb dangling from the ceiling, and the bloody sheets wadded up on a little cot in the corner. It was either that or go to Sweden. I never knew anyone who had one, but then I was pretty sheltered as a teenager and pretty oblivious and naive. Even though I never felt I'd be in that situation, I always felt very strongly that women should be able to control their own lives.

After Peter, our second child, was born, I began teasing Will on and off about wanting a third child. I can't figure out why I ever thought I wanted a third. Maybe it was because we are both from big families. Before we were married, Will always used to say he wanted five kids. He came from a staunch Catholic family where it was traditional to have many children. He has such fond memories of visiting one aunt with eleven in their huge rambling house on the coast of Maine. The cousins always had a great time when they all got together. I said to Will, "Of course it was fun for you kids. It's always fun for the kids because they're not doing the shopping or the cooking or washing all those dishes and making all those beds."

Will is usually very even-keeled. From the moment I started teasing about the fact that I thought I *was* pregnant with a third child, he got this very closed look on his face. He wouldn't talk. He didn't show joy at anything, not even with the kids. I think it was a sadness on his part, a sadness to think that we had let this happen, because we really had been very foolish. We had acted just like teenagers, risking fate. I had known it was a bad time of the month, but we had risked fate before.

I was very upset. I was ambivalent. But every time I tried to talk about my feelings about a third child, I felt Will distance himself. The only way he could approach the question about whether to have the baby or not was through logic. He got a piece of paper, and he drew a line down the middle. On one side he wrote "pros" and on the other side, "cons."

Our cons were clear. We were just coming out from under all the custodial care with Peter, who was four: all the feeding, the diapers, the constant supervision so that he wouldn't kill himself. We'd sold the baby equipment. I said, "If this had happened a little sooner, maybe I could deal with it, but I just can't go back to all of that." We both work, and the logistics of dealing with two children are already mind-boggling. We dreaded the prospect of loading a baby and all its stuff into the car to get to the sitter's at the crack of dawn; all those missed days of work for another round of childhood illnesses. Money wasn't the most important factor, but it was a factor. We're not sure how we're going to afford college for the two we have.

Another factor was that Will and I didn't have any supportive family nearby to help us. It was too hard going it alone. There was no grandmother to ever take them for a weekend. It seemed as if we never had any time alone. I hate to tell you how infrequently we have sex. When I read about these people who have sex so many times a week, I'm embarrassed. So many times a week! They must stay up later than we do. We've really lost the intimacy we once had. We are like two roommates who live side by side.

So there was Will with our list of "cons." On the "pro" side there wasn't one item. There wasn't one reason why we should have a third baby, not one.

Even seven years ago when I became pregnant with Missy, I wasn't sure I'd done the right thing. We were just beginning to know each other. We'd married, but then I had two operations, one on my knee and the other for a benign tumor on my back. Then we moved into our house and I became pregnant, all within an eight-month period. I knew, though, that the clock was against me. I was thirty-three and felt I had to get pregnant soon. Yet I have to admit that when the doctor announced I was pregnant, I almost fainted.

Then Missy was such a horrible baby. She was a *horrible* baby. She *never* slept. When she had her eyes open, she was crying. That was mental torture. I remember pacing for hours in the middle of the night thinking, I am going to die. I am not going to live through this. My friends would call and say, "You'll survive it. It will get better." I didn't believe any of them. I also knew that if I wanted to have a second baby, it had better be soon. So Missy was just over a year old when I got pregnant again.

When the doctor called this third time and said, "Louise, you are with child," I cried. He had just seen me the month before, and had said, "What are you doing for birth control? You still have many fertile years ahead of you." He had asked me then, "Do you want a third child?" and I replied that I didn't know. And here I was, only a month later, sobbing into the phone, telling him, "My husband is so unhappy. I don't know what to do." He said, "For your own sake, make up your mind by Monday morning. If you want to have an abortion, the sooner the better. You can come right to my office, and I will take care of you there." He wasn't at all judgmental.

It was an agonizing weekend. I spent hours on the phone with my sister who had had an abortion twelve years before. She felt she had no choice. She wasn't in love with the man, and she didn't feel she could make it as a single professional person with a child.

She told me how empty she felt when she came home alone after the abortion. She couldn't sleep. She had a balcony, and she went out and stood on it. The sun was just coming up over the city. She said, "I had a feeling then that that had been my only chance to be a mother." She felt like it was a prophecy. She's thirty-six now, unmarried and childless.

However, she was very supportive of me. She was like the voice of reason: "Look, your marriage is at stake. You're ambivalent about having a third child, and Will feels strongly he doesn't want one. You will be risking a lot if you decide to. Maybe you can learn to live with this baby, and maybe you can't, but Will is the primary caretaker in your family, and you really have to think about his needs, too."

She was right. I will admit it to anyone. I had carried each baby inside of me for nine months, and then I said, "They're yours." He didn't mind. He's very nurturing. He actually enjoyed all the feeding, the bathing, the dressing. He's very patient. Now that the kids are older, he loves to play He-Man with Peter for hours. I can't be bothered. He'll even play those board games like "Candy Land" and "Cabbage Patch to the Rescue."

He's also very easygoing. He doesn't care if Peter doesn't have his face wiped, or that Missy hasn't brushed her teeth in the morning. Her class was going to be on TV last week. It didn't bother him when she picked out clothes that made her look like an orphan. I wanted her at least to wear something that matched. He said, "Let her wear what she wants."

I'm particularly impatient with Peter. He'll be five in two months, and do you know, he still wears a diaper at night. I said, "Peter, you don't need this." I think he must have a little more control. But he doesn't want to. Will says, "Why push him? Look, he won't go to college in diapers."

I think Will has a funny thing with Peter. I think he wants him to stay a baby. They have this little ritual. After I finish reading stories, Peter calls for Daddy to play baby. Peter will lie down on the floor, then he wants Will to reach over and pick him up and carry him to bed. Then Will sings him a lullaby. It's funny. When

80

Will went away last week, both kids said, "Who's going to play baby with us?" I said, "I don't know. I don't play baby. There's no baby when I'm here." Because I don't want them to be babies.

During that agonizing weekend, my father called me on the phone. He said, "Whatever you decide to do, I completely support you. Another child really is a lot to take on." He added, "You know, your mother and I never had that choice. The doctor told her that she should never have had all those kids because she just couldn't deal with them." And she couldn't. She had these four little kids by the time she was thirty, and she was a nervous wreck. She started chain-smoking the moment she woke up. I remember that she would completely lose control when we wouldn't cooperate. She'd stand there and scream and scream, "Goddamn it! Goddamn it! Goddamn it!"

I kept thinking, if only Mom were alive (I often wish that). Dad is so different now. It's a shame she didn't have the opportunity to see the change in him. I don't know if he's changed as a result of women and society changing or whether it is because he had to housekeep for himself for so many years before he remarried, and realized that it's no fun. Now he shares the housework with his new wife, and does most of the cooking. I wish he'd been like that when my mother was alive.

If my mother was alive, I would say to her, "How could you stand it? Really, how could you absolutely stand it?" I think of Saturday mornings. My father insisted we all had to go to church. We all had to look just right, but he never helped her get us ready. We hated to go, so we just sort of slunk away and purposely took an extra long time. She'd start screaming at us, and then there was a long trip in the car where our noise level was deafening. After church we would have to rush right back home so that Mom could get the meal going. My father had to eat between two and three in the afternoon. That was his ritual. Then he watched football for the rest of the day, while she waited on him.

I think the stress was tremendous. I was twenty-three when she became sick. I quit my job and moved home during her illness. She had a brain tumor that caused convulsions, and she couldn't be left alone. I took care of her and my younger brothers, who were twelve and fourteen. It was very difficult.

They were so slovenly! There were only three things that I asked them to do. Instead of walking out of their undershorts and leaving them in the middle of the floor, I just wanted them to put them in the hamper. I didn't care if their beds were made neatly, but if they would just throw the covers over, that's all. And I wanted them to aim when they went to the bathroom. Here were these three men. They never aimed, and I had to clean up after them. I asked only for those three things, and they wouldn't do any of them.

Mom died at the end of that year. She was only forty-four. I stayed on another year. Then I got a job and moved away. My father convinced me that it wasn't my responsibility. He hired a woman to come in. He was right. I realized then, however, that motherhood was no bed of roses. It's a small wonder that even at the age of thirty-three, I had doubts about motherhood.

Anyway, by Monday morning I had decided that I had to have the abortion. I just couldn't start with another new baby again. I cried the whole way to the doctor's office. When we got to the parking lot, Will said, "Look, Louise, we don't have to do this. We can have this baby, and we'll somehow manage it." I said to him, "No, this is it. We have to do this, and I know it." That was the painful part, knowing that it wasn't just Will who didn't want this baby. I didn't want another baby either. But it went further than that: If I went through with the abortion, it meant I really was not going to have any more children. The possibility would be gone forever. There would be no more fantasizing about a boy or a girl, and what we would name it, and who it would look like—or any of that. This would be the end of my childbearing years, as well as the loss of this baby. It seemed so sudden.

The minute I walked into the doctor's waiting room, I started sobbing uncontrollably. I couldn't look at that room full of pregnant women. When I thought of all the times I had sat there. Oh, that was hard! The nurse saw me and grabbed me right away. She took me into a private room. I was quite incoherent, blabbering: "I can't go through this again. I've got these two I can hardly keep up with. Half the time I want to lock myself up in a room alone. I'm almost forty and I work full-time, and we can't afford it." I kept saying, "I feel so selfish. I feel so guilty. We're so fertile and Will's brother and wife want a baby so badly. They've been trying for years. They would kill for a baby. I mean if I really was a good person, I would carry this baby and give it to them. . . ." Lynn, the nurse, talked to me. She held me, and she stroked my hair. She kept saying, "Oh, Louise, you have to do what's right for you." I was so grateful to her, so grateful that she was there that day.

Then the doctor came in and explained the procedure to me. He didn't rush through it. He was very calm.

It was worse than I thought it would be. I don't know why I thought it would be nothing. I was awake, and I felt everything. Here it was, and he was just taking it all out. It was going into a jar. I wished I could have covered up my head and blocked my ears, so that I couldn't hear. It was bad enough to feel it. But hearing it and seeing it made it worse.

When it was over, Will came in. The doctor said, "Now that you have really made up your mind that you don't want more children, you should consider a permanent solution." Will told him that he'd been thinking about a vasectomy. Within two weeks Will went and had it done.

It has been two years since I had the abortion. About a month afterwards Will's sister announced that she was pregnant with her fourth. I said to myself: What is wrong with me? His sister can handle it. Lots of women can handle it, and even enjoy it. Why couldn't I just toughen up and have that baby?

But the truth is, I feel relief. I really do. There are so many things that I want to do, to learn, to read, to change. I want to become more involved in the community again. I want to work for our church and for the PTA. I also want to expand in my professional life. I want to enjoy my children as they are now. I am out of the baby stage. I'm ready to move on.

I'm a Tiger Scout Mom

MARTHA GRADISHER

On the day Max was born—and this is the gospel—I worried about two things. I worried about toilet training, and I worried about Cub Scouts. I had understood that it was difficult to toilet train a boy. My mother-in-law told me that when her babies were a year old, she would put them on her lap when she went to the bathroom. That way they would get the idea about what she was doing. That thought just didn't sit well with me in Freudian terms. I knew I wasn't going to do that—I didn't want to screw Max up for life—but I didn't know what I was going to do. I just wished he had come already trained.

But back to Cub Scouts. What I was worried about was being a den mother. It's nothing I aspired to. It was something I never ever felt I would be comfortable doing. Well, last spring my two best friends, Sally and Mimi, having full knowledge that I felt this way, signed me and Max up for the Tiger Scouts. I wasn't even there. Then they flipped a coin to see who was going to tell me.

I conveniently forgot about it over the summer. The other day Mimi reminded me that the first meeting was at six-thirty this Wednesday. "Be sure to bring a pair of scissors," she said. I asked Max no less than fifty times in two days, "Are you sure you want to do this?" and he kept saying, "Yes! I told you *yes!* I really want to be a Tiger Scout!" I couldn't get him to change his mind. I wasn't influencing him. I was just asking him.

The day before the meeting Sally asked, "Did you iron his little Tiger Scout decal onto a T-shirt?" I said, "What are you talking about? I didn't get any decal. Maybe we can't go if we don't have the uniform." Sally said, "I'm sure he can go. Mrs. Stoll at the school has all the information. You probably didn't get your packet because you didn't pay your five dollars yet." I said, "Okay, I'll call her."

I conveniently forgot to call Mrs. Stoll until three hours before the meeting. Max said, "What time are we going? What time are we going?" I said, "Excuse me a minute, I have to *stall* Mrs. Stoll." Now is that a Freudian slip or what? I called her, and she said, "No problem. He'll have the stuff for the first meeting. Just bring in a check." I said, "Thanks a lot, Mrs. Stoll."

Off we go to our first meeting. As the five little boys ran amok, the parents gathered. There is a woman I don't know named Milia who has a son Jason, and Mike, Sally's husband. Mike is the Tiger Scout parent because she gave him a choice. She said, "You can stay home and watch Spencer"—who is two-and-a-half—"or you can be the Tiger Scout parent for Griffen," and he opted for Tiger Scouts, which I might have, too, considering Spencer at six-thirty. There was Harriet, a very funny woman, and her son Benson. Mimi and Seth were the Tiger Scout cohosts for that evening.

Mimi had the Tiger Scout manual in her hand and explained that the meeting was going to go according to the book, which is exactly what happened. I started reading it because I hadn't gotten my copy in the mail, and discovered that it said that in order to be a Tiger Scout, your child must have either completed the first grade as a six-year-old, or be seven. Well, Max is neither. Of course I didn't say this blatantly in front of Max. I took Mimi aside. I said, "I don't want to go against the book. Maybe we shouldn't be here, though." She said, "It's all right. We already talked to Mrs. Stoll about it, and she said it was fine."

Mimi suggested we all get in a circle on the floor, which we did. She said, "Try to sit next to somebody you don't know. We're going to spend the next two minutes talking to this person and finding out something about them." I *hate* things like that! I *hate* them! It reminds me of church where you have to shake somebody's hand.

I've just never been able to do that. I'm always pretending I'm coughing into my hand, so that nobody wants to shake it.

I sat next to Harriet, whom I knew a little, and the kids all sat next to each other. I took the opportunity to ask her to come to Sally's surprise birthday party. After we were done chatting, Mimi said, "All right, now let's talk about what we learned." She started with her cohost, Seth. He said, "No, Mom, I'm not doing it!" "Well, maybe we'll start with Benson." He starts giggling. He was just not going to do it either. We all looked at Griffen, who literally hid under the rug.

My smile was faltering as I happened to catch Mimi's eye. She was staring right at me. She said, "Martha, why don't you start." I said out of the side of my mouth to Harriet, "I'm going to wing it," and I told them what I knew about Harriet—that she lives in a *beautiful* old house, and that she also has a daughter and, I believed, a pet. Harriet said, "Three dogs." Then it was Max's turn. He was very good because he got to talk to Mimi. He said he'd learned that Mimi was an only child like he is.

Then we went on to the next activity. Mimi had made a banner out of gingham, and she had cut out the letters in each boy's name. She said, "We'll put our names on tonight, and then we can add to this banner all year long as we do different activities." I guess it's a cute idea, and I'm all for that. She said, "Now, what do we want to do? Sew these letters on, or do we want to paste?" I pictured all of the little boys and us mothers and Mike poking themselves with needles, and was so relieved to hear this resounding *"Paste!"* I think with the exception of one, each little boy was writing his name in paste, and then hoping that the letters fit on top. I thought that was hysterical. Well, the pasting went on for about half an hour, which was twenty-five minutes too long.

After that Mimi said we were going to play some games. We'd start with the blanket game. You put a blanket down, and all the kids stand on it. Then they get off, and you fold the blanket, and they get back on it, then they get off the blanket, and you fold it again, and they all have to get back on. It got pretty funny when they started falling all over each other.

We parents were all standing around with our arms folded, chuckling. Isn't this fun, and aren't we having fun, and everybody was very up and very positive, until we had to play the ha-ha game.

The kids had all played that game to death. They said, "Oh no, not the ha-ha game," and "That's a dumb game," and "I don't want to play that game," and "Do we have to play that really dumb game?" And all the parents said, "Yes, one more dumb game, and then we're going home. Now shut up!"

So they got down on the rug. One kid lies down, and another kid puts his head on that kid's stomach, and the first one says, "Ha," and the second one says, "Ha-ha," except they are saying it in the boredest tone. "Haaaaaa." Then "Haaaaaaaa. Haaaaaaaaa." I think someone finally farted, and they all started laughing, and the ha-ha game finally worked.

Then Mimi said, "I think it's time for lemonade and cookies." I thought that must signal the end. It was a quarter to eight already, and not the best time to have lemonade and cookies, but I was a Tiger Scout mom, and I wasn't going to go against the book. So Mimi put out the cookies and the lemonade. The cookies were on a plate, and I turned around. When I turned back, all the cookies were gone. Everybody had a little pile in front of them.

Then Mimi said, "I think we should go over the pledge with the boys now." I believe it was to love God, your family, and your country and to learn about the world. The kids were not with it, and they were making fun of the pledge. They were very irreverent. "God. God who?" Then all of the parents got very upset. Mike said it the best. "Tiger Scouts is fun until we get to the pledge. There are some parts of Tiger Scouts that must remain serious." It was clearly time to go. It was eight, and the meeting had been going since six-thirty.

And so I came home and put Max to bed. He said he really enjoyed the Tiger Scouts. And I said, "Oh, then you want to go next month?" "Oh, yes!" he said. I felt I had done my duty. I felt responsible. I had just finished doing an idiotic thing, but I felt like a good mother. Max needed it, and I was there. I really didn't enjoy it, but I did it. I did it for him. So I actually came away feeling like a martyr, I guess. Martyr is a much better word than mother.

Isn't that amazing? Parents are always willing to embarrass themselves for their children. In order to give your children something —moral values—you sometimes have to make yourself something that you're really not. But you do it for your children. I think that is lovely. And you do it over and over again.

Inventing Motherhood for Yourself

BEATRICE SCHWARTZ

As a little girl I had a very strong drive to be a mother. It's what I wanted more than anything else. I was very attached to my dolls —I had six of them—and I used to line them up in bed next to me. I was so busy making sure that they weren't going to be smothered that I couldn't sleep. I remember being very uncomfortable lying on the edge of the bed, crowded by all these dolls, afraid they were going to die.

I had to take very good care of my dolls. I knew my mother was doing it wrong, and I figured I could do it better. Every time I felt my mother did something cruel to me, I said, "I am going to remember this, so that when I grow up, I won't do the same thing. I'm going to make sure that I remember how I feel at this age, so that I will not be mean to my children."

My mother was extremely critical. If she didn't feel well, it was our fault because we were a pain in the neck. She couldn't tolerate messes, and children have to make messes. So we would make a mess, and she would say we were ruining her life. This is one of her famous lines: "All I do is cook for you, clean for you, iron your clothes, do everything for you, and what do you do for me? Nothing!'' The other famous line was, "If I knew what it was going to be like, I never would have had children.''

My mother would have temper tantrums. She would explode into violent rages and go into withdrawals where she felt she couldn't function. I remember once when I was about five or six, she said, "I'm tired of being such a slave in the house. I'm going on strike!" She went into her bedroom for about three days. My father played a role in this, too. Instead of taking charge, he tuned out. He went around looking very sad and depressed. He was just like another helpless kid who couldn't handle the situation, either. I observed all of this as a six-year-old and thought: This is crazy. Grown-ups don't act that way.

I know my mother loved us, but I think she was unhappy and let it all come out on us. I don't think she understood the power of her cruel, hurtful statements on a child. She was a perfectionist, and we were constantly criticized. She'd want us to wash the dishes or help her. I'd do my best, and she'd say, "Well, how come you didn't clean the sink?'' She would have some complaint about everything, and we weren't allowed to talk back.

I had my own ideas. When I was about six I remember saying, "When I grow up I'm never going to wear high-heeled shoes or lipstick, like my mother, or smoke cigarettes and drink coffee." I had figured this out. High-heeled shoes were uncomfortable, bright red lipstick was ugly, smoking made me sneeze and cough, and I knew there was something about drinking coffee I didn't like either.

On every issue I had my own ideas. In eighth grade I didn't want to salute the flag anymore because it didn't make sense. Why should I be saluting this inanimate object? I refused, and everyone called me a Communist. This was the fifties, and my mother just about died. Her view toward life was, "What will the neighbors think?" I used to think: How could she care so much about what other people think when I am suffering?

She really wasn't happy being a mother. Sometimes I used to think I was imagining this, that I must be wrong. But now, when I see her with my children as a grandmother, I can see she had a difficult time. She can't tolerate the childishness of children: their free expression, or their irrationality, or any pleasure they may take in their bodies. She expects them to be like little grown-ups. It's almost as if she feels jealous that a child has the right to express herself and let out all these primitive feelings.

So I wasn't going to be a mother her way. But I also felt very afraid of being a mother at all, of making the mistakes she made. I delayed having children for many years, but I finally decided, okay, I'm never going to be a perfect mother, and also, I'm not my mother, so I'll take a chance.

I had some difficulty getting pregnant. I also had a miscarriage. I now believe all those things were related to my fear. Finally I gave birth to my first daughter, Lisa. It was a terrible shock into reality. Here I had been living in a fantasy world all these years about how I was going to be this wonderful mother. My adorable baby was going to be as fulfilling as the dolls I had loved. My idea of a baby was really like a doll, an unformed being, a sweet puppy. You would cuddle it and hold it when you felt like it.

I had no idea that this baby was going to be a fully developed personality trapped in an infant's body! I know that sounds funny, but when I looked into the eyes of this baby I saw a real person, and a person who wasn't particularly happy being a baby. She was an intense person who looked at me with tremendous depth as if to say, "What am I doing here? You better get busy and take care of me." She was very demanding.

She wanted mobility, and since she couldn't move, I had to provide it for her. Dr. Spock, and you can quote me on this, is a liar. In his book he says that newborn babies sleep eighteen hours a day. Well, this baby needed six hours of sleep, and never in one stretch. If she didn't get what she wanted, she would scream at the top of her lungs. I was like a slave to her day and night without a break. But I gave her what she needed even though I was a wreck.

What she did was force me to grow at a rapid rate. I had been the type of person who had to have all of my little needs taken care of: the right food, just enough sleep, a perfect household. I became stronger. I was forced to give up many of the things that I thought were so important. I gave up having time to myself and arranging my house. That was a big change because my house had been like a little work of art. Still, I didn't have a problem giving it up because I wanted this baby badly.

It was the second child that did me in. She was just as demanding and difficult as the first. I had thought: This can't happen to me twice. But I was wrong. The second one was just as strong an individual, plus neither one was sleeping at night. There have been studies showing that people who don't get enough sleep become crazy. That's what happened to me.

The incident that stands out in my mind as the turning point occurred when Lisa didn't want to get dressed to go to nursery school. I needed her to go because when I had the two together, I couldn't take care of the baby. Lisa wouldn't let me nurse Molly without attacking me. She was a very, very strong child and absolutely refused to get dressed. So we were in a battle. I became a maniac, just like my mother. I started screaming, "Okay, if you don't want to get dressed, then you can go out naked!" I threw her out in the hallway completely naked and locked the door.

That frightened me. I started crying. I said, "What's happening to me? I'm becoming just like my mother." I came to see that I was so afraid of making the mistakes my mother made that I went to the other extreme of expecting perfection from myself. I glorified the idea of motherhood. I wasn't allowing for any negative feelings. And I had accepted the idea that a perfect mother would produce the perfect child—a really ridiculous idea.

When I was having trouble with Lisa as a baby, people would blame me. "Well, it's your fault she doesn't sleep. You spoil her. You give in to her." Now I realize that each baby's different. It wasn't my fault. The kid was genuinely difficult.

I began to realize that it's perfectly normal to have the negative feelings about your child's behavior. The hard part is not to act on them. I had to work at developing more tolerance and patience. It was not something that came naturally to me at all. I found that I had to build on each success. I would say, "Look, I didn't lose it that time. I can do it again." I'd say to myself, "Remember what it feels like to be in control. It feels good."

Just yesterday I had the most torturous hour with Molly, who is now six. She had an hour-long temper tantrum over something so small. We only have one bathroom, and I wouldn't let Molly go first. I knew Lisa couldn't hold it even though she's older. I said, "Okay, I'm making the decision that Lisa's going first." Molly was furious. She was screaming at me, "I hate you. I hate you. You're so mean."

I used to get right down on her level and fight. I still have those feelings. I wanted to strangle her. I'd bent over backward to accommodate this kid. We'd been to the shoe store where she tried on twenty pairs of shoes. I'd let her make up her own mind. We'd had ice cream afterwards. And now she's screaming at me, "I hate you. I hate you." I wanted to kill her, but instead I said to myself, "I'll just try another approach. I'll try being rational with her." I simply said, "Your sister has a problem. She really can't hold it as well as you can. Your body's a little stronger in that area."

Another trick I use when they are screaming and yelling and acting out is to tell myself, "It's going to be over soon. There's got to be an end if I can just hold on." That's a very useful tool because children are like that. They'll go from one mood to another very quickly. While they're screaming you can't imagine that it's going to end because it's so painful. My kids have endurance. Their fits can last a long time. But if you try to remember ten minutes ago they were laughing and smiling and having a good time, then it's just as possible in ten more minutes that they'll be having a good time again.

While they are screaming, I say, "Well, one person here has to be the adult, and it better be me." I feel much better about myself. I say that to my husband when he loses it and screams at them. I say, "Look, you can't all be the children." He says that that has really helped him. His parents were like my parents. They would just rant and rave and let go and take it out on us. So we had to learn this new behavior ourselves. I still let go now and then, but my goal is to maintain my reason, to speak to them in a reasonable way. I also try to let them know, when they're acting out, that even though I don't like what they are doing, I still love them.

I have become much more sympathetic toward other parents. Before I had children, I had been a foster care worker with abusive parents. I always identified with the children: How could these parents be so cruel? But now I say, "My God, what a fool I was!" Those poor people. Not only did they have several young children in the family, but they were also living in the worst poverty. No wonder they lost control. I wish I could go back and do that job over.

I've also gained a lot of sympathy and understanding for my own mother. She must have been suffering terribly. She really was an extremely insecure person. Her parents were Eastern Europeans

93

who spoke English poorly. They settled in a small all-American town. My mother felt she didn't belong, and that everyone looked down upon her. That was partly true, because there was anti-Semitism. No wonder she wanted us to belong, to be all-American girls. She gave us very all-American names, Sally and Becky—short for Beatrice. We were supposed to be popular in school and fit in, and then she could live vicariously through us.

One of her other problems was that she was a girl between two brothers. Of the three, she was the most ambitious, yet everything went to the brothers. They were sent to college, and she was told she couldn't go. Then she wanted to be a beautician, but she became a secretary to please my grandparents. My mother thought of herself as stupid. She used it as a way to block herself from understanding things. She would say, "Well, I'm too dumb to understand modern art," or "I can't understand classical music."

Her mother was no role model for her, either. She was like a child, a very charming, loving child. She had a lot of love to give, but she had little mental ability. Something was missing. She had the intellectual development of maybe a five-year-old. For instance, she thought the images of people on TV were really tiny people inside the television.

My grandmother came from a poor family in a little village in Eastern Europe. They had a dirt floor. She was the youngest of thirteen children. And there wasn't enough food to eat. She also had typhus as a young child, and that may have affected her mental development. She saw the world in terms of doom and gloom, maybe because of the whole Jewish background where they were afraid of the next pogrom. She never felt safe, and she didn't make my mother feel safe, either.

I don't feel angry at my mother anymore. That is who she is. That is her history. I'm past that blaming stage. That is a true sign of becoming an adult. But it has been a struggle. It doesn't happen all at once. I am almost forty-two years old, and I spent many years blaming her. I'm very happy I'm over that because you could do that for a lifetime. And that gets in the way of your own development.

I have had to invent motherhood for myself. For instance, I've been thinking about praise lately. I always praised my children whenever they did something well. Then I started thinking about how people praised me as a child because I was smart in school. It didn't make me feel particularly good about myself. In fact, I've decided that too much praise has the opposite effect. Then the kid starts to think, "They only love me because I'm smart, or I'm pretty or I'm popular."

My latest discovery is that I do way too much for my kids; my tendency has been to wait on them. I've noticed that several of my friends encourage their children to do things like put their laundry away or make their school lunches. Just yesterday Lisa was watching TV, and she said, "Could you please bring me a glass of water, Mom?" I was very nice about it. I have to bring it on them gently. I said, "The waitress is off-duty. She's not serving today."

I realize that I've got to start working extra hard with Lisa, who is in such a good period. Pretty soon the hormones are going to hit, and she isn't going to be so good. She's going to be attacked again with all these intense feelings she had when she was younger. She's probably going to have emotional outbursts like the ones I had when I went through puberty. I've got to be prepared for it and be able to accept her. I loved her when she was good, and want her to know I'll love her when she's having difficulty.

She's giving me little hints. She'll say, "Oh, you look disgusting in that outfit," just to get me prepared. Then later I'll tell her, "You know, you really hurt my feelings," and she'll come over and hug me and say, "I'm sorry, Mom. I was in a bad mood." I appreciate that she can do that. Another thing I try very hard to do—my mother could never do it—is apologize. When I make a mistake, I can say, "Look, I overreacted. I took it out on you. It wasn't your fault." They're learning to do that, too.

Part of my personality is I have a lot of anxiety about what is coming next. I don't like to be taken unawares. I want to be prepared, so I've been thinking a lot about adolescence. It can be very rough. It can be a time when many problems show up, and you can blame yourself. Other people can blame you, too. It's your fault that your kid takes drugs because you weren't a good mother. I'm preparing myself right now not to feel guilty. I am not only saying, "I'm not my mother," I'm also saying, "I'm not this child, either. This child has a right and a need to be whoever she is."

I've also decided I'd better start focusing more on myself. I'm going to have these beautiful, sexy teenagers just as I'm going into menopause. The wrinkles are starting, and I have two daughters who are going to be gorgeous. I've got to work on feeling good about myself at every age.

One of the hardest things about being a mother is that every stage is different. You just master one, and you're hit by the next. In one stage you've got to give everything, and in the next you have to let go. You have to be flexible, and I'm not a particularly flexible person by nature. But I'm working on it!

I Was a Child Mother

KATHY LEONARDI

I was born and raised in an Italian area. I got married at nineteen. All the young girls I knew turned out the same way. If they didn't get married at nineteen, they did at twenty or twenty-one. I met Anthony in high school, and we were engaged at seventeen. I was scared, but it was the easiest route: a young man pursuing me who was very intent. He saw me every day, was always with me.

Perhaps I was just trying to get out of my home. Marriage was the easiest way. Other routes weren't sanctioned at all—my parents' values didn't include education for women. Since you were getting married, what did you need an education for? And I didn't have the emotional strength or enough experience to break away on my own.

I remember my wedding day. When I got to that hour, I told my father, "Dad, this is not my thing. I know it. There's something wrong." I was having doubts and questions before the wedding day, but I couldn't decipher them.

My mother kept saying, "This is the way life is—marriage and family. It's wonderful." It was such a positive thing to her. Marriage was such a good thing to do that even the thought of not doing it frightened me. Everyone was saying, "Isn't it wonderful about

97

Kathy and Anthony!" If I hadn't gone through with it, I knew I would have been considered very, very wrong.

After we were married, we moved into my in-laws' house. My mother-in-law lived on the first floor in her apartment, my sister-in-law and her husband and child lived on the third floor. My friend from work lived with her husband and baby next door. After a few months of marriage, maybe three, they started asking, "Anything yet? Anything yet?" With my Italian background, the whole reason to be married was to have a child. Everyone else conceived within three or six months. I wanted to wait a year.

When I did get pregnant, I started having pain in my vaginal area. I don't know whether it was psychological or physical. My doctor wanted me to stop working, but I didn't. I thought he was off his rocker, and I didn't tell anyone what he'd said. After six months, Anthony found out that the doctor wanted me to quit, and I had to stop.

All of a sudden I felt old. I mean, I felt totally old. Staying home and lying down all the time depressed me. It wasn't at all what I thought having a child would be like. The only thing I could think about was what crib and carriage I'd buy for the baby. I didn't think about what was going to happen to me.

I did start reading Dr. Spock and thinking about how I was going to bring up this child. I thought about what path, what conditioning I wanted to give the child. My ideas were there, but they weren't very sophisticated. I knew I didn't want to be rigid. I wanted the child to have some freedom. It was confusing because my own identity was not at all completed. I knew there were different views that I'd never had a chance to learn about.

When Thomas was born, I was thrilled. I remember saying, "I'm a mother now," almost in a joking sort of way. "One minute you're not a mother. The next minute you are." It's a miracle. When I first saw him, when I knew this child came from me, had been within me . . . it was the most . . . I can't explain it. It was the most *wonderful* feeling. He gave me some kind of a belief in God. At the same time, it was the most frightening feeling. It's like here you are with a responsibility to develop this child. It was serious, very serious.

In my life, everything had to be perfect. Anthony and my parents were very anxiety-prone. Everything had to be just right. That's why I read directions over and over again. I was really conscientious because I was so afraid that I'd do something wrong. I had to be perfect, and so did my baby.

I became a supermom. I had nothing else to do. What I loved best was feeding him. If he woke at one in the morning, I used to stay up until two or three, just holding him and rocking him, looking at his tiny fingers and feet until he went to sleep. A baby's body is so beautiful! But there was always this other side of me saying, "Oh, you're going to spoil him!"

The experience that ended my whole feeling of being a good mother occurred when he was about two months old. He woke up in the middle of the night and started crying and crying. It wasn't feeding time. It was too early. There was something wrong. I walked him, but whenever I put him down, he'd scream. I woke Anthony. He walked him, but the baby would scream if he put him down. I thought perhaps he was spoiled and just wanted to be held. I had rocked him too much. He cried all night.

At about six o'clock he finally stopped, and Anthony and I fell almost unconscious. Well, the baby started to cry, and we didn't hear him. We awoke to a room full of people—my mother and all of Anthony's relatives. We were on the first floor, and they broke a window. At first I thought it was a dream, but then I was furious. I said, "What are you, nuts?" Imagine lying in bed and waking up to a room full of people!

They were yelling, "The baby! Oh! Oh! Oh!" Their carrying-on was very dramatic. I thought it was a fire. "He's crying. You didn't hear him! We thought you were dead! That someone had come in and killed you, and the baby was left!" When we explained what had happened, they said, "Why didn't you call us if you were having such a problem? We would have walked him for you!" It was as if I was an awful mother: "You didn't even hear your own baby!"

It turned out that he had an ear infection, and this pushed the perfect-mom button in me. I became very nervous about this affecting his development. Before, I had been loose with him—watching him develop and letting him do his own thing. The infection triggered a lot of overprotectiveness in me. Every time I'd go out, I would wrap him and wrap him. Then I'd pass my mother-in-law on the way to the front door. She would check the baby. Then my sister-in-law and my own mother, if she was visiting. They were always there, looking over what I was doing with the baby.

As he grew older, I became more and more trapped. My relatives were always telling me, "You should do this. You should do that. You don't give him enough discipline. He's too noisy. You let him into everything. He destroys everything he touches." If I felt he wanted to touch the table for a reason, whatever it might be, and as long as he didn't hurt anything, I respected that. I felt the freedom to explore just had to be there. But they would be at him, "Take your hands off that table!" I would tell them, "You can talk to me like that, but don't you talk to my kid that way! Don't you dare yell at him! That's my role." I didn't want anyone to discipline him except me and Anthony.

When we were alone, we always had fun. I just loved doing things with this kid. I'd read to him and sing to him. I used to take him all over the city. We'd ride the trains to the parks and beaches. I really enjoyed being a mother at that time because I knew everything I was doing was developing him as a person.

Anthony was happy that he had a son, but at the same time he was threatened, because the kid was bright and outgoing. In the old Italian way, Anthony thought he was doing his job as a father as long as he brought the money home. That and being the disciplinarian—and his sense of discipline was, "Do what I say right now!" He was very rigid. He couldn't let loose and have fun with the kid. There was no laughing with him or playing with him. He wasn't like a father who rolled on the floor. Underneath, he was a very caring, gentle person, but he couldn't portray that. He wasn't allowed to.

When Thomas was about three, I wanted to have another child. I was so obsessed with this kid and knew I was overprotecting him. He was the *only* enjoyment I had in my life. I also felt that he needed companionship. Another child would bring out another side of Thomas. He would also have a family for the future.

I didn't have any fears about having another child. I felt I had learned a lot about myself and wouldn't repeat the things I had done wrong. I felt very proud of Thomas's development, even though he was always getting yelled at by my in-laws. I told him, "Use your own head. You'll be able to tell what's right and wrong from your feelings inside. You've got sense. If you're not sure, you can always ask someone."

When I became pregnant with Patrick, Thomas was almost four. After the baby was born, my feelings toward Thomas must have changed. I had always been with him, meeting his every demand, but now I couldn't. The exhaustion! That whole spring I was just exhausted from getting up during the night for Patrick. When summer came, I decided Thomas should go to day camp. I had to keep him busy and give him some space because he didn't have it where we lived. He was an active child, but he wasn't allowed to ride his bike. He used to get yelled at by my mother-in-law if he brought kids in the house to play. He couldn't play ball in the alley.

It was a very down period for me because I found out that Anthony was having affairs. I was depressed. I've always felt this was a deficiency for Patrick because I didn't give him the love and caring that I had given to Thomas. I was half dead. What Anthony was doing destroyed part of me. It just didn't make any sense.

I wanted to leave at that point. I said to myself, "This guy's off the fucking wall. Here I am with two kids in this lousy environment, and he's going out looking for someone. I'm the one who needs love and understanding." He kept saying it was just sex he was looking for. Half the time I was too pooped to have sex. All day my mother-in-law would be knocking on the door. "Oh, you're going to the store? Get me some milk. Oh, you go to the bank? Pay my bills." I also had to mother two kids and take care of the house and cook. By the time Anthony came home, there was nothing left to give. I was drained.

I kept saying we needed therapy or marriage counseling. At first he said he wouldn't go, but I convinced him. The nights when we had our counseling, my mother would have to come over at eight o'clock. Our appointment was at nine. By the time we got my mother home, it would be eleven, and she had to go to work the next day. It used to get me so angry that his parents, who lived right in the house, wouldn't watch the kids. They would say Thomas was so bad they didn't want to watch him. That's the label the kid got.

The marriage counseling straightened out a lot. The answer was to get out of that house, away from his family, something known without talking to a marriage counselor! I kept saying to Anthony, "No matter what, no matter where, we will get our own apartment.

We will do it." I used to tell him, "I don't care if it's a shack in a bad neighborhood. It would be better than this. I would rather have that kind of life where I would fear I would be killed than this, where I feel I'm being slowly tortured by these women." He couldn't see it. His attachment to his family was so great.

We would look at houses and apartments, but Anthony always came up with a reason against them. The place was too small or too large. It was in the wrong neighborhood. It was too close to the neighbors. It was too expensive, or he just didn't like it.

Money was a problem at the time. I think he was making eighty-nine dollars a week as a clerk. What bothered me was he didn't seem to want to better himself. He had opportunities. My uncle was in contracting and wanted to train him as a civil engineer. No interest. He met the man who was head of the computer system for Woolworth's, computerizing the whole inventory. He wanted to train Anthony. "Go there after work and learn," I used to tell him. "So you sacrifice six months. It's not going to be like that all the time." He didn't do that, either.

Finally, he took a test for the city and passed it. The day he was supposed to go for a job as a tow truck driver, he wouldn't go. I was wiped out! He was afraid of the people whose cars he towed coming after him and getting mad at him. I couldn't believe it. I went bananas. I walked out. I left him with the two kids.

I said, "You can take care of them. Where are you going to make money? You take care of the two kids. Get your mommy and your sister to help you. I'm leaving." I didn't know where I was going, but I wound up staying in church until about seven or eight that night. Then I went home again.

Every opportunity that knocked at his door, he closed the door to. So there was never any money. I'd have to take the kids to eat at my mother's three days a week. We were living in poverty. There was no way I was going to get out of there! I felt like I was in prison.

Finally, I got a job at the pharmacy just a block away, two nights a week, from six to ten. My mother would come straight from work to my house. I would have dinner ready. She would feed the kids and put them to sleep. When I got back, I'd take her home. I was very grateful for her help. At the same time, I wished that she would be strong enough to help me to leave. But she was against it.

When Patrick grew older, it was like an instant replay of what my relatives had done to Thomas. Sometimes I had thought there *was* something wrong with him. When negatives are all you hear, it's easy to start believing. But they did the same thing to Patrick. He'd ride his bike. They'd yell, "You're making too much noise!" He'd run in the house, drop his coat, and yell, "Ma! Hi! I'm home." They'd yell, "Too much noise!" Never, "Hello, how are you?"

I found myself getting very withdrawn. I didn't want to go out because then I knew I'd have to come back into that house again. It was better to just stay there. All I could do in the morning was get the kids dressed. I didn't even feed them their breakfast. My anger for being a mother was tremendous. I had all the responsibility, not only for the house, but when they were sick, or when they needed something for school. When I would reach out for pleasure of any kind, there wasn't anything there. I was thinking of suicide. I saw myself as such a bad mother that I felt it would be better for the children to be without me.

But somewhere deep inside, I knew I had to develop myself if ever I was to get out. I had started school that summer. I knew somewhere that I was going to get positive sanction for myself. I'd leave the house and kids very, very depressed. When I'd come home, I could deal better with the kids. I was also still working three nights a week at the pharmacy.

Then I started realizing, "What the fuck do I need this guy for? For nothing I needed him." He was doing nothing for me, and was fooling around again with another woman. I wanted to get out. It wasn't only for myself, but it was for the kids. They weren't getting anything, either. The kids were fighting; they'd say, "Well, that's the way you and Daddy fight!"

I had started to go to therapy on my sister's recommendation. Anthony wouldn't go, but my sister kept saying, "You can't wait for him. You have to go yourself." Patrick was about four and a half and Thomas nine when I got the gumption to leave. I explained to the kids that their father and I didn't love each other anymore, but we still loved them very much. Since we didn't love each other, it wasn't good to go on living together. There was an apartment available on my parents' block, and I took it.

I was fearful. I'd never lived on my own before. I was going to school at night and working at night as well. It would have been impossible without my parents' help. However, they were shocked that Anthony and I had broken up. We had seemed the ideal couple. They were afraid I was doing the wrong thing. My mother was so upset, she had a heart attack after two months. What held me together during this period was the children, being their mother. Seeing the children continue to develop and being able to adapt to a new situation—I had felt they couldn't do it, and they did—this gave me strength.

It was hard on me when they went to visit Anthony on the weekends. It is still very hard for me. It is a physical feeling within, like a deep sorrow that they are leaving me and going to him. When they come home, I'm so happy to see them again, but they're sad because they've just left their father. Patrick has the hardest time. Leaving me, then leaving his father, leaving me, then his father. Thomas is able to cope with it a little better because he is older.

I've been separated six years now. I would do it over again. I would have the children again, but I never would have gotten married so early. I was much too young. I was too close to them. The children were the only positives in my life, and that's not healthy for the child or the mother.

My kids are not that loving or warm with me. They have to act like babies in order to let me touch them. Thomas is almost impossible—there's no touching or hugging or showing affection. I think they're holding onto their own feelings because of what's happened between me and Anthony: They're afraid if they show they love me they might get hurt. After the separation Patrick had problems with his speech, and Thomas was blinking and had a lot of facial twitches. I sent the kids to therapy for a year and a half, though Anthony was totally against it, and it helped.

But all in all, I feel very proud of both of my kids. Thomas is fifteen, in a school for gifted children. He is very responsible. He's at an egotistical state right now, but I'm hoping he'll come out of it and become more giving. I'm especially pleased with his sense of life, his enthusiasm for people. That's a real pleasure.

Patrick, at ten, is coming along well. He was five when the separation occurred, and he experienced the bulk of our anger. He's got this label in his head that he's retarded or something because he went to speech therapy and had psychotherapy. He thinks there is something wrong with him. Here in this neighbor-

hood, nobody goes to therapy. I'm trying hard to give him a positive image of himself. I compliment him on how he looks, on his
homework. I try to encourage his special abilities. He has a fantasy
head, he'll go off into daydreams. I'm trying to steer him into art
or writing.

This week the nun yelled at him for not going to church. I told
him, "Why didn't you tell her you were at your father's, and he
couldn't take you?" He said, "Oh, no! They don't know you're
separated." I said, "Patrick, the reality is that we are. You can't tell
them that you have this happy family with a mommy and daddy, the
way they picture it. It's time your teachers should know, and be
more understanding."

As for myself, there are different choices I can make. I was
supposed to graduate in January, but I dropped a course, which was
too much with the house, the kids, and a job. At one time I saw
myself graduating and becoming a CPA. But what's the rush? I'm
thirty-six. If I start when I'm older, I can still have a good, long
career. I don't have too many more years to be with the children.
In the last five years, I've spent so much time on me, that between
the separation, school, work, and starting to date again, I've had
very little time for them.

I took a new apartment last month. This apartment is very important to me, and I want to give the kids this space where they can
be who they are. It's the first time in my life that I don't have
anybody looking over my shoulder telling me what to do.

I want to take time out. I want to just enjoy the quiet pleasures
of life. This apartment has a porch. I love sitting and relaxing on
it. I've always loved plants. I want to fill the porch with plants. If
it takes me a while to decide about my career, that's okay. For what
am I killing myself?

Right now I want to be here for the kids.

My Mother Never Sat Down

MAGGIE PHALAN

At the moment I'm angry with my mother, first for dying so suddenly and second for seemingly bringing it on herself. My mother had opted to take care of my grandmother at home, and I think that is what killed her. She worked herself to death.

Grandma was physically fine when she first came to live with my parents. She had started developing some memory problems, but the doctor's attitude was, "What do you expect? This is a little old lady." (He never really evaluated her. He patted her on the head and took her blood pressure. "She's fine. She's fine.") Then her arthritis became more severe, and she stopped coming downstairs. She became very withdrawn. It was a fairly rapid slide. When she had become really senile, the doctor said, "Now it is time to put her in a nursing home."

My mother refused. She said, "I couldn't live with myself if I did something like that." In the old country, you just didn't put your parent away. Family problems were *family* problems. And she'd say, "Besides, even if Grandma is in a good nursing home, I'd have to run up there and feed her all her meals. If I have her at home, it's easier."

My mother demonstrated that she cared by fussing over you, by doing things to you or to help you. Michael was the first grandchild, and she really enjoyed him. This was before Dad or Grandma got sick, and she had time to come up and help me. The work involved! It made me tired to look at her. There was a right way and a wrong way to bathe and dress a baby. First she would take warm oil and rub his skin. She'd do this while she was exercising his joints. He must have been a week old when she got him on the changing table, taking his arms and lifting them up and down, going, "One, two, one, two" and then the legs, "Three, four, three, four." The interesting thing is that a lot of the stuff she did is now being done in formalized programs. Look at the baby exercise classes.

Then you know how babies have their toes in? She'd massage Michael's ankles and toes, and then she'd twist them out this way and that way, and turn his knees out, so that he wasn't bowlegged. She'd rotate the hip one way and then the other, and then she'd put both legs out and put on sixteen diapers to keep the legs straight, and then flip him over on his stomach and rub his spine, rotate his shoulders, and turn his head from side to side as if he were crawling. That is what they do with brain-damaged kids. It's called patterning, where a whole team comes in and puts a child through the motions of crawling.

I'd laugh at her. I'd say, "Mom, I'm just going to let him grow the way God intended." But Michael seemed to love it.

She was wonderful with my children. She thought kids were kids and were supposed to have fun. She was always very vital and full of enthusiasm. I remember once when they had "Grandparents Day" at the elementary school. Michael was in the first grade. Since she lived two hours away, I didn't bother to tell her about it. But she found out about it herself. She got the directions and the time. Well, Michael came running home from school, and he was smiling from ear to ear. She'd already surprised him, and she was going to surprise me, too. She was hiding behind the screen door. She was always doing silly things like that.

Grandma was a sweet old lady, and good company for my mother. However, when she came to live in our house, she was totally removed from her roots. She was an immigrant from Russia and had never learned much English. She didn't read or write.

If we'd still been in the Ukrainian neighborhood where I grew up, she might have fared better. Everybody knew each other there. They all walked to the same grocery store and the same butcher. They all belonged to the same Catholic church. All the old ladies got together and had coffee down on the sidewalk where they kept a good eye on the kids. You had forty friends and neighbors up and down the street. You had relatives around the corner, upstairs and downstairs, so that if you wanted to go to the store, there was an abundance of people who could stop by to watch the baby or sit with an older person.

Grandma was isolated in a contemporary split-level house with no neighbors that she could relate to. I think this hastened her senility. There was nothing to stimulate her, and she had no place to go. My mother would drive her to her Ukrainian church, but it was a good half hour away.

Soon after my father died, this turkey of a doctor put my grandmother in the hospital for phlebitis, which he had diagnosed by phone. He never even examined her. He ordered bed rest for six days, and not surprisingly, after a week, when they tried to get her back up on her feet, she couldn't walk. The doctor then said to my mother, "Well, now you have a reason to put her in a nursing home." My mother said, "I told you, doctor, I never intend to do that." He said, "Well, now you have no choice." My mother said, "Like hell I don't."

She got a hospital bed for the house. She knew that caring for a sick person was something she could do well. My grandmother just slid right in and took Dad's place. I think taking care of Grandma buffered her from thinking about other things. It was her safety place where she hid and never dealt with Dad's death. She concentrated one thousand percent on caring for my grandmother.

If you think of a newborn baby and how much care it needs, well, this was twenty times worse. Besides feeding her, bathing her, fixing her hair, giving her medicine, Mom had to lift her out of bed and hitch her across the floor to the bathroom several times a day.

Getting down there to visit was hard for me. It was a two-hour trip; and, since our divorce, I couldn't just drop the kids with their father. But I went as often as I could. I would say, "Go out. You need some relief. Go shopping." When I would arrive, Mom would run out for an hour or two, then run right back. I am a nurse, but she was the only one who could take care of Grandma the right way.

It made me feel angry that she didn't get more help. She was near a school of nursing. So what if you have to pay seventy dollars a day so you can get away once in a while? Her answer was, "By the time I get back, there would be two days' work to do. And the house would be a mess, and I wouldn't want anyone to see it, and I've got valuables I don't want anyone to steal." Her house was spotless, and there weren't any valuables around. She had squirreled everything away.

My mother didn't have much money, but what she did have she was always saving so that my twin sister, Mary, and I wouldn't have to do for her what she was doing for her mother. She'd say, "Hope I drop dead. Then put me in a hole. I don't want to be this kind of burden." I would say to her, "If you find that this is so unfair, why are you allowing it to happen? Are you saying to all these grandchildren, and me and Mary, the whole bunch of you don't matter as much as this senile old lady?" I said, "Mom, it's unfair." She said, "Fair has nothing to do with it. I could not live with myself, otherwise. This is the only way I can deal with it, so please drop the subject." So I stopped talking about it.

With her mother an invalid, Mother never sat down. She used to say, "You'll see, I will never lift a spoon or a finger once Grandma is gone." My mother dropped dead at the age of sixty-two. When she dropped dead, knowing her, she could have been having chest pains and not done anything about them. She just didn't have time to deal with things like that. She was immune.

Grandma is now in a nursing home, which I find difficult to accept, since I think Mom literally killed herself to keep this shell of an old woman out of one. Now that is where she is, and we don't have Mom.

I have a cousin who is a nun. At the funeral she said, "Maggie, try not to be angry. Think how much you care about your mother. That is exactly what your mother was doing for her mother. If you can understand how strongly you feel now, that is how strongly she felt about her mother."

Goodbye

LISA McMULLIN

It has been nine months since Nicholas had the accident in the swimming pool and died five days later. He was twenty-one months old, and a child who absolutely lived to the hilt in his brief time. He was the kind of child who, when he'd fall, would get right back up. He was bitten by dogs three times. One time a dog got his teeth on two sides of his cheeks, but it didn't faze Nicholas. He never had a fear of dogs.

He was always on the track of Birch and Katherine, which I guess is the third-child syndrome. He especially loved to roughhouse with Birch. They loved to play chase games all through the house. He, much more than the other pregnancies, was the wild man inside of me.

On the other hand, he loved books. He climbed out of the crib earlier than the others had and would toddle into our room in the morning. I would say, "Nicholas, go get some books." He'd come back with an armful and sit happily on our bed for a long time. Kim always said maybe he was the most intellectual of our children.

He also *loved* music, absolutely loved it. Music boxes fascinated him, and as a baby he would point to our collection until I got one down. We had a china music box that he especially liked, and

111

starting from the time he could walk, I could trust him to carry it pressed against his ear. He was always dancing.

He was very appealing looking, with a broad face, straight blond hair, and big oval eyes like Kim's. He had a wonderful way of dealing with the world, enthusiastic, friendly, and trusting. He was just a very loving little person.

When he died, I felt there was never going to be pure golden joy again. There was no escaping the sadness. I felt I could never be unqualifiedly happy, or experience one of those rushes of "Isn't life wonderful?" I've changed in these nine months. I don't feel that way now. My sadness is interspersed with other feelings. I think of grief as waves of sorrow. The waves don't stop coming. It's just that they get farther apart.

There are events that unleash my sadness. A child's birthday party is a predictable one. Something very unexpected can also trigger the sadness. I was sitting at the dentist the other day having my teeth cleaned. I was talking to the nurse without a second thought. Then she put the suctioning device in my mouth, and I suddenly remembered Nicholas lying unconscious with a similar tube in his mouth. I got very teary. I don't think that will happen the second time I go back to have my teeth cleaned. It won't be so painful. By the third or fourth time I may not feel a thing.

My sister, Katie, said to me, "You must feel like smashing plates." That isn't my style. My reaction would be: I'll still have to clean them up, plus I won't have any plates left. I still feel angry, I guess, but it's somehow subtler. When I see parents driving with small children sitting unprotected in the front seat, that makes me sad and angry. I want to roll down the window and yell, "Put that child in a seat belt! Let me tell you, I can tell you from experience, if you lose that child out of sheer carelessness, you are going to feel *awful!*"

Lots of people have misconstrued ideas about how I feel. They think I don't want to be reminded of Nicholas. Especially in the beginning, he was my only thought. I wanted to talk about him. I do not understand the mentality of never mentioning the child's name, or immediately removing all the possessions. I cling to some memories and to some objects. I know that there are some things, odd little things, I do that are definitely holding on to Nicholas, or not letting go of him. I still have a card from Children's Hospital in my wallet with his name on it. Why should I have that? There is no reason to. I know that there will be a time when I will say, "Okay, I don't need this."

It took me a while to put Nicholas's clothes away, and I suppose there were people who thought that was bizarre. Katie came over on his birthday, which was two months after he died. I said, "I'm ready to do it." And that is when we did it, that morning. We took his clothes upstairs to the storage room and put them into the drawers. When you are ready, you are ready.

A few weeks ago I couldn't remember what Nicholas had been buried in. That really bothered me. I thought, I am losing my memory of him. Even remembering the funeral and his death brings back Nicholas.

I am letting go, though. I think that the process of living through your grief is being able to say, "I accept this person as being gone." And those little things which we hold on to are signals. When I cry, I no longer totally break down. Five minutes later I can be laughing and talking about something very mundane and be fine. The teariness is even kind of nice; it's nice to know that I am still feeling. It is not unpleasant. I don't want *not* to feel.

We were open with our other children. When it was clear that Nicholas was close to dying, we told Katherine and Birch. Their reactions were very different. Birch was just five. We expected him to ask a lot of questions. We thought Katherine at three and a half would not really realize what was happening.

Birch completely denied what we were saying. He knelt down on the kitchen floor and turned away and started to play with his trucks. He still doesn't talk about Nicholas too much. If I say, "I'm feeling sad about Nicholas today, and that is why I'm crying a little bit," he tries to change the subject. He will say something like, "Mommy, do you remember when we went to the circus and we sat in the first row, and the clown came over and shook my hand?"

Katherine immediately asked a lot of questions. "How does Nicholas eat? Can he come and have breakfast with us?" We said, "No, Katherine, he is not coming back for breakfast." She started to cry. Then she said, "There should have been a wall around the pool, so he couldn't fall in." She got very frightened. "What if I fall in?" Kim put his hand on her ankle and said, "We won't let it happen to you, Katherine." She went on, "If there was a wall, and it got a hole in it, and I got through . . ." Kim said, "See, I've still got your ankle. We *won't* let it happen to you." He held on to her for a long time.

Katherine has talked a lot about Nicholas since then. One of the things we've tried very hard not to do is to sanctify him. For instance, we talked about the biting stage he went through. It became almost amusing, even a little embarrassing: In front of visitors, Katherine would say, "It sure is lucky Nicholas isn't here biting!"

But there have been moments when Katherine's questions have been very, very hard. "Mommy, how did it happen? Why wasn't someone watching Nicholas? How could he have fallen into the pool?" All I can say is, "Oh, Katherine, I don't know. I just don't know."

Why weren't we watching Nicholas? That is the question I still back off from.

Kim was in the kitchen, and I was busy being sociable. At some point I looked around to find my four kids. Katherine and Birch were facing me. Christopher, who was only three weeks old, was asleep in his basket. I looked over my shoulder for Nicholas and saw him running toward the house. I turned my back on the pool, sure that he was in the kitchen by then, and if not, what could happen with six adults on duty?

Garth, one of the friends present, has been very firm in saying his attitude toward this is if there are children around, whether they are yours or not, you take responsibility for them at a gathering. Garth felt very responsible for Nicholas's death. Even Kim's brother felt guilty. He is a doctor, and was supposed to come up to the farm for the weekend, but didn't. He thinks if he had been there, maybe it wouldn't have happened.

These friends have been very helpful, but they have not finally changed my feelings about responsibility. Ultimately it was ours, Kim's and mine. We were his parents, and he was our responsibility. You watch little children around the water, and we didn't. That ultimate sense of responsibility will *never ever* go away.

As much as my upbringing makes me prone to guilt, my attitude has been that a surfeit of it is really destructive. I did go through a very difficult period right after Christmas of beating myself, whipping myself. That was something I told myself I wouldn't do. I haven't had one of those attacks in a while. But if I allowed myself, I would work myself into a real orgy of guilt.

I also worry about being too overprotective as a mother. I used to think my kids were totally invulnerable. Certainly that notion has been shaken for me, and for them. They know another child can die. I have read that when tragedies like this happen, parents can become too overprotective, so that a child will do things almost too safely.

When we were in Maine shortly after Nicholas died, we were climbing a mountain. There was one place where the land dropped off very steeply near a lot of bush. I had heard about a child getting lost there for several hours. Our children were running around, not doing anything unusual or particularly dangerous. But it was almost unbearable for me—to the point where I felt physically ill. I was sweating. My hands were trembling, and I felt slightly breathless. It is going to be very hard, I suspect, to know when I have a legitimate concern about danger, and when I am overreacting.

The horror is that it is very unnatural for a child to die before you do. A young child is so utterly dependent.

I did hold Nicholas one night in the hospital. It was nice to hold him, and I had felt that I would just want to go on holding him forever. But one of the surprises was that he felt so different. When you cradle a sleeping child in your arms, there is a certain form to their bodies. Nicholas didn't feel that way, and I can remember after a while feeling that it was tiring. There came a point when I was ready to stop holding him.

I had already said goodbye to him. We took him off the respirator because the doctors had explained to me, and this is my real acceptance of it, that he was brain dead. He was getting intravenous fluid and food, and the respirator was bringing in oxygen. Finally, on the sixth day, I was ready to say, "Okay." I felt that keeping him going, hooked up to all those machines, was only for our benefit.

We had an open casket at home. I know some people thought that was kind of morbid, but we felt it was the right thing to do for the sake of our children, and those present at the accident, and for our own sake. It was important to be clear, to allow Nicholas's death to be as real as possible, as opposed to mysterious or abstract.

The children's reactions were totally natural. Every child went in and touched Nicholas and said, "Goodbye."

I still feel that we are extremely fortunate, extremely fortunate. Kim said it so well. He said, "People talk about this as being so extraordinary. But death isn't extraordinary. What is extraordinary is the life that has been given us. That is the miracle, that life goes on."

I Earn My Vacation

PAT PILGER

There are some women who are meant to be mothers, who enjoy it, and I think I'm one of them. Being a mother is what you make it. I was always going to have twelve children. My mother looks at me now and says, "You're bound and determined to do that, aren't you?" Well, I'm not even close.

Fred has been saying since Andrew, our seven-year-old, was born, "No more children! I have enough!" Fred has three by his first marriage, but only one of them, Cynthia, lives with us permanently. So when I accidentally got pregnant with Patrick, I was a little afraid to tell Fred. He was good about it, though. His answer was, "Oh, what the hell! What's one more?" But that was absolutely it. No more kids! We both agreed.

Then I changed my mind. I said, "I really want to have *one* more baby, Fred, just *one* more." Fred was mad. He said, "Then go out and buy one!" Little did he know that I would find a way. That's when I talked him into becoming a foster parent. From the very beginning Fred said, "We are *not* keeping any of these children, right?" and I said, "Right, we're absolutely not." That was just a way to have a baby in the house, and it was a nice way. My friends would say, "Why are you doing it?" and I would say, "It's purely

117

selfish. I haven't reached the point where I'm content not to have a baby around. I do it for me."

Becoming a foster parent is quite involved. Social Services checks into your background, your finances, your family's medical history. They even check your marriage license. They do a home study, and then they meet with each parent separately. I said to Fred, "Don't you dare say anything that would make this impossible for me to do! You better be nice and charming." Of course, he snowed them. They thought he was wonderful.

Fred was not at all sure about being a foster parent at first. As a matter of fact, we hadn't finished our orientation when they called me in. They had a baby for us to take. I was so excited I said yes immediately. Fred came home and said, "No way. I'm not ready. We haven't even finished our training." I had to call them the next morning and say, "I hope you haven't got that baby in your office yet, because we can't take it." They knew how reluctant Fred was.

The first baby we got was a premature boy. He was with us for four weeks. Then he was freed for adoption and went to his new home. That was very nice. It's hard to explain. I knew he was going to somebody who had been waiting eons and eons to have a baby, and I knew this kid was going to have everything in the world that he could possibly want. I thought it was just great.

The next little boy we got was six weeks old. He was retarded. He had been sick, and his mother, who had two other little ones at home, and her own problems, just couldn't handle him at that time. He stayed for about six months. From the very beginning, I knew he would go back home, and that was okay. It was like an extended baby-sitting job. Then we got Neil, who was almost two. He had been abused. Neil was a true test of whether we really wanted to be foster parents or not. That's when I figured out whether I was really being selfish, or whether I was doing it for the kid. Neil was a handful. He was big for his age. He did not talk, and he also had motor problems.

Our kids really wanted to like Neil. They would go over to hug him, and Neil would grab a handful of hair and literally pull it out. He was also a biter. Everybody else in the family would have liked me to say we couldn't handle him, but my feeling was that he had already been bounced around enough.

He wasn't a cute child, but somewhere there was something

likable about him. A social work student interviewed my seven-year-old for a paper on the effects of foster children on natural children. When she asked Andrew, "Who was your favorite of all the babies you've had?" Andrew said, "Neil." "Why?" "Because he had the most problems." I think that's how I felt.

He was here for five months. The pediatricians felt Neil would improve when he came to a so-called normal home. There was some improvement, but not a whole lot. I had to fight and yell to get some help for this kid. Eventually he did get some therapy. Now he is back with his mother.

Supposedly, I was only going to care for infants. But then I got a phone call from Social Services. They were desperate. Another foster mother they were counting on had to go away for a few days. Could I possibly take a nine-year-old girl? I said, "I really don't have room for a nine-year-old, but I'll take her on an emergency basis."

Lois had a seizure disorder, her younger brother had rickets, and the two-year-old, who had fallen out of a window but survived, suffered from fetal alcohol syndrome. The parents were receiving counseling and alcoholic treatment.

Well, Lois came in April and stayed until October. She was a real sweetheart, a real good little kid.

About a week ago, I got a phone call. There was this little voice. "Hi, Pat! I miss you! Can I come over and play?" I spoke to her mom, and it was okay. Lois lives close to us, and I said, "Fine, I'll send Cynthia and the boys over." They went traipsing down to pick her up. She came over and spent the afternoon. We all had pizza. It was nice to see her again.

We then got a newly born black boy. It was the day before Father's Day, and I said to Fred, "Gee, I didn't know what else to get you for Father's Day, so look what I got!" I thought he was going to die because he didn't know another was coming. He had no name other than "Baby Boy Smith," so we called him Adam.

Adam weighed four pounds and six ounces and was only seventeen inches long when he came. He was born addicted to heroin, so he was going through withdrawal. I felt an instant bond with him. Almost right away I started thinking, wouldn't it be nice if we could keep him, but I didn't say anything. He had not been freed for adoption. His mother had disappeared without signing a release. I was never really convinced that she wouldn't come out of the woodwork.

He was almost six months old before the withdrawal symptoms disappeared. He was a very irritable baby, but not in the usual whiny way. Ordinarily you can touch a baby while it's sleeping, and it usually will stay quiet. Well, a touch would send Adam into spasms, real tremors. He also had a runny nose all the time, and sneezed. They say withdrawal is very painful, but my pediatrician said Adam's wasn't nearly as bad as it could have been. Within the first two weeks, I could see an improvement.

Adam was not freed for adoption until after his first birthday. When they called me and said he had been released, I asked Fred, "Okay, now what are you going to do? If we don't adopt him, he'll probably just be in foster care forever." He was a little old for adoption at that point. What they do with older children is photo-list them in the "Blue Book." There is a small photo and a blurb about each adoptable child. It has older kids, too, handicapped ones, everything. If you see a picture you are interested in, you can call up and make an appointment.

I said to Fred, "How could you take Adam out of our house, which is a total loony bin, and put him in a quiet family where he would be an only child? I mean he would suffer a nervous break-down. They wouldn't know what was wrong with him." So Fred said, "Oh, go sign the papers!" Adam just happened. He just came into our lives, and there he stays.

We are still in the process of adopting him. I just talked to our case worker yesterday, and we've run into a few snags. Two of my references don't approve of what we're doing. This is a *friend,* and her mother, whom I have known all of my life.

They both feel Adam should be in a black family. My girlfriend thinks that it will be hard on Patrick and Andrew when Adam goes to school. There will be name-calling, and the kids won't be able to deal with it. I am sure he will get a lot of flak, but my hope is that by the time that might happen, whatever we've taught our kids in this house will have been implanted so strongly that they will be big enough to ignore those who choose to be nasty, and be able to support Adam.

Our adoption worker had brought up all the negative things to make sure that we had seriously thought about what we were doing.

"What are you going to do when Adam's sixteen, and the guy next door says, 'Keep that nigger away from my kid!' What are you going to say?" and, "Do you have any black friends?" and "How are you going to deal with his black heritage?" "Ten or fifteen years from now, what's he going to do about dating, what's he going to do about his friends?"

My answer is that fifteen years ago the situation with black and white was very different than it is now, and fifteen years from now, who knows what it's going to be? I can't live my life based on what I'm going to do fifteen years from now. I am a firm believer in taking each day as it comes. I'm not planning for next year. I'll take one day at a time, and eventually fifteen years will have passed, and however I've dealt with it will just have to be the way it is.

My girlfriend's mother thinks that we haven't thought it through financially. She thinks Adam's going to be a burden. Frankly, Andrew, Patrick, and Cynthia are going to be a financial burden when it comes time for them to be in school. In fact, I don't know where I'm getting the tuition to pay for Cynthia to go to Catholic high school next year. But I don't see that that's a criterion for not keeping a kid. I'm sorry. Somehow there'll be scholarships. They'll work. They'll help themselves. They'll get through school. We will make do. Yes, I realize how much it costs to raise a kid, but that's not a reason for not doing it.

Adam's medical history has also come up. It's questionable. We don't know who his father is, and his mother has disappeared. My answer to that was, "Well, I've got diabetes on both sides of my family, and Fred's mother is diabetic, so somewhere along the line, Patrick and Andrew might have a good chance of having a crummy medical history, too." That wasn't going to stop me from having kids, either.

I guess in the last five years I've gotten to the point where I don't care anymore what other people think. I am going to do what's right for me. All my life I had to listen to my parents say, "Well, you should do this, and you should do that." It was the same with my brothers and sisters who were all a lot older than I, telling me how things should be.

If they had all had their way, I wouldn't have married Fred. My brother called me the night before I got married and said, "How can you marry a bus driver?" I said, "Listen, he's had the same job for ten years, have you?" My brother practically dropped in his tracks because at that point he was on about his tenth job in that same amount of time. I said, "What's wrong with a bus driver? People have to ride buses." I had been dating a fellow at the time who was single, had money in the bank, owned a house and all that. "What about him?" my brother wanted to know. I said, "There is only one problem. I don't love that guy."

It took my mother a long time to accept Fred, and it doesn't surprise me that she has also been very unaccepting about Adam. The first day she saw him, she said, "Oh well, he doesn't look black." That was her very first comment! He did have much lighter skin and straight hair then. She said, "He looks like he could be Indian." When he was about three months old, she said, "Well, when does he start to get characteristics?" That's how she put it. I said, "You mean, when does he get frizzy hair and a flat nose?" She said, "Patricia!" I said, "Well, Mother, that's what you're asking."

I guess he was about four and a half months old when she finally came around and carted him off in his little basket to visit a friend. That's when I knew she was hooked. He's eighteen months old now, however, and she's still asking, "Have you heard anything? Haven't they found a nice home for Adam?" I keep saying to her, "Mother, they already found a nice home for Adam." She knows, but she doesn't want to know. I think she feels he will cause problems that I don't necessarily need to have. But my answer to that is, "My own children give me problems. I don't know what's to come. Life is full of surprises."

Now we have Elizabeth. She's our first baby girl, and I'm enjoying her a lot. When I heard she was coming, I called my neighbor who has two daughters and said, "Quick, get me a box of pink things because I don't have any." I enjoy playing dress-up with her. I've bought her a few things. Fred said, "Oh, this kid is going to cost me." I said, "Fred, I promise I'll be good." And I've tried.

When I picked her up, she weighed only five pounds, and she was three weeks old. She's much improved now, but she used to look like a little old lady, all eyes. Fred called her "my favorite Martian." She was born with hepatitis to a very young mother who did not know she was pregnant. Elizabeth's had several setbacks, a virus and an ear infection that were very difficult to clear up. So it's been a little slow going.

Now she is seven and a half pounds. She's doing all the things that she should be doing for her age. She's just small. She may have a liver problem, but there is no way of telling because a liver biopsy is too risky now. She may develop problems, and she may not. This makes her more difficult to place. She will probably be listed in the Blue Book.

The nights I work, Fred has to get up to feed her. She drives him crazy. He says, "I'm too old to do this and go to work." I said, "I do it on the nights I'm home, and I work all day." I haven't told him yet, but Social Services called me this morning to say she would be here at least another two months, which could stretch to three or four. But I walked in the other day, and Fred was sitting with her on his lap. He was stroking her head and singing to her. I said, "Excuse me. What are you doing?" "Well," he said, "her hair was knotted up." I said, "What hair?" He's such a softie.

The other day Cynthia asked, "Are we going to adopt Elizabeth?" Fred was on the stairs. I thought he was going to have a heart attack and fall down the rest of them. He said, "Cynthia, be quiet!" I said to her, "Do you want to share your room?"

My friends ask if I am not getting attached to her. I say, "No." I say, "She's very nice to have, but I really don't have any desire to keep her." She is going to turn into an adult female, and I already have one adult-type female child in the house. I don't want another. That could be because Cynthia and I have the problem of my being her stepmother. Or it may be the fact that she's thirteen. I don't know. But I do not want to go through this again.

Cynthia has two older brothers who, at different points of their lives, have lived here. They were never like Cynthia. They get mad. You yell at them. They're ticked off, and they make no bones about telling you. Ten minutes later, they're friendly again. Three months later Cynthia is still mad at me because I told her some outfit looked stupid. Girls are very nice, but only when they're babies.

I like Cynthia. Basically, we have a good relationship. People ask me, "How many kids do you have?" and I say, "Three—and we're adopting a fourth," or they ask, "How old are they?" I say, "My daughter is . . ." I never consciously say, "Well, she's my stepdaughter." Very few people know. In fact, they see us and they say, "She looks just like you, Pat." We laugh, just laugh. I don't consciously think of her as my stepdaughter, and yet there's a difference.

I try very hard to be fair with all the kids. When I had my first baby, all three of Fred's kids lived here. I stayed in the hospital a full four days. My friends said, "Why are you doing that? It's so expensive." I said, "Because this is the only four days in my life I'm going to have this child to myself and not have to be conscious of the fact that I have to be fair to other people." I've always made an effort to see that what one got, everybody got. But Cynthia will always tell you the boys get more. I say to her, "You're the only girl in this family, the only child to get her own room. You're the only one who doesn't wear hand-me-downs. How can you say they get more than you?" That's her biggest fear, that they're going to get more than she does.

She still thinks the sun rises and sets on her mother, but do you know that she has lived in my house since she was seven years old, and she's seen her mother only once in all that time? That makes me angry at times.

I also watch four other kids during the day. One little girl is here at six-forty in the morning. Her mother's a nurse. So my day starts real early. By eight-thirty at night I don't want anything more to do with kids. I say, "Go to bed, and leave me alone!" And there are times when I get discouraged because Fred's not here. He leaves for work at six-thirty in the morning four days a week and gets home at ten o'clock at night. On the fifth day he goes to work at ten in the morning and gets home at one A.M.

I know I do a lot. I went back to work at the hospital when Patrick was six weeks old. He was sleeping through the night by then. I worked nights twice per week. "How can you leave your baby?" my mother asked. "I'm leaving him with his father." She said, "You're what?" I said, "Well, Fred knows how to give a kid a bottle. I hand him the bottle and say, 'You're on, Fred.'" I say to her, "I'm trying to buy a house, and I have to have a paycheck in order to buy a house and get a mortgage, and this is just part of my life."

I do get out. I bowl on Mondays. I'm not going to just give up everything that I like to do because I like having kids around. I want

124

it all. I take them with me, Elizabeth, the nine-month-old I watch; Adam; another two-year-old I watch; and Patrick, my five-year-old. There is a nursery at the bowling alley, and they have a great time.

I think nothing of piling seven kids in the car when we go to the supermarket. I'm in the store and someone will ask, "Are all of those yours?" I say, "Well, no, not all of them. Only three of them." "Which three?" and I'll say, "Well, can you pick them out?" They, of course, never pick Adam, and I say, "Wrong, that one is mine!" I get lots of strange looks.

We get away. We do things. For spring vacation I'm taking the two little boys to Washington. I'm doling out the rest of the kids to my girlfriends. Then I'll watch their kids for a week when they want to go away. It works out real well. My kids are good. I can take them anywhere. We went to Disney World last winter, then drove seven hundred miles home in a snowstorm.

When I got out of that car at three o'clock in the morning, I said, "I'm never getting in the car with a child again, *ever, ever*." But then last summer we got back in the car to go to Canada. I said, "Fred, why are we doing this?" We went fishing. The high point of the trip was when Patrick caught a seagull. They're good kids. They really are. We can take them anywhere.

Fred and I finally did get smart, though. We take a vacation in the fall, a week with no children. Not for anything will I give up that vacation. One year there was some question whether we could afford to go. We had started to renovate the kitchen. It was all torn up. The costs were getting out of hand. I said to Fred, "I'm going. You want to stay home, you can stay home, but I'm going. I will do without this, this, and this." I did without a finished kitchen for a long time.

Some people say, "How can you do that? I could never leave *my* kids for a week." Well, I can leave them. I see my kids fifty-one weeks a year, seven days a week. I earn that week. And I go, and that's it. I really don't miss them. Oh, Fred does. About the fourth day he's going, "I wonder . . ." I say, "Fred, I don't want to hear it. I don't want to wonder. I just don't care," and I don't. I really don't. I know they are being well taken care of.

Oh, it is wonderful, truly wonderful. I do *nothing*.

I'll tell you, though, this year we almost didn't go. We dropped Patrick off the night before we left at one of my girlfriend's. But

125

we had to go back to leave something on their porch the next morning on our way to the airport. I got out of the car and looked up. There was this little face pressed on the window at six o'clock in the morning. This little hand started waving to me. I said, "Fred, I can't leave." He said, "Pat, we *are* leaving!" And we left.

We Learn by Example

MARY ROBERTSON

Right after Dad died, Mom started talking about buying another house. With Dad gone, she felt the farm and barn, orchards and fields had become too much of a chore to take care of. But I think it was mainly the loneliness. On Sunday, when I called, she told me she hadn't been able to sleep. That is often the case with older people. Well, she'd gotten up in the middle of the night and re-arranged all the living room furniture.

When Mom is at the stove, she has a certain line of vision through the dining room and into the living room. She's very much like I am. Once I find a comfortable arrangement for the furniture in the room, I don't want to move it. Also, I don't suppose she changed that room around for years and years, which meant that my father sat in the same chair, his chair, to watch TV all that time. That was his spot. And she was always conscious of him there. Every time she turned in that direction, she could catch a glimpse of him.

She found herself still watching for him because it was her habit to turn that way. To break herself of the habit, perhaps to take one more step to separate, she rearranged the room. When she did, of course, glancing that way she would see a totally different image. When she told me, it struck me. It's such a simple thing, yet I can't seem to get it out of my mind.

127

We all feel a loneliness without Dad. Even though I am now a woman in my mid-forties with a husband, a ten-year-old daughter, and two grown stepchildren, I hadn't realized how much I counted on knowing he was always there. I can't turn to him anymore, and because Daddy is gone, a certain stability is missing. A part of my life is over. I am grateful, though, that I still have my mother. No matter how old you get, it's nice to be mothered a little bit.

It has been a big change for Mom. She has needed time to mourn and to begin adjusting to living alone. But my sisters, Ginny and Carol, and my brother and I said, "Why buy another house and take on that kind of responsibility, that burden, at seventy-two?" That was about two years ago, when Tom and I began talking about having her come to live with us. Our house lends itself to sharing. My mother could have her own apartment at the far end. There would be plenty of room for her dog, her constant companion, to run outside, and a space for a garden. And she would be within three hours of my two sisters, instead of eleven or twelve hours as she is now.

When we suggested this plan to her at first, she said there were some things in her life she had to resolve first. Her best friend, Norma, was dying of cancer, and we did not think she would live the winter. Mom wanted to stay nearby. She also has a twin sister who is quite dependent on her, and she wanted to be sure she, too, had relocated near other younger relatives.

Mom will be needed here, but I am not sure she knows exactly how. And that may be something that is holding her back. Even now there's so much I don't know in terms of running a household. I always felt Mom used her time so well. She seemed to be able to get everything done. When I think about having four children over eight years and not having an automatic washing machine or dishwasher or any of the conveniences that I have, I marvel at her.

I remember her scrubbing floors, cleaning upholstered furniture, and how I helped her stretch curtains back when they had those gigantic curtain frames. She was able to tackle a job and finish it. She didn't seem to be distracted. I don't use my time very efficiently. I don't *like* to keep house that much. I don't imagine she did, either, but it was something she accepted very matter-of-factly as something that needed to be done.

She was a good plain cook, too. Dad didn't care for any fancy food. He was basically a meat and potatoes kind of a person. I wouldn't mind at all learning some of her tricks in the kitchen. She pickled, canned, and made jellies. She never truly sat me down and taught me how, though she always expected us girls to lend a hand.

My mother sews beautifully. In fact, I can remember being upset because I didn't have a single store-bought dress when I went off to school. She even made our baby brother's snowsuits, our winter coats, and my father's work shirts. I can picture Grandma sitting at the machine whipping up clothes for my daughter, Mary. It will be fun for both of them.

I am really eager to have another generation in the house. In fact, I think if I had my life to live over, I would try to locate my family closer to grandparents. I think Mary will benefit a great deal from having an older person in our home. If you are involved intimately with someone who is aging, and you have a positive relationship, it's a lesson. It teaches you that growing old is perhaps something that isn't so terrible or frightening. After all, all of us are growing old each day that passes. We may not want to think about it, and there's no sense dwelling on it morbidly, but it's part of the process of life and death we're all going to have to experience.

Right now Mom is in good health, and she's very active. She wants to do some traveling. She'd like to go to Hawaii. We all said, "Mom, go!" But she said, "Not yet." She told my sister Carol, "Once I get to Mary's house where I can leave my dog, then I can go off and not worry about a thing." She's always been nervous about leaving an empty house. She won't have to worry about those things here.

She is also a realistic woman and has said that if some day she is not able to take care of herself, she will be grateful to be near us. After years of taking care of us, now we can take care of her if she needs it. All of us will be involved in her aging and death. I'd rather have her with us than alone, just as when that time comes for me, if I don't have Tom, I'd like to be near our Mary.

I think my mother is feeling, too, that in her last years, however many that may be, she would prefer to be nearer her own children and spend the time she has left knowing her grandchildren. She will bring another dimension of love into our home.

I know we are going to have some difficult times, some difficult moments. There are little things that we do that get on one another's nerves. When we're working in the same kitchen, I do things a certain way, and she does things her way. Neither way is wrong or right. But I want to run my own kitchen. She'll have her own apartment, so I hope we can avoid that kind of a situation.

I also anticipate occasional criticism of the way we live our lives. My parents were both very frugal people. They came out of the depression. My father was a man of simple tastes. His favorite clothes were bib overalls and flannel shirts. One of the funniest things about him was that he would take out of the back pocket of his overalls a roll of cash that could make a horse choke. He never felt comfortable unless he had a good deal of cash with him. My parents never had a checking account, or a charge account. Their house and our college educations came out of expenses, not out of their savings.

My parents saved and saved for their children and their old age. They thought three times about making any kind of a purchase. So my mother may feel that we carry too much debt, that we spend our money too freely. But who can put anything aside nowadays?

I do think, though, that we agree on child-rearing. Hers was a comfortable house. Mom had a wonderful attitude. She said, "The kids aren't going to remember when they're grown whether or not the house was perfectly neat and clean. They are going to remember that the cookie jar was full, that there was good food on the table, and whether or not you had time for them."

Mom had time for us. As I grow older and watch my own child grow, I feel much more appreciation for my mother. I remember when I was in high school how often I stayed late for club meetings. I didn't have a car, and I remember Mom coming by to pick me up and then going back an hour later to get my sister Ginny, or across the town to pick up Carol at Girl Scouts. I'm doing the same thing now with my kids. I have a few friends who complain, "It's so much running around in the car!" Cris, my stepdaughter, didn't understand this when she first came to live here. Her mother worked and wasn't available. She was surprised that I would take her places and pick her up. But there is absolutely no resentment on my part. This is part of my job as a mother.

When a neighbor heard that Mom was coming to live with us, she said, "Oh, marvelous! You're going to have a baby-sitter for little Mary." But that was the farthest thing from my mind. If Mom occasionally says, "I'll be here when the bus drops Mary from school, why don't you go shopping if you want?" Okay. That'll be fine occasionally, but I like to be here myself.

For years the argument about mothering has been that it's not the quantity but the quality of the time you spend with your kids. I'm beginning to feel that's not true at all. When the kids come home from school, I like to be here. Sometimes there is really no good reason. They come in: "Hi, how are you? Had a good day at school, but now I have a lot of homework." They have a snack and immediately put their noses in the books. Other times we sit around over a glass of milk for three-quarters of an hour discussing a problem with a friend or a teacher, whatever. If I weren't here, we might never ever have that discussion. It would be shelved.

We're still waiting for Mom to sell the farm. She's lived in Ohio for seventy-one years, and to move in with us is the end of many chapters in her life. We haven't pushed because we aren't ready with the house. We never seem to have the time or the money. There has been progress on her part, though. When she last visited us she said to me hesitantly, "Well, you don't know very many older people, do you?" I said, "Wait a minute, Mom. Sure we do." I made a point of taking her across the road to meet Margaret, who is in her sixties, and Olive, her mother, who is eighty-three. Olive and Margaret will introduce Mom to all the members of the LX Club in Pennington.

Now only last week she said to me on the phone, "How is the work going on the house?" I said, "Slowly, as usual." She laughed, "I think I'm going to be dead before your house is ready for me." I thought: We better spend the winter finishing up her kitchen. She's really getting ready to come. We need to set a deadline now and meet it.

This Time with My Mother Has Been Like a Gift

KATHY ALCORN

The morning I was going off to surgery my daughter Abigail was staying with friends. I called, but I had missed her. Well, Abigail got to school and she went into her teacher's office, and he let her use the phone. It was eight o'clock, and I was being put on a stretcher. The telephone by the bed rang. It was Abigail. She said, "Mommy, I miss you." She was crying. I wasn't in any condition to be very upbeat either. I said, "I miss you, too," and started to cry, but then I started trying to reassure her that it was going to be okay. "I'm going to be fine."

Somehow we got cut off. They were wheeling me away, and I had left her crying on the phone. I said to my mother who was there with me, "Mother, you've got to call Abigail." They're wheeling me out of the room, and I'm trying to give her the phone number of the school. My mother was so upset by what was happening to me that she followed the stretcher down the hall to the elevator. She was saying, "You're going to be all right," and she was crying.

We're holding on to each other, and I'm trying to tell her to call Abigail to say, "Mommy has gone for surgery now, but it's going to be okay," when the elevator door closed.

My mother is here taking care of me after my hysterectomy. The time together has been a gift. Having the reason to have the time has created a special interlude. In the past, particularly since my divorce, our relationship has been quite strained. I felt my mother became very judgmental: When you marry someone, you stay married your whole life. We never had an open conflict over this, but there was tension. I was defensive and short with her.

But when we were together for my operation, everything else got pushed into the background. I was very sick and very scared. I thought maybe the tumors were malignant. I was afraid I was going to die, that I would not get to see Abigail grow up and, much worse, that she would not have a mother.

I am forty-one years old, and my mother is seventy-six. She is still the person I turn to. You feel you're imposing when you ask friends to help. But you don't feel that way if you ask your mother.

My perception of my mother has changed. My earliest memories of her were that she was sick herself. She had a heart condition and was a semi-invalid. From the time I was two until I was six, we lived with my grandparents because she couldn't manage her own home or take care of me.

I remember getting up from my nap when I was little. My mother couldn't go up and down stairs, and my aunts, her younger sisters, would get me dressed. I remember being afraid that if I misbehaved or was too noisy, it might cause her to have another heart attack.

Now for the first time I appreciated the seriousness of what she went through. The day before my operation, she talked to me about her own hysterectomy when I was four. She had her first heart attack when she was pregnant with me and then another one shortly after I was born. Even though she genuinely feared for her life, my father pressed her to have another child. The doctor agreed that she shouldn't have more children, and the operation was a great relief to her. Later, when my father found out that the operation was done not only because she had endometriosis, but as a form of birth control, he was very angry. He felt that he had been tricked. I am sad that their sense of communication and support of one another wasn't there on an emotional level, even though on the surface my parents always had a happy marriage.

I was so grateful that my mother was with me the night before my operation. She was very loving, and very positive that I was going to be okay. I had a conversation with the doctor that morning when I realized that the health risks were too great to save my uterus, and I would need a full hysterectomy. Then Juri, the man I was involved with, called me on the phone. I had hoped we would get married, and maybe I still could have another child. So when he called, I told him that I had told the doctor not to go to heroic efforts to save my uterus. That would mean that we really could not have a child. Didn't he think that's what I should do?

He said that I had done the right thing. I felt that was a message that he still loved me, even though I couldn't have a baby with him. That made me feel very close to him, but it also made me feel really sad. Because as I felt closer to him, it was most sad that we could not have a baby.

When I hung up, I started to cry. I looked at my mother. I just felt so bad that I wasn't ever going to be able to have another child. I said, "To have it be this final, to know that there will be no more children, is so upsetting."

In the past, whenever I had said I might remarry and have another baby, she'd expressed disapproval. Now that the end of child-bearing was a reality for me, she was able to empathize. We both cried and held each other. I realized that I might not have much more time with my mother. She's in ill health. She has Parkinson's disease. Most of our visits in the past had been rather formal. I was trying to please her, to make sure she had a good time. This occasion freed us.

What's most interesting is that I don't feel we have to resolve all the other issues that we disagree on. I was telling my mother how ambivalent I felt about Juri. She said the kind of thing that always used to make me furious: "If you ever have another relationship, it would just kill me." In the past I've confronted her very directly. I've said, "Mother, do you hear what you're saying? You are saying that I have to stay in a relationship that may not be workable or never have a man in my life again. Is that what you want for me?" She feels that it's damaging to Abigail because each time I have gotten involved, she has become emotionally involved with a father figure whom she has then lost. Also, now that Abigail is getting older, my mother feels it's inappropriate for her to know that I have a sexual relationship with a man I'm not married to. I'm concerned about these issues, too. I mean my preference would be that my relationship would work out and turn into marriage.

I realize, though, that my mother will never be able to accept the fact that I would not consider marrying a man unless I'd lived with him. Now, rather than argue with her, I'm able to say, "Well, let's just stay in the present. I'm nowhere near the point of becoming seriously involved with another man. Let's not get into dire predictions." She's generally quite pessimistic. This visit I was able to see her pessimism as connected to her fear of the future. When she stays in the present, as she did when I was sick and needed her, and it felt like a real crisis, she was loving and supportive, and that was what I needed. I needed my mother.

Motherhood Burnout

CATHY MUTTER

I felt totally consumed by the kids. I was doing everything for them, trying to be supermom, being so organized, with all the cookies baked and so on. My house wasn't dirty as much as it was messy. That didn't bother me. It was just . . . I would have enjoyed motherhood if I'd only taken the time to enjoy it, but I always felt that I should have been more than a mother.

I didn't want to be like my mother—a Mother Earth. I wanted to be a career lady, too. I wanted a profession. But I didn't have time. Back in Australia, I tried to do a law degree part-time, plus work, but I didn't have an extra eight hours to do all the reading for school, plus take care of Gordon, who was two, and a new baby, Nicole. I felt I was pulled in too many directions. I had to put career on hold. It's as if the woman has to put everything on hold, and that's what I started to resent.

I enjoyed the birthing. That was a real joy, and I did well at breast-feeding. But I never felt that I got enough pats. Nobody ever said, "Gee, you're doing a great job." Nobody came home and commented, "The floors are nice." There was no feedback, nobody telling you you're successful.

And then I had the third child, Andrew, when Gordon was eight and Nicole was six. Andrew was not planned. Afterward, I felt like I had fallen into a black pit. I was physically exhausted by sleepless nights when I had to get up to nurse the baby. Like my other kids, Andrew wouldn't take pacifiers or bottles. He had to have Mummy. I was so tired, I had to give up jogging, the one thing I did for myself. I had no one to help. I never had my mother around like my sisters do. I've always lived away from my family. I had to be self-sufficient. My husband was the kind of person who felt you solve your problems by yourself. I tried to be like that, but I couldn't. I felt so angry, and it all came out at him.

I didn't think John was there enough. I was doing everything alone with the kids. He worked. He supported us. I think back now: I should have been happy. I had everything, but something was missing. I felt that John was having a glamorous life, doing everything he wanted. He's an oceanographer, and he was going to sea in the company of adults, and I wasn't getting anything. I felt he wasn't there enough for me.

He knew I was unhappy, but he has a hard time dealing with emotions. He said he would do anything he could to make me happy, and then he seemed to withdraw even further. I said I needed some emotional support. He said, "Well, I can be there financially, but I can't be there emotionally." He'd never seen anger like the kind I was expressing.

I used to fantasize that he was having affairs. The young women graduate students he worked with really got to me. I'd see them at parties at John's laboratory. They would say, "What do you do?" I felt I wasn't interesting, that I was less intelligent because I had children. I began to ask myself, "Well, what do I do?" I was out of touch with what I needed. I depended on him instead of making decisions for myself. I always deferred. I was taking care of everybody, and there was nobody to take care of me.

I should have known from watching my mother. She had five kids, and she was exhausted and angry, too. As I got older I realized it. Her family was her life. She was fanatic about housecleaning. She had to have everything spotless, and we would come home from school and just mess it up. The same scene happened over and over again. Her way of dealing with it would be to rant and rave, "Nobody cares! Nobody cares! Nobody does their part!"

She gave up work when my father was ill, to take care of him, when she really should have kept working because she enjoyed it. She would always be there for somebody else.

Now I appreciate how she felt. Nobody said to her, "Hey, you're doing a really good job! You keep a nice house. What a great shopper you are." We just took it all for granted, and then I couldn't understand why she would be nagging all the time.

I fell into the same pattern. You are supposed to love every minute of motherhood, and you can't when you're so tired. All the advertising says you're such a wonderful person. You're always so glamorous, and sexy, too. Well, I didn't go to the hairdresser's for years, and I never bought myself any new clothes. My mother wore shredded underwear. That symbolizes so much to me. I always thought, "I'll never do that to myself," and I did. You fall into the same patterns.

You get out of the habit of thinking of yourself. I just read something in a women's magazine on "motherhood burnout." It started me thinking: That is exactly what happened to me. You really have to have your own time. The problem is that even if you realize you need the time, you know you have to take it away from somebody else, and then you don't. You never say, "No." That is the fallacy of motherhood.

I had high expectations, and when I kept failing to meet them, I tried harder and harder. Why wasn't I able to teach my children to be rational? You'd see these models of wonderful children on television. There is never any teasing or needling, and you feel bad because your kids aren't that way. We all think someone else has the secret. How come her children are so good in school, and her house is spotless, and she has the cookies baked and the finger paints out? Why can't I be that way?

I used to call up my sister back in Australia and cry. I was so exhausted, and she would say, "You can't please everybody. You've got to start pleasing yourself. What do *you* want?"

I wanted to work. I would say to her, "I want to do something for money, so that people can actually see the dollars, so that I will feel I am worth it." My sister, who is a working mother, said, "That's not what it's all about. You're pulled in so many directions if you're working, that you end up being mediocre at both things because you can't give all your time to your career and then short-change your kids."

If you don't take care of yourself, the ramifications are serious. My husband walked away because he couldn't take my anger.

I got some counseling. I wish I had taken more time for myself and kept myself mentally healthy rather than falling into depression. I had a hard time seeing that I really was ill. I thought, "I'm intelligent. I should be able to cope. I have an education. I should be able to combine everything." Now, of course, I know that there are no "shoulds" in this life. I also learned that I'm not the cause of everything—that it's not my fault, for example, that Gordon has difficulty making friends.

What shattered me more than anything was when John served me with the divorce papers unexpectedly. He accused me of child abuse. I was accused of beating Gordon. The fact was he came home from school one day, and I said, "What homework have you got?" and he threw his books everywhere, and one book hit me. I said, "Don't do that," and I threw it back, and it caught him in the face. Now I was told to undergo forensic psychiatric evaluation.

Today, after two years, my anger toward John is subsiding. We are finally able to talk again. In the separation agreement the lawyers are working on, I have asked for "rehabilitative maintenance" money so that I can go back to school. He said, "The whole idea of rehabilitative maintenance is terrible! You could have gotten a job and gone back to school three years ago."

I looked at him, and was able to say without anger in my voice, "Three years ago, think about it. Andrew was a small baby. What could I have done? I didn't want to give him up to someone else to care for him. I wanted to be with him. Maybe I could have gone to school, sure, but where were you? You were at sea a lot. You were at meetings. Do you remember that I used to take the baby to meetings at the bottle-recycling program? You didn't feel comfortable baby-sitting him. I'd already taken the two older kids every place I had to go, and I wanted some time away from all of them to be with adults. But I had to take the baby." He did remember that.

I have come to realize that I never really had lived a life of my own. Even when we went down to Immigration, they didn't want to know anything about me. I said, "I'm a teacher," and the lawyer said, "Well, that's not important. We've got a lot of teachers in this country." It was as if I didn't exist. John was the eminent scientist, and I was the Mrs.

The same shit is going on with the lawyers right now. His lawyer happens to be a woman, and she's very condescending. John would like joint custody of the children, so that they live half-time with him and half with me. I think they are too young for that right now. But here is this woman lawyer talking to my lawyer about "quality time." She says, "Your client wakes up with the children every day, and that's quality time. The father would like to have that, too."

I looked at this woman and said, "Oh, that's nice to know, that it's quality time." Then I'm looking at John, whom I spent most of my adult life with, and I say, "You can't be serious, to let this woman sit here and say those things, because that is not what having kids is like." He's shrugging his shoulders and looking kind of embarrassed. I said, "John, will you advise your lawyer as to what the mornings in our house are like? 'Get out of bed! The alarm went off twenty minutes ago! You've got five minutes to get down here for breakfast! Right now! Up! I don't know where your sneakers are! Come on! You're going to be late for school!' "

I can laugh about it now because I think I've come to terms with a few things. But it has been a wrenching experience.

I Am an Endangered Species

ROSEMARY SCHARRENBROICH

What are the mornings like in my house? We both have things to do to get everybody off to school. I'm lucky because Ingo helps a lot. He usually makes the sandwiches and fills the Thermoses while I'm still getting up, washing my face, getting dressed, and waking the kids up on my way down. He's poured my coffee, too, and I drink it as I stand and make three different kinds of breakfasts.

Then while they're eating breakfast, I run back upstairs to get the clothes for the two little ones. The oldest one, Sylka, can take care of herself. Dressing the little ones, there are always endless disasters along the way. Maxy pinches his finger in the cupboard door, and then I have to get a chair so he can stand with his hand under the cold water while I tie Illya's shoes. Then Illya is screaming because he didn't want bananas in his Corn Pops even though he had said he wanted bananas in his Corn Pops. I remind him he said it. He said, "I didn't, either!" So I fish the bananas out and get a Band-Aid for the other one, whose sleeve is now soaking wet.

Meanwhile, Ingo's asking, "Where are the checks? I need checks! I don't have a single check in my wallet." "Okay," I say, and put down the kid with the Band-Aid, and race upstairs and get him a check. He's out the door and yells, "Did we ever get that bank statement?" "I'll call," and Sylka is screaming, "Where are my barrettes?" I'm trying to buckle Max's belt, so I stop and search the kitchen counter and find the barrettes on the breadbox. "Could you put my hair in barrettes, Mom?" "Then get the brush." "I don't know where the brush is." "I don't know, either. I didn't use it last." "Oh, forget the barrettes." Then she needs money because she's going to an after-school activity that costs two dollars. "Get my pocketbook from the hall." The phone rings, and it's Dotty Spellman calling about the food committee for the school. "It's the wrong time to talk. Goodbye!"

Everybody's finally dressed. We walk out and close the door, but I've forgotten my pocketbook. "Sylka, watch the boys for me." I run in. While I'm looking for the pocketbook, which I finally discover on the breadbox, the two little ones have torn apart a garbage bag and are now covered with wet coffee grounds, and their lunch has fallen down into a puddle. The bag is wet and torn. And I race back inside to find another paper bag.

It's endless. I can plan to be out of that house an hour and a half before it's time to leave. I could be ready to go out, and by God if something doesn't come to fill that hour and a half. I end up being late all the time. And I don't even have diapers to change anymore. It used to be when I did, somebody would move their bowels right before we were ready to go out. Off would come the snowsuit, the boots, and the overalls. Upstairs for another pair, while the other child had gotten into the dry cleaning I'd just set down on the chair.

Then I drive everybody to school, to nursery school, picking up another child on the way, and then on to Sylka's school. I drop them and realize I have to be back at her school by eleven-thirty for a teacher's conference, so I rush on to the supermarket and the bank. And then finally, as I turn down my own street, I see a neighbor whose husband was taken to the hospital. I can't just pass her by. I pull over. "Marjorie, how is he? When is he coming home? We were so sorry to hear." Now it's ten when I finally pull into my own driveway. What I have to do is running through my head.

I stop the engine and consciously sit perfectly still for a moment. I find I have to do this. Yesterday, for example, I parked the car and waited a few moments. Then I got out and walked very, very slowly across the grass. As I walked, everything began to look so beautiful to me—the greens, the sun coming through the leaves all dappled on the grass, the porch, the way the rocker sat on the porch, the pink and white begonias in the copper pots.

Coming up the step to the door, I always pause and take a deep breath, a renewing breath, before I come into the house alone. I have a friend, Lois, down the street. She works. She once said, "When I walk into my office, and I see my papers, my phone, my desk, and my chair, the work I have created for myself, all serenity enters my life." This is the way I feel when I come back into my home, which is my office. No one is there, and it's very, very still.

It's only when you are alone that you have some time to focus on yourself, or to experience yourself, to come back to your core. I give myself maybe twenty minutes. This is my time. This is the time where I experience my own wishes, the things *I* want. When you are in service to other people, which being a mother is, you don't have time to do that. Everybody is telling you what *they* want. It's an interesting thing. When they are all here, I only see what I have to do, the dishes in the sink, the pajamas on the floor, the shoes, the cereal scattered around in bowls, books, magazines. I see those things, but when I'm alone, by myself, I don't see them. I come in and see only what's beautiful and pleasant and cheerful. That's all I see. Nothing intrudes on this few minutes of . . . it's a kind of communion, I guess.

Maybe I'll sit quietly in the kitchen, but often I'll just walk through the house. I begin to see the colors, the shades of rose on the rug, the dried flowers in the vase, a paler rose by the window, and how the morning sun expands the room. I only bought things I really loved, needed, but really loved. The things in my house aren't only functional, and so they give me a great amount of pleasure looking at them.

I love the color of the wood on the turned spools of the maple bed. I have a hand-crocheted bedspread that I love. It's probably a hundred years old. Every time I pick it up, I love the woman who worked on it. I just love her because she . . . *she* has given *me* such pleasure. And I admire the time and *love* that went into it. She must have been like me. She loved beautiful things, and she loved to put them together, making a home. She must have spent hours creating this by whale-oil light.

I may then decide that the curtains aren't right. I think, what can

I make to replace them? Then I'll remember that I picked up an old lace tablecloth at a yard sale two years ago. I may take it out. Can I get four curtains out of this? Then I've started to create something. That's sort of the way it goes. Or I may step outside on the terrace where the sun filters through the reed awning. The light comes through in an irregular pattern. It's cool back there. The greens are so deep, and the pink tablecloth looks so nice with the greens and the white and the bench I painted pink. And the first daylilies are out, orange against the white fence.

Then I can start my day.

I can come back to wash the dishes, pick up the Corn Pops, shake out the wet towels, hang up the clothes, find the lost shoe, sort out the dirty from the clean, make the beds, sweep the porch, call Dotty about the food committee and the bank about the missing statement, and think about dinner. I'll start to defrost the lamb chops. Or if it's something that involves long cooking like spaghetti sauce, stew, or soup, I'll start that early. Because I'm always keeping schedules. There is never a time that is uncounted. I constantly look at my watch and know that this one gets picked up at this time, and I've got to start that soup now because I'm not coming back after I pick her up. I have to take her to the allergist.

Nothing ever really gets finished. The feeling of completion is literally limited to tasks, certain tasks like cleaning out a closet, emptying the dishwasher, folding that laundry, vacuuming a room, changing the sheets, making a pot of soup.

When you are a housewife and mother, none of it's really your time. You can say, "I'm having a lunch out with a friend," but you're looking at your watch. And those two hours go by so fast. Yes, every minute is valuable and precious, *full*.

When Sylka was a baby, eleven years ago, there were a dozen women at home on our block. We spent a lot of time together out in the street—little ones on this busy street need constant supervision. Sometimes we would gang together and take them to a park or to the zoo. We'd pack snacks and juice, and then come back for lunch and naps. That would be the time when you'd run around and do all the things you couldn't do when they were awake.

On rainy days we would visit each other for coffee. We could spend a whole morning in somebody's kitchen while the kids played in the next room. We all had backyards, and we'd sit outside and drink iced coffee in the summer and let the kids play in a wading pool or with the hose. We'd just talk, trade recipes, joke, just talk. At that time nobody thought about a meaningful life, or that this was not important. Many of us felt tedium, which is why it was so good to have each other.

When the children turned three, they went to nursery school, so we wouldn't see each other so much in the morning because we'd be involved in our own tasks. In the afternoons, after the naps, we'd be back out on the streets again. It was very nice. I was never lonely. There was tremendous support, and a lot of sharing of baby-sitting, dropping kids off so you could run to the department store alone.

By the time Sylka was six, I was about the only one in the group who hadn't had a second child. I didn't seem able to get pregnant again. I became a part-time real-estate agent. I liked it, and I was very good at it. I love houses and really enjoyed finding the right home for each client. It's an extension of my own nesting instincts. But the work was so part-time that it just wasn't financially rewarding enough. I started writing for the local paper. I went to school part-time. I felt I was groping. I'm one of these people who never really decided what I wanted to be when I grew up. But then it didn't matter again. When Sylka was eight, I got pregnant with the boys. I'm still working on making peace with my life. In my best moments I think I have it all solved. I say, "This is the best of all possible worlds. I really love what I'm doing. I'm so incredibly busy now, how could I possibly take on a career outside my home?"

I don't want anyone else to take care of my children, either. I feel they are too valuable, yes, valuable! I surprise myself with how large an ego I have. I'm the only one who can do this even if I am in a lousy mood and we have a bad day. An occasional baby-sitter is okay, but if the kid is sick or has to be taken to the emergency room, I want to do it. I don't want to be in a conference room. I've also found when I do leave my kids with a baby-sitter for too long a period of time, I lose contact with them. It's an interesting thing. The more contact you lose with them, the easier it is to relinquish the time with them. It's easier to give it up.

Being a housewife nowadays is not an honored profession, however. Sometimes if you say, "I'm a housewife," what happens is people go away, or they look right through you. It happens. They don't take you seriously. I'll go to a party and someone will say, "What do you do?" Sometimes I treat it as a joke. I say, "Well, I'm an executive, and I work fourteen hours a day, and I'm pretty tired at night."

They ask, "What do you do?" never, "What are you interested in?" I want to learn a hundred things. Let me see—I'd like to take a couple of different cooking classes. I want to learn how to do something called candlewicking, and a kind of cross-stitch embroidery where you count the stitches. I want to learn to upholster a chair. We sail, and I'd like to learn to navigate by the stars, and how to do some simple repairs on my car. I want to study art history, a history of Europe through its literature. I want to read poetry, and learn a computer language. I'd like to learn more about business, say, be at the side of someone who is a very clever deal-maker, a manipulator. I'd like to write a book.

I know I have a much better chance of doing all those things than that man at the party who is working sixty hours a week. I am really lucky to be able to do what I'm doing. There are so many women out there who don't have the luxury to even think about what they want to do, no less learn. Hey, listen, I'm a true housewife, a rare and unusual person! In twenty years people will ask, "Are you really a housewife? Can I touch you?" Being a housewife is a dying craft. It's an art, too.

Can you imagine the Housewives' Hall of Fame for those of us endangered species who are desired, sought after, admired, elevated? I can see it now, the diorama of my kitchen with its dirty floor, sugar Corn Pops all over, the little jockey shorts in a heap, a manikin, the stuffed image of Rosemary Scharrenbroich, one of the last of her species, with her pot of soup on the stove. Hand on hip, a howling baby in arm, a stuffed baby, ladle in hand, the phone squinched on her shoulder, the unfinished needlepoint on the table, the station wagon out the window. The clock is set at five-thirty. There's an anguished expression on her face because it is the classic hour of disintegration in the American housewife's kitchen.

Oh, I joke about it, but do you know what? It's not a bad life. I'm my own boss, and I'm important. They need me, and I like that. That makes me feel good. If I was a big executive in a corporation, that would probably also make me feel good. But this is what I do.

* * *

148

I Am an Endangered Species

I find that I am picking the boys up a lot lately. I love that intimacy with them. I really do. It's the way they feel, the way they fit against my body, the way they speak, too, the sound of their voices. It's what holds their attention at any one moment and what they tell you. You're getting it in a very physical way. They smell. They sort of taste almost.

Maybe it's because I feel they are the last. They're going to kindergarten next year. They are my last babies. Maybe it is a wisdom that says, "Stop wishing these hours away because you have something important to do. Stop wishing them away because pretty soon they won't be here." Perhaps that comes from having another, older child. You don't always learn it the first time around.

We had such a nice time last night. Ingo was out, and it was just the kids and I. We were waiting to go to Sylka's soccer game. We had finished eating. I had put away the food, but hadn't done the dishes because there wasn't time. We went outside, and Maxy said, "Push me on the swing." I said, "Okay." They didn't want to take turns, but I straightened that out. I gave them each a couple of big pushes. Then I said, "I'm really so full. I have to sit down." I'd been on my feet a lot that day. I took one of them with me. I said, "Come sit on my lap. Keep my lap company."

You almost have to leave the house for those moments to come, because the house cries out, "Do this, do that, do it now." And you forge ahead with another task. You tend to ignore the kids, and you miss some of the opportunities for the good things.

We sat in the rocker on the porch and just talked. I don't remember about what. Then the other one came and sat on the other knee. The three of us rocked and looked up at the trees. It was nice, those few minutes rocking on the porch. In fact, it was the best. That short time was really the best that life has to offer.

You Can't Control It All

JANET SONNENBERG

My daughter, Jami, was four and my son, Joel, was almost two. Mike had worked all summer, and we needed just a short vacation. We were heading up to New Hampshire with my sister-in-law, Kathy, and her husband, Doug. We'd split up into a two-car cara- van with the men, Mike, Doug, and little Joel in one car and Kathy and I and Jami in the other. We were only twenty minutes from our destination when a tractor trailer loaded with thirty-six tons of cargo rammed the line of cars we were in at a toll booth.

I could see fire coming from the rear bumper of our car. Think- ing it was going to blow up, my sister-in-law, Jami, and I ran in terror. Then the car with my husband, Doug, and Joel burst into flames. I stopped in shock. Kathy and I were widows. I did not believe any of them had gotten out.

My glasses had been knocked off my head, and I hardly recog- nized Mike when he staggered up to me in a stuporous state. His clothes were torn, and he was completely covered with soot. Blood was oozing from the back of his head. I said, "Where's Joel? Mike, where is Joel? Where's Joel?" "Oh," Mike said. "He was such a neat son, Jan. He was such a neat son."

Then this guy came running up to us. He was screaming! "I saved your baby! I saved your baby!" He had gone through the toll booth, found out that he'd taken a wrong turn, and was backing up to turn around when he saw the accident occur. He ran for a fire extinguisher in the toll house. When he got to our car, he heard a baby screaming in the back seat. With great difficulty he opened the door and yanked out the infant seat with Joel in it. He slammed it on the ground because it was so very hot. His hands were burned from the melted seat. This man had never finished high school and had run away from home and had a very rough family life. Here he was saving my child.

My sister-in-law said, "Look, Jan, it's Joel." No, it couldn't be, because when I looked down, there was this black thing. There was this black body. Everything seemed to be gone from his face that was recognizable. There was no hair. The top of his head was white. The nose was very—oh, just swollen and shrunken at the same time. His lips were burned off. His blackened arms, crisp with carbon, were outstretched and quivering. No, this was not Joel!

The only things that I recognized were his clothes that I'd dressed him in that morning. The "Oshkosh" brand label was still there on the pocket of his denim overalls, and his baby shoes were intact. It was an awful sight, not just visually awful. Burnt flesh smells awful.

At first I was angry. This guy came up to me and said, "I saved your baby! I saved your baby! He's going to be all right." I knew his statement was so absurd. As a nurse, I knew that very few people survive sixty-percent-and-over burns. Joel looked totally charred. Why had this guy saved him to suffer horribly and die anyway? Just a few more seconds and he would have been at peace.

But then I started thinking as a nurse. I said, "What can I do for Joel?" My mind went from wishing he would die to promoting life. I couldn't see his chest rising or falling. I bent over him, and I couldn't feel any air on my cheek, so I gave him mouth-to-mouth resuscitation. He started coughing and choking. Then he started screaming and screaming and screaming and screaming, and he just kept screaming. Actually, it was great for his lungs. It was the best thing for him to aerate those lungs, but it was an awful thing as a mother to experience that screaming and not really be able to do anything.

An ambulance attendant rushed up to me and said, "Let's pick him up and carry him to the ambulance." So we picked up that hot infant seat, I on one side, and he on the other, and we began to run. Maybe it was the adrenalin—the rush of picking up Joel and running as fast as we could because he had to get somewhere for medical treatment very, very fast . . . but as I ran I began thinking more like a mother. Instead of only saying, "Let's get him to the hospital," I started saying to him, "Just live! I don't care what the odds are. I want you to live!" As I ran I was saying, "I want you to live! You are going to live!" That's when that push, that process, that race to save his life began for me.

We got to a small, local hospital and things started happening. From there we went to Boston, where Joel was given a five percent chance for survival.

It was a mess, an unbelievable mess. Mike was in the hospital back in New Hampshire with a head injury and a badly burned hand. My daughter, Jami, had become separated from me. But when I look back at it, it's unbelievable the way things were taken care of. People were so kind. A lab technician offered to take care of Jami, so that Kathy could contact relatives and see to the myriad details. I had no money at all. A stranger poured coins into my hands for the pay phone in the hospital. An off-duty fireman drove me to Boston because the ambulance had rushed off without me. As I got into the car to leave, someone else thrust a twenty-dollar bill into my hand, saying, "Here, you will need this."

People reached out and sustained us. I believe it was also our common bond of faith, which provided a network of support and prayer throughout the country. Mike teaches at a small Christian college, and our lives have been very much involved with our church. People just started helping us. Friends of friends from our college days came to visit us, offered us housing, brought us new clothes and suitcases because ours had been burned. Later, our church replaced our car and sent us checks every month because we were strapped. They knew Mike couldn't go out and get a part-time job. I couldn't go out and get one. We made too much money to go on welfare. The church was phenomenal. It got us through.

Weeks and weeks and months and months went by. Joel was in the Boston hospital, wrapped like a mummy in splints and bandages. He lived in a plastic, bacteria-free tent. He suffered tremendously. He lost his fingers and a hand. He has one toe. He had a deep, deep burn in the skull. The doctors had never seen one as extensive on a living person. The fifteen percent of his body that hadn't been burned had to supply the skin grafts for the rest of his body. For this he underwent—and still undergoes—many, many, many painful operations. As one plastic surgeon put it, "If your son survives, he will always look like a freak." Joel's face *is* severely disfigured.

The guilt, the grief, the sense of loss . . .

Four and a half months after the accident, we brought Joel home. We still had to sustain him through a tremendous amount of physical suffering, dressing changes on his head, Ace bandages rewrapped, emollient cream on his body. For a good year, we had to feed him constantly. He needed those calories.

Joel could be very stubborn. He wanted to trick us into doing things for him, which is a kind of smarter mentality. I had to discipline him. I had to say, "Joel, you're going to walk over there." or "Go get me that candy." Just to get him to walk. Sometimes I had to spank him. I would *have* to! It was imperative that he walk, or he wasn't going to function as well. It was a matter of survival! I had to say, "Joel, this is the way it is! Do it!"

Our daughter, Jami, had to be part of our total effort to rehabilitate Joel. She had to play with him and try to teach him. She showed him how to pick up toys with his wrists. "See, Joel, do it this way." She was there to help Joel. She couldn't exist for herself. At the time there was no other choice. We were in such a survival state. She really couldn't say, "Well, what about me?"

I had no time for her, but again, other people were wonderful. They took up the slack. I never had to ask. They saw the need. Friends ferried her to and from nursery school and invited her over to play. The teacher worked with her closely. They did a lot of play therapy with dolls reenacting the accident.

I think Jami has grown up faster than she would have because she has had to rely more on herself than on Mike and me. I think she resents that. She also receives much of the negative attention of having a handicapped sibling. When she walks down the street with Joel, people stare at her too, but she doesn't get the same positive

154

attention. Joel has been on TV, and he's been written about. "Oh, this is Joel, the hero."

Yet, Jami is very much of a heroine in her own right, not just because of Joel, but because of who she is. She is in the "Gifted and Talented" program at school. She sang a solo in front of the whole student body. She was on the cover of the school magazine because the editor said, "I think she needs that." I never would have thought of it. She was cast in the college play where Mike teaches. She was great. She was billed as a star and loved taking those curtain calls.

I had no time for her, or Mike, or myself. I was totally consumed with caring for Joel. Besides the physical care of a handicapped child, there were also the constant directives to other people to get things done. There were physical therapists and occupational therapists and nurses who helped with the dressing changes coming and going in and out of our house. The constant mobilizing of people to perform the service and to do it well requires tremendous energy.

A student who lived in an apartment in our basement did all of my housework and laundry. My good friend Barb had arranged for meals to be brought in every day for months and months. That's how disabled I was as a mother: I was just taking care of Joel.

I was exhausted. Joel was up in the night screaming, sometimes four or five times. During the day I was changing those dressings on his skull. This was extremely draining. The horror of the screaming and the pain! I hated ripping off those dressings. I hated watching the blood rush down his face. I hated his screaming. I hated the fact that the doctors weren't doing anything to clear it up, which was why I had to go through it in my house. I hated the fact that my daughter had to listen to it! This went on for two and a half years.

But what was the alternative? I could get a nurse to come in so I didn't have to do it, but we'd still have the screaming. I just had to say, "This is it." I accepted it, and accepted the fact that I hated it.

The person who has a handicapped child hates . . . No, that's not true. You're ambivalent. You love your child, but you *hate* what it's doing to you. You *hate* that it's dragging down your family. You *hate* the dynamics in your family that have changed. You sometimes *hate* yourself because of what you can't do, what you're too tired to do, what you don't want to do. You *hate* what has happened. It's being able to love and hate at the same time and to accept that, and then to let the guilt go. You have to let that guilt go.

I had a dream about Joel once. He was in our backyard when a big dog came along and chewed his face and pierced his jugular vein. He was bleeding to death, and all of the grafts on his face were wrecked. Those grafts can't be done again, a whole nose took a year to put on, and the eyelids. There was nothing left of his face but blood. It had all been chewed away by the dog.

What did I do? Do you know what I did? I thought, "I don't want to go through this again. And I don't want Joel to go through this again." I said, "Joel, I am not going to put pressure on your jugular vein to stop the bleeding." It was a matter of letting go. I said, "Go in peace." That was my dream. When I told this to my husband, he was horrified to think that I was dreaming that our child would die.

Our church was the first place where Joel really emerged into the outside world. Everyone knew about him and had prayed for him. We had not known how to pray for him: We didn't know if we wanted to pray for life. We simply asked that God's will be done.

Everyone had seen his picture. When I think about it now, he looked awful. To me, as his mother, he looked beautiful. He had survived, he was walking, he was going back to church. But now, when I see the pictures, I think, "Oh my gosh!" He was red, lobster red in the face, a very shiny face because it was full of grease to keep that skin moist and stretching, a face that had fresh surgery on the eyes. He had only the rudiments of a face. His mouth didn't have an upper lip. He had no nose, just two holes going into his face. Only the color of his eyes hadn't changed. They were still very dark brown.

There were many tears. At the time I interpreted them as a sign that people were glad Joel was back. Now that I look back more objectively, I can see different responses—sadness, horror, even fear. One little boy screamed. All that he could think of was that Joel was fire. Here was fire in his class. Fire had touched Joel, and Joel was fire, and fire was going to hurt him.

It is a matter of perception when you see Joel walking down the street, and if you focus on what is the same about him, it is much easier to deal with the differences. When you see him as an active seven-year-old on the playground, climbing the jungle gym, running and laughing and having a great time, you can say, "So what! He's having a riot." You can learn from people like that.

What do you learn? All I know is what the parents who have children who play with Joel have told me: Their children don't see him as being handicapped, and don't see any differences once they know him. What becomes important is how they can have fun together, how they can learn together or even fight together, not what makes them different. It's what makes them the same. I am learning this. Joel goes to the hospital frequently and I go with him. Days before we leave for Boston, I start agonizing. The kid has to go through another surgery where the doctors shave skin off to graft the scars. They excise the scars, just to keep Joel moving, to keep his arms moving, to keep his mouth opening, to keep the eyelids functional, just basic bare-bones surgery, they call it. It has nothing to do with cosmetics.

I say "Joel, you're going up to the hospital soon. What do you think, honey?" I'm gulping because I don't want him to have to go, but it's part of his life and I know he has to. He says, "Mom, do you think this time you could leave me at the hospital and not come in for the whole day?" Here I am, the mother who must be there to fight his battles for him, and the kid is saying in effect, "Mom, just leave me by myself for a while. I'm seven. I'm trying out new waters. I can do this now a little bit more on my own." He's looking forward to playing PacMan in the computer room with the teacher he likes so much, and here's the mother saying, "But you're a handicapped child!" It's almost funny. Here he is so normal in that respect, and I'm focusing on the abnormality.

When people see me with Joel, they see me as someone who has gone through something *so awful!* They wonder, how could she get through it? They feel like my problems are so much greater than theirs, how dare they talk about how tired they are? How dare they talk about their kid whom they can't potty train? This is how they feel: "Oh, gosh, my concerns are so petty."

Beyond this, there is a deeper fear. I remind them of their greatest fear, which was also my greatest fear. What if something happens to one of my children? For me, this fear was realized. Something did happen to one of my children, so demobilizing and so debilitating, and yet still very much an enrichment in my life. Yes, there is pressure in my life, but there is also excitement in that pressure. Life has given so much!

When I talk to other mothers about Joel, I offer them a journey that sometimes frightens them, but it's a journey that is life.

People say to me, "I would die if something happened to my child. How do you get through a crisis like that if it happens?" I say, "You live your life to the fullest that you can, and you draw on the resources that make life meaningful and energized and deep and vibrant, and if something happens, those resources will sustain you."

We don't know in ten or fifteen years, when Joel is a young adult, how our society will cope with this new frontier of the handicapped, that is, people who look so different, but who can walk, run, talk, people who are not in wheelchairs with normal faces. Can he wait on people at McDonald's? Can he maintain a service profession? Can he get out in the world and mingle with people, which is one of the smallest steps toward becoming independent? Will Joel be able to do that? We don't know.

Now we are focusing with him on vocations that he might be able to grasp hold of if a public vocation will not be his. One area is computers. We've bought our own, and we already have him working on it. In other words, we try to control these things with a little more intensity than we would with a normal child. Rather than wait to see where the child excels, you guide him toward what we feel might be appropriate.

We cannot protect Joel emotionally. We cannot control people's stares, and the fact that some people want to hurt him. We wish we could! As a mother, I may say, how dare that person hurt my child, how dare they! But then I have to move beyond that. I really have to believe he's going to grow and learn something. I do believe we have the power to allow those reactions to not control us.

I say to Joel, "When people laugh at you, what do you do?" He says, "I don't say anything." I say, "If I were you, I would say,

'What are you staring at?' " Joel says, "I don't want to do that, Mommy." I say, "That is your decision."

Sometimes I will watch him look in the mirror. I say, "Joel, what do you see?" He goes, "Me!" He smiles at himself. That is who he is. That is Joel.

When I Grew Up, I Wanted to Make Sure My Children Loved Me

NARRADA SANCHEZ

I grew up with my grandparents. My mother left me with them. She was very young, about fifteen. She felt I would be better with them than with her. I didn't know anything about her until I was older. My father couldn't take care of me because he had left Puerto Rico to work in New York. He had another wife and kids to support. It was like he forgot me.

I enjoyed living with my grandparents in one way and in other ways I didn't. They were nice to me. They were very strong and very strict. My grandmother is the one who used to love me. I was the only small one in the house. It was nice in the country in their little house. My grandfather had a piece of land that he worked on. He used to grow beans and vegetables and sometimes rice. He had a cow, horses, and chickens. I like animals.

He worked cutting sugar cane. I used to take him his lunch in the field. I went to school; we had no cars, and I had to walk a long way to get there. I liked that: up and down the hills, through the trees, and past the sugar cane fields. The sugar cane looks like green leaves on a big, long pole. I used to stop and eat it on my way to town.

My grandmother died when I was five or six. It would have been better if I wasn't alone with my grandfather, because he didn't teach me much. He was a religious man, and he did teach me how to pray. But it's not like having a mother, who is always there to tell you if you are doing right or wrong. What I mean is, I was running wild like an animal. He was always in the fields, so he couldn't take care of me. So I was like an orphan by myself in the house. At the time I didn't feel uncared for. It's only now when I look back that I can see it. I don't have hard feelings about it, you know.

When I was about twelve, my mother came to Puerto Rico looking for me. I was at my aunt's house. When she told me, "This is your mother," I was surprised. For me it was like the Virgin coming from the sky. I'd never seen anyone so pretty, all dressed up in silk stockings and high heels. She was so well dressed. She made a big impression on me.

I would have stayed in Puerto Rico, but my grandfather decided he didn't want me to go to school past the sixth grade. The school was way in the city, and I had to travel. He didn't like the idea of me walking all the way to the city. I said, "Well, I want to learn more. I want to go with my mother." He said, "If you want to go, okay."

After I came to New York to stay with my mother, I figured I would rather have stayed back in Puerto Rico. We lived on Tenth Street and Avenue C in a railroad apartment. It was a shock coming from Puerto Rico. I didn't understand much about the city. I didn't speak English. I didn't have many friends.

My mother didn't have much love for me. She had four other children, and she didn't know me that well. She was very hard with me. How she would beat me! She had a very young husband. She was very jealous. When I came, she thought I had an affair with him, which was very difficult because I didn't have anything to do with him. Then he left her.

My half sister was jealous of me too. Everything my mother bought for me she would take the scissors to or break. If I had jewelry, she would take it away from me. The older boy used to run away and come home late. Then he had a drug problem, and my mother had to put him in a home.

I felt very trapped. I went to school, but I had to be home by a certain time. Other kids did their homework and went outside and played or entertained themselves. Well, I couldn't do that. I was supposed to take care of the little ones, Edwin and Bisbee. I did my mother's work. I had to cook. I had to wash the diapers because they didn't have Pampers in that time. I had to feed them, and clean the house, everything. I was twelve. I was afraid of my mother, but I didn't dare say I wanted to go back to Puerto Rico.

When I was fourteen, I met my husband. He was twenty-nine. I met him near the school. He used to hang around where the girls were. I would go to my friend's house and meet him there. My mother found out. She said, "You don't know how to do anything." She always complained that I didn't do her work right. She said, "How are you going to go and get married if you don't know how to do anything?" I didn't answer her. I never used to answer her. I was very quiet, shy. I kept to myself.

Finally, I couldn't take it anymore. One day she told me to make some potatoes. She didn't tell me how much, so I put the whole bag of potatoes in, and I cooked it along with the bacalao, codfish. She came home. She was furious. "You used all the potatoes! You used all the potatoes!" she's screaming and yelling. Oh, how she beat me and beat me! I didn't talk to her for three or four days. Then she said, "Do something in the house or get out. Get a job." I said, "Okay, I'll get a job." I left, and I never came back. I thought, if I ever grow up and have kids, I'll make sure they love me.

I went to live with my husband. It was easier for me being a housewife in my own house than in my mother's because there nobody beat me up. I would do whatever I wanted. Then I got pregnant. In the beginning I felt okay. But then my husband changed. He used to go out and leave me by myself. He used to gamble. There were other women, and my friends would tell me, "He's going out with this girl, and you don't even know it." We used to have fights. But then I decided to drop all that. I thought if he wants to stay outside, let him. I don't care anymore. In a couple of years, he did stop. Maybe he got too old to keep up with us both!

I was fifteen when I had the baby. It was hard for me. You have to get up in the night and do all those things for the baby. He had ear infections. He cried all the time. My husband loved the baby, but he used to have to go to work the next day. The crying made him very nervous. He used to say, "If he doesn't shut up, I'm going to take that baby and put him outside." I felt very mad. I didn't want that to happen. I was going to run away with the baby, but then I decided not to. Then I was pregnant again. The next baby, Gloria, was very quiet. She was a good baby. They were a year apart. Then came Else and Jose.

I loved the kids. I always loved children because kids are still good. I was used to taking care of them. It was something common like an everyday thing. I decided I was not going to be like my mother. I wanted to be a different person. I wanted to understand my kids more, and give more love to them than I got. If you hit the kid all the time, it won't love you. It will end up getting frightened, and hate you when it grows up. You have to love in order to get love.

I think I had a lot of patience. My church helped. After I got married, I started going, and I got more faith. The nuns were very nice to me. I used to go with the kids to the church group and enjoy myself. I make sure they go to mass every Sunday. It's educational. They learn about God, and feel what is going on in the world.

The girls are Daughters of Mary. They wear white dresses with blue ribbons and have medals of the Virgin on them. They go places—ice skating and to Disney World. They both went away to Marydell camp, and they took a trip to Canada. I became a minister, a Eucharistic minister. I went to classes. I help the father serve the wine or the Eucharist.

I trust my kids. I always taught them what is right and wrong from the beginning. I say, "You don't do this because it's wrong. You do this because it's right." They haven't gotten involved with anything that is wrong. I had to learn that for myself by looking around me, by seeing the environment. When you grow up in New York City, you see a lot of things. You see drug addicts, people smoking and shooting up. You see gangs. You see prostitutes. I wanted a different life for my kids.

My kids respect me. I guess it's because I am fair with them. They have a problem, they come to me. They need something, they come to me because they don't trust their father. He starts screaming at them. They feel more free talking to me. They ask me for my advice: "Mommy, should I do this? I have to do that." I say, "If you have something to do, you do it. Tell me, and do it. That's that."

My husband is very strong with them. He's very strict. He never gives them enough freedom. He thinks by keeping them in they will never learn from the bad things in the world. They will stay innocent, clean.

I feel differently. They have to grow up. If they stay in the house, they won't grow up as bright as they're supposed to. In Puerto Rico some parents won't send their kids to school because they don't want them to leave them. They grow up with their parents, then they come to a certain age, and they can't leave them. They are too attached to them. That's frightening. They stay stupid all their lives.

Now Fred and Gloria are going away to college. I am very proud of them. Already they have achieved more than I have in my life. I would like them to be something, have a better life than I have had. My husband disagreed in the beginning; he said, "I'd rather have them nearby where I can keep an eye on them." But they can go anywhere, and I know they won't do anything wrong.

I love my kids like they are babies. But I don't think they are spoiled. They're lovable, and they are kind. They have tempers like their father, but I can handle that. Their lives will be better than mine. I think now women have the same opportunities that men do. Already they have a higher education. They won't marry so young. They will be their own person. I always tell them, "First school, then marriage." I tell them, "You see my life, how it is. Would you like to have the same kind of life?" They say, "No, Mommy. We don't want that kind of life. We want to live free and do what we want. We want an education." Else, my smaller daughter, makes me laugh when she tells me, "I will not marry a macho Puerto Rican guy like Daddy."

I stayed with my husband because I didn't want to be like my mother. I wanted to have kids with one father, all of them from one father, and that's what I did. And it's no good to be on welfare. Most of the young girls have been on welfare since they were little. They say, "Oh, if I get married and my husband is no good, I'll just go to welfare," and that's it. They don't think if you get married you should try to make it work, or get an education or a job. They say, "Well, my mother went to welfare. Why shouldn't I?" They feel like welfare is always there, like a mother to support them.

Now I work as a baby-sitter for two different women, Frances and Sheila. I like it. I like the kids. I get involved with them. I give them lots of love like they are my own kids. Maybe I spoil them. I do it, too, because I need the money. What I get from Social Security is not enough to support a family. My husband's disability is $600 a month. It's not enough for rent, telephone, utilities, and food. Then the four kids need money for school, clothes, books. Where am I going to get all that money? That's why I decided to baby-sit.

They can't always have what they want. They've learned the value of what they have. I say, "Don't ask for more than what I can give." For me it's difficult because I don't have that much to give. I tell them, "I'll try to do whatever you want me to do, but if I can't, I can't. If I have the money, I'll do it." They understand.

Frances and Sheila say to me, "You have the brains. You should go back to school." They want to help me. Jose is twelve. When he's eighteen, I'll be forty. I wouldn't mind going back to school to be a nurse or a midwife. I think my husband wouldn't like it, but maybe I'd quit him too.

I always wished to have another baby. But Jose was my last one. It was my idea to have my tubes tied. It was clear to me at the time that I didn't want to have too many kids. I can hardly afford the ones I have. My husband disagreed with me. The church disagreed with me. They all wanted me to have more kids. But I said, "I am not going to leave this hospital until I have it done."

When I got on the operating table, I was afraid. I was afraid I was going to die on that operating table. But it turned out okay. There's always kids to take care of. Sheila, who I baby-sit for, says, "Oh, Narrada, you can't quit on me now! You can't quit on me now!" Her next baby's due in a month, and I know she needs me.

I'll Pay Anything to Make You a Winner

ELIZA BLAKE

Grant has always been a person who made his own decisions. When he was four, he went up the street to a little nursery school. After about two weeks of it, he said, "I don't want to go there anymore." Eventually we listened to him, and I took him out. Even then the teacher said to me, "You'll regret this as long as you live. He will always dictate what he's going to do." And I said, "Well, that's okay." I explained to Grant, "When you're five, you *really* do have to go. It's the law."

To me, there are two ways to bring up children. One is to train them by force. Some people train their children to be like adults, and in the process they don't have much respect for that individual kernel of a person. Other people are in awe of the beauty of that individuality, but they don't try to train them. In an earnest, naive way they may try to just move with the child to get them to a certain point by always respecting them. That might be the mistake we've made with Grant. We totally respected his individuality. "What do you want? Oh, you don't want this? All right, tell us how you would like it."

This spring we suddenly found ourselves with a six-foot-four thirteen-year-old boy who has never been forced to do anything. Adolescents can be hard to live with, but this guy was really horrible. My husband would wake him up in the morning, and Grant would say, "You fucking asshole! Get out of my room!" At seven o'clock in the morning, you say to yourself, "Is this what it's all about? Is this where we are?" He wasn't doing well in school, was sticking to himself, and was out of step with the rest of the family.

One night he came in for dinner. I looked at him. His pupils were very dilated, and the whites were bloodshot. I said, "Grant, look at your eyes. What's going on?" He never lied. He said, "I'm high." I said, "Well, what are you taking?" And he said, "Pot." I said, "Why are you doing this?" He said, "Because I guess I like it." His directness was encouraging, I guess. At least we were talking.

I confronted him again. I said, "Grant, I don't think we can live with this. When you're eighteen and you live by yourself, and you pay your own way, I guess you can do whatever you want. But when you're a child in our house, I'm not fixing dinner for anybody who comes in here high." He said, "Oh Mom, you really don't know anything about it. I've been doing this for a long time." And then he said, "I've thought it all over. I've made my decision, and you're not going to stop me." It was a direct, strong, calm statement of where he was.

I said again, "This is something we can't live with. I want you to know that I'm going to take some time to look into all the possibilities—programs, treatment centers that deal with this." I called various programs here in the suburbs, but there was nothing for a child as young as thirteen. The only program that would take him was a place called Phoenix House on the West Side of New York City.

I decided we would go there first just to gather information. I wanted to tell them what had happened and find out whether they would be interested in us, and if we would be interested in them. The director explained to us that their approach was definitely that drugs don't stop once they start. The problem just gets worse. You have to step in. He told us it would be very fortunate if we intervened now rather than when Grant was seventeen. They do not believe in using any chemical substances, and their approach is to get the whole family off chemicals. If Grant were to join their program, Jim and I would have to give up alcohol for six weeks.

At first my attitude was, "What, me?" I don't have a problem with alcohol. I enjoy a gin and tonic or a glass of wine with my dinner. That's culturally acceptable. But then you realize these children are watching that pattern, and they're hearing us say, "Don't take drugs." It's a cross message. There's also the pressure from their peers, who are saying, "Take pot," and God knows what else. I don't think I have a problem with alcohol, but I thought if it will help my kid, there's no question about giving it up.

In the car on the way home I asked Grant, "What do you think?" He said, "Do I have a choice?" I didn't pick up fast enough on that remark. I think it really showed us where the power was. This kid probably would have liked us to take control. I probably should have said, "No, you don't have a choice. This is what we're going to do." But I wasn't there yet myself. I hadn't really made the decision that the strong stand Phoenix House takes would be the right thing to do.

For the next ten-day period I would say things like, "Grant, I just want you to know we're still looking into all the possibilities. All I can tell you is that we have our first crisis, and we're not prepared to live with you using drugs. We're taking our time to evaluate what we're going to do, where we're going to go, and as soon as we make our decision, you'll be the first one to know." He said, "Okay, okay." He was agreeable enough. He didn't say too much. He was respectful that we couldn't live with it, and that we wanted to do something about it.

Then all hell broke loose. A few nights later he was dressed at nine o'clock at night and said, "I'm going out." I said, "Grant, I'm sorry. You're not going out. It's a school night, and you're not going out." More of "You fucking asshole." He started down the stairs fully dressed, and I jumped out of bed and ran down after him. I said, "Grant, if you touch that doorknob, I'm calling the police." He stopped, turned and gave me another blast, and went back up to his room.

Three days later, he was dressed to go out again. He said, "I'm going to do what I want. You're not going to stop me." I stood in front of him. He came toward me. I pushed him, and I remember ducking in the upstairs hall, but he hit me in the head. I'm tall, close to five-ten, but this child happens to be six-foot-four. I got hit by the ear on the side of my head. I had never been hit that hard in my life by anybody. That was a horror. I was crying. My daughter came running out of her room screaming, "Grant, Grant, stop, stop!" The situation was out of control, and I knew we had to go for help. We called the police. The other children were crying. The police came, but Grant had run away. At that moment Phoenix House was looking pretty good.

He didn't come back that night. We went to bed. We closed the doors, and I said, "Lock them." My husband said, "We can't lock them. He might come back." I wasn't interested whether he came back. I wasn't worrying about what was happening to Grant. "Lock them," I said. When he showed up the next day, it was almost like looking at a stranger. I said, "Are you all right?" I wasn't angry. When you know you have a real problem, there's nothing to talk about. I said, "Grant, you really hurt me last night." He said, "If I hurt you, I'm sorry." I said, "We're going for help. We're going to Phoenix House. The situation is out of hand." He said, "It's not going to work. Just don't worry about it. It's my business. I'll do what I want, and it's not your concern." I said, "It is our concern because you live here."

Jim said, "Grant, you are going to Phoenix House. It's three days a week after school. I'm going to leave work early to pick you up at the junior high." Grant didn't say too much about it. When my husband came to school, the principal paged Grant out of class. He came down the hall and said to the principal and his father, "Oh, excuse me, I have to get a book out of my locker." They waited like fools for twenty minutes. Then they realized that he had outsmarted them. He was gone. That was day one.

On day two I said, "Well, look, I'll try to get him. It will be less of a confrontation." I was always trying to give him a little side door to protect his dignity and his feelings. It was a repeat except that he had left a period earlier. He'd cut French and fled the school grounds. I went around the neighborhood looking for him in the car and finally found him two streets away.

I pulled up in the car. There was Grant crouched in the bushes with two boys watching. I got out and said, "Grant, get into the car." He said, "No, I won't." More foul language. Then I took a step toward him. He said, "Don't come near me, or I'll hit you." I reached over to grab his arm, and he twisted my arm behind my

back. There I am on the street in my own town, upset and in pain
and yelling to the other kids, "Jake, what's happening? You kids
are out of control. Look at this!" They just snickered. I said, "Jake,
I need your help." I got into the car crying, and backed down the
street. I came home knowing that we had a fight on our hands.
Getting him to Phoenix House wasn't going to happen with words
or persuasion. It was going to be force.

I walked into my own home, and I said, "There's going to be
some trouble. This child is going to come back here and fight.
We've raised a monster. We have raised a kid who is out of control." I have some eighteenth-century English coffee cups, really
beautiful cups. I laugh about it now, but at the time I thought,
whatever happens, the windows can break, the paintings can fall,
but I don't want these English cups broken. I packed them up as
if the A-bomb was going to drop on the house.

Sure enough, within about twenty minutes of getting them all in
a box, in walked this six-foot-four angry kid wearing his father's old
army shirt. "It's not working. I'm not going!" Jim said, "Grant, I'm
sorry, but you can't live here anymore." And he said, "Now get
out of our lives. Get out of here." Grant sort of shrugged his
shoulders, turned and walked out of the house.

I got mad at Jim. "Look, don't tell him to get out of our lives.
Tell him he has to go, that he can't live here." I laugh now, but Jim
went running down the street after Grant yelling, "I don't mean to
get out of our lives! I just mean you've got to get some help." Grant
is screaming, "Fuck you!" and throwing rocks from the driveways
at Jim. This is four o'clock in the afternoon. They're running down
toward the Hudson River: "Don't get out of my life! I just mean
you've got to get help."

That night we did lock the doors. I remember thinking, in another century a fourteen-year-old boy could be on a freighter heading across an ocean. He could be stoking a furnace, apprenticing
for some job. I thought this guy is six-four. Even if he leaves school
. . . I really came to the conclusion that we were doing him the
biggest favor by saying to him, "Grant, we wish you all the luck.
Goodbye and good luck." We were prepared to do that.

At three A.M., there was a knock on the door. It was the police.
"You Mrs. Blake?" "Yes." "Where's Mr. Blake?" I went to wake
him up. "Is this your son?" "Yes he is." "Mr. Blake, this child is

a minor, and you are responsible for him. There's a curfew here at nine o'clock for a child his age. If this happens again, we'll issue you a summons." At first I thought, he's won. He can see we are responsible for him, and we can't throw him out. But then I thought, he must have been pretty uncomfortable out there on the street until two o'clock in the morning. He wasn't hiding in anybody's garage. He was standing out where he could get caught and picked up. I decided that allowed us to tighten the bolts for one more round.

The next morning we didn't wake him up for school. I went to the school principal and asked to have Grant suspended. Then I went up to Grant and said, "Take a shower. Come down and have your breakfast. We'll talk about it in the kitchen." When he came down I said, "We're going to visit your grandmother in the hospital, and then we'll talk about this on the way to Phoenix House." There was some resistance. "It won't work." I said, "Look, Grant, you owe me one. Because of what we've been through, you owe me one. You're going today."

We got in the car. The rock and roll was on, and I said, "Grant, do you want to talk with the music on or off?" I tried again to give him some little technical out. He said, "With the music on." Well, at least he was in the car, and we were on the way. I then told him that the school had suspended him for his behavior toward the principal and his father, and I said, "You have a week at home, anyway. I'm asking you to go for this week. At the end of one week, you can give me your decision." And then I said, "If you don't agree to go, we'll have to take more procedures with the family court."

He was pretty quiet. He did visit his grandmother in the hospital, and I must say I think it's nice when other members of the family get involved with the problem. You have a tendency to hide it, to say, "My God, I can't let anybody know this," but to make that child face his grandmother is one more way of influencing him. Here's this old lady flat on her back. She looked at Grant at the end of the bed and said, "Grant, I wonder if you'll go into medicine." I'm watching this and thinking this kid is so far from going into medicine. He's totally off the wall, but still someone is seeing him positively. That positive encouragement alone might be an influence on him. She reminded me that you can never give up on a child.

We came out of the hospital and didn't talk too much about that. We walked across the East Side to the car. It was a long ride through Central Park. There was nothing to be said. He was in the car. I was in the car. We were going. I can say, though, that the moment we actually walked into Phoenix House is frozen in my mind. It felt like a victory. He'd walked into that building, and that showed there was some doubt on his part.

The director met us in the hall and said, "Grant, welcome to Phoenix House." I thought, whatever will come of this, I think we have taken a good stand. Then I turned and left. As I told a friend, "I felt like I've won the war, but I'm bleeding to death."

For the rest of the term he went three days a week after school. Either Jim or I would drive him in, and we got nothing but swearing. I never asked him about the program. The first day I dropped him I said to Jim, "When you pick him up, wait in the car. Let him walk out of that place on his own." We never asked, "What's going on?" or "What are you doing?" or "How do you like it?" It was his business.

Grant continued to go to Phoenix House through the end of the year. The violence had stopped. There was no more hitting, but we were still living with the language and a very angry child. He had stopped speaking to me. He said, "I'm just not going to talk to you anymore." One morning I was fixing orange juice for everybody, and I yelled up the stairs, "Do you want juice?" I had handled the first weeks of no communication, but that morning at seven o'clock when I was asking someone who lives in my house a civil question and got no response, I went into a rage. I ran up the stairs and said, "I'm asking you a question! I expect an answer!"

He was lying in bed looking at me. He only said, "Oh, you fucking asshole." I reached down and grabbed him by the shoulders, and I shook him! He got up and raised his hand at me. Jim, who is very kind and nonviolent, came running up the stairs. I would say he boxed Grant with his arms more than his fists. For the first time Grant controlled himself. He said to Jim mockingly, "Oh, you're so violent!" I was happy that that happened. I think that I had a right to get in a rage over not getting an answer. I think it

173

was great that Jim finally showed some real anger. It was our turn to act out.

One of the things that finally got Grant speaking was that I saw Dustin Hoffman on the street near Phoenix House. When I mentioned that to Grant, he said, "Oh." Two weeks later we're coming up the West Side Highway, and Grant said, "Didn't you mention you saw Dustin Hoffman?" I said, "Yes, I did." He said, "Well, I saw Dr. Spock today." This suburban kid was impressed with city people. And then I think he said, "Let's get an ice cream cone." The thaw was coming.

At the end of six weeks we had an evaluation with Phoenix House. They felt that we were very lucky to have had Grant at such a young age admit he was into pot. They felt that we had made a lot of progress. The violence at home had stopped. But they also felt that any kid who is into drugs has low self-esteem, and the only way to build up his esteem is to continue to find out why he was experimenting in the first place. The director turned to him and said, "Grant, we're going to see a good deal of you this summer. We're going to see you every day from ten until six. We're going to have fun: We're going to go to museums, and shows, and spend time in the park." Grant had his head down. He looked up and said, "That's not my idea of a summer. I want to get a job." The director said, "Grant, you'll have plenty of time later to get a job. This is the most important thing you can do right now."

Jim and I were very quiet. We were not really dictating the terms. Phoenix House was. We sat there listening to them tell our kid what he was going to do for the summer. Their approach to getting this young boy off drugs was to keep him busy, and control every bit of his time. The reason they know the kids are off pot is they will do a urine test at random. Marijuana is traceable in the urine up to three weeks after only one cigarette. The kids succumb to this kind of control.

We were not convinced it was a good idea for him to spend the summer supervised from ten until six every day. I wasn't so sure that that was going to solve his problem. I even began to feel that by forcing a decision at this age, we might force him to get wilder.

I asked myself, do we really have a drug addict on our hands, or do we have an adolescent boy who happens to be very tall, who lives in a culture that has drugs all around him? He doesn't know

174

which way to go. He's trying to figure it out, and he's made a mistake. The Phoenix House approach is the hard-line approach of saying, "What, you're using marijuana! Well, we'll stop you!" I thought, well, maybe we're in for a long road to hell, but we have to let him make this decision himself. We decided if Phoenix House could convince him, we'd stay out of it. But the first day of the program, he took the bus and spent the day wandering around the city and was back home at two o'clock.

I said to him, "If you're not going to Phoenix House, you've got to do something this summer." He said, "Look, I'll go to summer school. Tell me to go to summer school." I said, "All right, you've got yourself a deal. I'll back you up. I'm willing to see what you do with this. But at least go to Phoenix House and tell them that you won't be coming anymore." He said, "No, I'm not going. They will just trick me about what I'm saying." That made me feel badly because I thought ultimately he did feel cornered. I'm not so sure that's how someone is going to change.

The next day he signed up for three summer courses. But two days later he said, "You know, I guess I don't really want to take English." I said, "Wait a minute. You decided no Phoenix House, and now all of a sudden it's no summer school. I want you up in the morning. I am not going to tolerate you just doing nothing. You're going to do something. At some point today I'd like you to mow the lawn and clean up the kitchen."

I went off all day with the younger children and came back to the sound of the lawn mower. It looked damn good. The kitchen was in order and the floor was clean. I said, "Grant, how much do you get for an allowance?" Without turning around he mumbled, "Four dollars." I said, "What would you think of a raise?" He turned around and said, "Gee, that would be great." And I said, "Well, you washed the floor and picked up the kitchen, and I think you've done a very nice job on the lawn." I said, "How does ten dollars sound?" He said, "Yah. That would be great." He was really almost a little enthusiastic. I felt we had more of a partnership.

A couple of days later it was still no summer school. I began to feel that he was going to win by dictating all the conditions. I suppose I even bribed him. I sat down and said, "Look, Grant, I realize you want a job, and if you can get one, fine. But if you can't get one, how about taking typing? That's not like summer school, and I would pay you to go. You've got to get up. You've got to get there. I would expect you to attend and do a good job." He reluctantly agreed.

The next morning I knocked on Grant's door and said, "Grant, time for typing." He was stretched out in the bed. He looked up and said, "I still haven't made up my mind whether or not I'm going." I said, "Grant, we've been through this." He said, "You tried to trick me at the last minute. You're offering me a bribe." I said, "You bet I'm offering you a bribe." I said, "You're going!"

He got up and took a shower. I just kept yelling up from downstairs. "Grant, I'll be in the car." And at fourteen past eight he got into that car. Going up the hill to the high school he said, "Ten dollars isn't enough of a bribe." He said, "Fifteen." I really felt extorted. "How ridiculous can you get?" I said, "You brat! You want fifteen. I'll pay it." I said, "The rest of the world believes in force, so they think we should break your back to get you through this." I said, "I'll give you a fifteen-dollar bribe any day, and I hope you learn something from this." I said, "I'll pay anything, Grant, to make you a winner."

I've Got Respect

PEARL BROASTER

My grandchildren love to listen to me talk. My grandson, James, is writing my life into a book for his history class. He says, "Nana, any time you remember, you tell me, and I write it down." I tell him, "You see an old, hard-workin' woman. But when I was a little girl, back in British Honduras—it's Belize now—I had things pretty good. I used to be something like a princess compared to my cousins, who had it so poor. My father was a bootlegger. My mother had a big white house. It had a big kitchen with a great big wood stove with a chimney throwing out the smoke. The house was set into the foot of a hill. To the front was the sea, and the poles of the house was in the water, and you could hear the water lapping in the night on the poles. The boats used to come and pick up copra, dried coconut, and my mother used to sell food to the sailors."

I say to James, "You see how hard I had to work when I become a woman? But I never know anythin' about work when I was a little girl. My mother used to drive me out and say, 'Go, Pearl, go out and play.' She was always keeping me so pretty. My hair was combed with a bow in it." James is writin' so fast to get this all down! So I tell James how I used to go out to my trees and climb up and look at the sea.

I loved those trees. My mother told me, "Your father had wanted a son so badly. And I guess he was disappointed when you were born." My father planted a plum tree because he said, "That is for my son," and another tree that used to put out beautiful yellow flowers that looked like cups. He planted those two trees because he said I was going to be a boy. He didn't think a girl would want a tree.

I was not even fifteen years when I had my first baby. The father was my boyfriend. In my country when you were twelve years old, you could marry, and my mother had liked the guy, so she just talked to him, and we got married.

Going through the nine months I used to always have problems, pains. I was so exhausted. It must have been the weight. The men were away working, building roads, so the women had to back the water. We used to have wells, and we back the water in these big kerosene cans. We nail a piece of broomstick in the can, and we lift it to our head. But my mother said after I got pregnant, she wouldn't let me do it. She used to go and do it for me. She lived right in the house with me.

I'll never forget Cecil's birth, and it's forty-five years now. I had washed the clothes, and I had cooked. I washed that whole house. I scrubbed that white pine. I took all those curtains down, and I washed them, and then I ironed all those clothes I'd made for the baby. It was December 14, one of the royal birthdays. I don't remember whose, but everybody was out singin' and dancin', and I'm in labor cryin'. "Ouch, this hurts. I don't want a next baby!" Oh that pain in my back and belly! I think of it as iron through iron. I'll tell you, when you have a child, your feeling for your own mother grows. You understand what she went through.

The midwife wouldn't let me lie. She made me walk, my mother on the right and she on the left, and they kept me walkin' and walkin' until my water bag burst, and then they got me up to the bed. From there I couldn't bring that baby, so the midwife she boiled thyme leaf and anise seed and ginger and she gave me that, and that's when the labor start comin' faster and faster. The baby's head crowned, but it was stuck. It was too big. Oh, that pain! The midwife she gave me a wash cloth to bite, and I bit right through it. She had to take the baby. She greased her hand with sweet oil, and she caught that baby somewhere by the shoulder, and pulled him out. I passed out.

Oh, but it was worth the while! As soon as that baby was born, oh, the joy! That baby was the beautifulest thing I ever saw. Cecil was so big, thirteen pounds. You look at him, and it seemed he'd been born a long time. His head was right up like he was lookin' at me, looking right into my heart, so I said to the midwife, "Can this baby see?" She said, "No," but I figured he was seeing. I believe that to this day.

The midwife dressed the baby and gave him to my mother. She fed him anise seed and sugar, and that make the baby bring up the mucus. And then they cut the navel string with a candle. They light the candle, and then they burn the string and put the wax from the candle onto the navel, and that heals it. And how that first baby did thrive. I used to give him flour porridge. I used to take that flour and knead it and boil it in a big lump and then grate it, and that baby was so fat! Then when he was four months old, I gave him mashed potato and butter, and I gave him the breast also. He walked from eight months on.

I would give him a bath in the morning. Then I'd make the fire and put on the beans and sweep and make up the bed. By that time the baby would be takin' his first nap. Then if he woke up, and there were no flies around, I bring him outside, put him in a box with a pillow, and put him right down there and wash. We didn't have plenty of clothes, so we washed every day with a scrub board and wash pan. Sometimes I'd be at my fence, and the next woman at her fence washing, and then we'd talk. There was plenty of women around me, and I was never lonely.

My kids come right behind each other. The next baby, Erroll, was only ten pounds, and Joan, after that, was only nine. With Joan, the midwife never got there in time, and my mother helped me. She know how because she helped her own mother deliver. She was the oldest sister of twelve. Her father used to work on the coconut plantation, and many time he wasn't home when her mother was ready.

She got me a bottle, and she told me, "Blow in the bottle," and she took a binder, like a baby napkin, and wound it around my big belly. When she saw the head she told me, "Push, push!" and she

179

kept pulling on that binder while I pushed. Before I knew it, I heard that baby bawlin'!

My mother adored my kids. They were part of her life. She was something like me, hard-workin', very friendly, a bold person, more bold than me because I'm kind of shy. She was a friend with everybody. They could be high or low. We were close, just like me and my daughter, like friends, more than a daughter. And what I didn't know, she showed me.

When all the kids were walking, I used to take in ironing to make money. Sometimes I ironed for the soldiers, the Home Guard we call them, and sometimes for the police. Then this other woman took my husband away. I had to go on the road and start cookin' for the gang building the highway. I used to cook for about fifty-two men. That helped me to buy my own place. I bought a house on top of a hill, and I had about three to four hundred chickens. I had so many that I used to have to keep an exercise book to keep up with them. The kids used to help me pick up all those eggs in a bucket in the morning. I'd sell them. That help me buy clothes for the kids. I loved that livin' on a hill. I could see a green pasture with cows and horses, but then I moved back to the city to put my kids in school. And then, finally, I came to live in the United States.

I was very strict with my kids. Up 'til the time Cecil was seventeen years old I'd take a strap to him. He was so humble. To this day my kids respect me and listen to me. When I first came to the United States, he got involved with the first girl. I think he was nineteen. She was a beautiful Indian girl, but she had a husband. I scolded him, I put my law down, and he broke off with her. My boy Erroll got involved with an American girl, and he loved her so much. He find out this girl is cheating on him. Well, he hit her. She got on the phone to me, and said, "Please, Miss Pearl, come and get him out of my house. I'm scared he might kill me." So I tell her, "Okay, I'll come over and get him." My daughter Joan drove me over there. I went into the house, and I said to him, "Erroll, why did you hit Flora?" He said, "I forsake my kids back in Belize. I work two jobs, and I give her all the money I earn." He said, "Look how I fix her house for her, and she's cheatin' with another man. I caught her, and now I want to kill her."

I said, "No, you're not going to hurt her." I said to Joan, "Open the door, and open the car door." And I tell you I don't know where I get the strength from, but I catch that grown man right on his pants, and I pitch him clean out the door and into the car. He was around twenty-seven, and I throw him right in the car. I say to Flora, "We'll be back for his clothes tomorrow." Oh he was plenty mad! But he listened to me. You know what he said? "You are my mother. You could do me anything. I respect you, but nobody else could do that." Then I sent him to live with his brother, Cecil.

Today it's a different time, and the younger generation feels like they know best. Jacqueline, Joan's daughter, tells me plain, "Nana, I'm not trying to be upstart or sassy, but I think I should live my own life. I'm seventeen years old, and I should pick my friends." What can you say? Times have changed.

But I've still got respect, right down to the little ones. When I speak, they listen. They come upstairs to my bedroom, all of them around. I play with them. I joke with them. We watch cartoons and movies together. I spend my life around my children and my grand-children. I work cleaning houses for them. You know, they don't have a lot to give me, but the greatest thing what they give is love, and that beats all the money or anything. They always show me love. In the night before I go to sleep, Cecil always comes up and checks, "Mother, are you cold? Do you want the heat higher?" And every year at Christmas my daughter, Joan, buys me a ticket to Cleveland, and sends it to me. I didn't want to go this Christmas, but I didn't want to let her down. And I need the rest, so I went. They wait on me hand and foot. They make me waffles in the morning, and they want to bring it to my bed. But I say, "Oh no, I'm coming down." Every evening we go driving. We do simple little things. We go shopping. We take pictures. We go to church. We sit down and laugh a lot.

I am the peacemaker in the family. Last year Erroll got a young woman pregnant. He says he didn't want any more children be-cause he's got three grown boys. He tells her, "Get rid of it." Well, I didn't know she was pregnant, but she called me up and she was hysterical. She tells me she's going to commit suicide. I say to her, "If you know the Bible, you wouldn't try to kill yourself." I say, "When you tell others your business, they talk it out, but when you go straight to the Lord, it's between you and him. You read the Forty-sixth Psalm, and call me back." Well, she called me back in an hour and said, "Thank you, Miss Pearl. I feel such peace."

That night Erroll called me and said, "This morning Paulette was going to the doctor to get rid of that baby, and on account of the way you talked to her, she didn't." I said, "Baby, which baby?" and he said, "Didn't you know she were pregnant? I told her to get rid of it." I said, "Erroll, you make good money. You can afford a next baby. Why do you want to get rid of it?" He said he's forty-three and he doesn't want to be tied down. I said to him, "Well, let her bring that baby, and I'll take it." He says to me, "It's only on account of you that I'll let her bring that baby." Well, she had that baby, a girl, and I'll tell you, Erroll don't have eyes for anything but that little girl. He love that baby, so it was good that they keep the baby. She is named Pearl Marie, after me.

That's my youngest grandchild. That makes twelve. God give them to me, and I love them.

We Are Too Busy for a Family Life

PATTY SIMPSON

Several years ago I went to a women's meeting at church one night. One woman was complaining about how her son was playing football, and her daughter was playing basketball, and her ten-year-old had taken up the flute. She said, "I spend my life in the car. My husband and I hardly see each other. The whole family hasn't had dinner together in two weeks." I just looked at her. She said, "And when your kids get older, just kiss your weekends goodbye." I said, "Oh, that's never going to happen to us." At the time we only had the two older boys, and David seldom traveled. We would spend these wonderful Saturdays in the park having family picnics and togetherness.

Now I am just like that woman I deplored. With four kids, one parent or the other is constantly running. There is always some child who has got to be taken to the dentist and another picked up at the Y. You would think, too, that when they are older you would get your full night's sleep, but you don't. You're waiting up for them if they've gone to a party.

David and I hardly see each other. Last night, for instance, I had to go to a PTA meeting. David rushed home. We've developed a system. I start the meal. He's fairly domesticated. He takes over with the cooking, and I take the two little children and bathe them. I've fed them early, then they read books on their beds while the four of us have dinner. I rushed off to the meeting, and when I got home, David went back to his laboratory for a few hours more of work.

On Saturday nights when the kids were little we used to make a habit of having dinner late by ourselves after they went to bed. We did that every week religiously. Now with teenagers, if you aren't driving them to their hockey game, they are around, and they want to talk to you.

It's gotten to the point where I never see my own husband, so I find I'm calling him at work just to talk about decisions that have to be made about the family. I can hardly talk to him at home because we get interrupted by this barrage of kids.

What happens is that I tend to take over a lot of the day-to-day logistics. I don't resent it really, but sometimes I feel it's too much. I'll get extremely frustrated if one more person says "Mommy" to me.

Last night David said, "Come to the airport with me, so that at least we can talk in the car." I'm thinking, this is insane, as we're racing down the thruway to meet these Egyptian scientists he works with. Is this the only way I get a chance to talk to my husband?

I remember my father coming home for lunch every day. We all came home for lunch. We had breakfast, lunch, and dinner together. Then after lunch my father and mother would go into the living room and sit down and talk about us and household-type things. In this day and age, people don't have time for that.

David and I are fortunate. Our backgrounds and values are similar. We both have the same philosophy of child-rearing. We always wanted children. He had done a lot of volunteer work in the Big Brother Program, and I grew up next door to an orphanage. When we first got married, we missed having contact with kids. We used to take our friends' three children ice skating every Saturday morning. It was great fun. Our kids don't bother to play one of us off against the other because we almost always agree on the solution to a problem.

I don't think people realize that you have to work at having a family life. My mother used to drill it into me, from the time I was a little girl. She would say, "Marriage and family are a woman's idea. It's up to you to make it work." I know it was a sexist view, but now I'm beginning to think she's probably right. You have to give a lot. I think women have to give maybe more than men, though men don't want to admit it.

My mother also said two other things. "Never live your life through your children. They are not extensions of yourself. Remember that you are you, so that you have something of your own." And then she would say, "Remember, too, that your husband's the one you married, and he's the one you're going to end up with."

Her life was geared for my father. Daddy was a doctor, and Mother felt he saw all these sick people all day, so life should be calm for him when he got home. She also felt you should be available whenever your husband wanted you, even when he came home at three o'clock in the morning and wanted to talk or make love. I've said, "The only problem is all that was for him and not you."

I do think, though, that you have to work at intimacy in a marriage when you have children. When we were younger, we used to swap our kids with friends and get away three or four times a year. Now that we have four kids, it's harder, but we do try to take at least one trip a year. Last year I went to a scientific meeting with him in San Francisco. I slept late and shopped. We rented a car and drove to Los Angeles. I didn't have to worry about what time it was. It wasn't just taking care of myself, but taking care of our relationship. It's just not being rushed, either physically or mentally.

At home there's always someone coming into our room at night. It doesn't bother us too much. We're very easygoing. We joke about it. One time I told him, "I'm coming down to your office, and we're going to lock the door." You know, there are so many articles in the women's magazines about couples having sex all the time. The truth is that they aren't because there's just not time.

I think everybody's too busy nowadays. There are lots of families now where the mother and father leave the house at seven-thirty, before the kids, and they don't come home until after the kids, and I don't see how anybody can function that way. Everyone is going in a different direction. There is no center because no one is there. It doesn't matter what anybody says, it's laid on the mother to be the center unless you have one of these reversed situations where the father's at home and the mother's out, and those are still rare.

I think women are trying to be too much, and I think it's really scary—because we're paying for it. The product is messed-up families. We've got a lot of emotionally disturbed kids. We've got teenagers jumping off the bridge into the river. We've got druggies. I see this firsthand, because I work part-time for the school system as a tutor. I get into homes for extended periods. In some of these homes, where the parents are working long, long hours, there are more video recorders than people. These are upper-middle-class kids, lonely kids. And the ones who are disturbed seem to be getting younger and younger.

Looking back, I realize how much time my mother spent with us. Maybe that's why I try to be around home quite a bit. I look back to those conversations she had with me about marriage and family, and they usually took place after I came home from school. She'd be cooking dinner, and we'd be hanging out in the kitchen.

Now I'm looking at my daughter, Jane Ann, who is only seven, and I'm thinking: What am I going to tell her about marriage and family? When am I going to start on her? I remember when I had my first child, Timmy. This was fifteen years ago, back when Gloria Steinem and Germaine Greer were very active. I had a friend named Mary Alice. I remember her saying to me, "How am I going to bring up my daughter to be happy? If I encourage her to be a physicist or an engineer, she will not be happy as a woman because she'll be constantly competing with men." I said, "Don't be ridiculous! Of course you should encourage her." She said, "You wait!"

Now I look at the women who are scientists at David's laboratory, and they *don't* seem very happy. They pretend they are, but science is a man's world. They are competing with men, and at the same time they have the same desires that most women have—to have babies and to take care of them. But they won't admit it.

I don't mind admitting it. I always wanted to be a wife and mother, and I enjoy it. We really have not achieved complete equality, and I'm not so sure it is possible or even should be possible. For a while there, it was like you were doing a disservice to the women's movement if you were a mother, but you know, it's okay to be married and have kids.

186

Can You Make It to the Top and Still Be a Good Mother?

EILEEN KINSELLA

I went back to work five years ago when Darcey was five. To be perfectly honest, I found staying at home with a child very boring. But I did it because no one can nurture a child like a mother. I think until children can walk, talk, and shit in a pot, and express what they feel, they should be with their mother, whether the mother hates it or not. I didn't hate it, but it was not the nicest part of my life. I believe that if you leave your child with somebody else, you will have somebody else's child. Their values will develop in that child.

I am very successful at what I do, which is making deals with *Fortune 500* companies for a bank. I make over eighty thousand dollars a year. I work in a department with one thousand people, and I'm the only woman on my level who is married with a child. I am very unusual.

I love my job. I took it because when I stayed home when Darcey was small, and I saw my husband walk out the door, and then I saw my child walk out the door, I was very frustrated. I was not going to be left behind. Underneath I was very depressed.

There was also pressure for Howard to produce. I have very expensive tastes in food, clothing, and entertainment. He said, however, "If that is what you want, at least you can help support it." Now I get up at five and am out the door by six-thirty.

I love to go in and make a deal. But believe it or not, I do not think somebody who is married and a mother should be doing what I do. I work under tremendous stress and pressure. Often I'm away on the road selling, and even when I'm in town I am not home before seven or eight. Howard works twenty minutes from home and he is able to be there. To tell you the truth, he is more suited for parenting than I am.

I honestly think that two people cannot both work the way I do and have a normal child. I feel badly saying that because I am very much for women succeeding, and very much for my own daughter succeeding. Even though Howard is available, my daughter still would prefer to have me there. She could call him when she gets home from school, but instead she calls me. She tells my secretary that she has to get me out of a meeting because it's very, very important. I think preadolescent girls have very complicated feelings toward their mothers. She comes home and wants to bitch about all the kids in school and how much homework she has; and she wants me to be there to listen.

On the other hand, I think she is proud of me. She comes to my office and sees that I have my own secretary. She flies around the country with me. She likes that.

I want Darcey to have the opportunities that I didn't have. I think I am a good role model for her. I want to do what I don't think my mother did, which is to relate to her that she is smart and can succeed and build a career. Then you can find a man and make a decision about whether you want to be a mother. That's not what I did. My mother, who was a graduate of Vassar and had a master's degree from Columbia, never encouraged me to be successful. She considered it appropriate for me to be a debutante and marry young. Howard was twenty-three, and I was nineteen, helpless.

In order to maintain the kind of responsibility I have in my job, I have to compete constantly with men. I have to live in their world, and that affects the way I am a mother. I don't, for instance, have a picture of my child on my desk. My job does not allow for me to be sick. I can't call up and say, "I won't be in because my kid's got chicken pox." A man would never do that. A man would also never say, "My child has a play, and I would really like to see her in it." I have to be honest. There are many times when I would really like to do that, but I don't. My husband goes instead.

I always have to juggle. Darcey asks, "Can you come to assembly at school, Mom?" I tell her, "You can't ask me this morning! You've got to tell me *three weeks* in advance because I have to plan everything." I am very regimented and controlled. That's the only way you can really be successful at a job like mine. I am able to close deals successfully because I'm persistent. I'll find out all the answers.

I come home from work physically and mentally exhausted. I tell the men I work with that I don't go home and relax the way they do. I go home and do all the things that my husband and child have missed while I'm gone. I listen to Darcey. I draw her bath for her, and I comb her hair. I ask her how her school work is going, and I browbeat her into doing her homework. I find out how Howard is feeling, and what he needs to make him comfortable. There is no slack, *none.* And do you know who misses out? Me. I miss out. I would love to relax. I don't get the time to just relax.

In fact, the last time I relaxed, really relaxed, was more than six months ago. I had come home from a business trip on an earlier flight than I'd planned, but it wasn't worth going into the office. The mother of one of Darcey's friends happened to see my car in the driveway. She came in and dragged me out for an ice cream cone. Now this seems goddamned stupid, but I hadn't done anything like that in a year. I just left my house spontaneously, knowing I had a million things to do because I'm never home to do them. We walked to the ice cream store, chatting all the way. Then we came back to my house and had a couple of glasses of wine while the kids played. I never do that. *Never!*

Six months ago I was offered a big, big job. It was much more responsibility than I now have. I would have been in charge of offices in New York, Boston, Chicago, San Francisco, and one soon to open in Atlanta, with sixty-five professional people reporting to me. The headquarters was in Boston, but the bank was willing to let me stay in the New York area, which would have meant flying out of Westchester Airport three days a week to Boston.

I did a total soul-searching. I could have been one of the top five players in the organization. I would have made well over a hundred thousand a year, even maybe had my picture in *Fortune* magazine! I had to think about where I was going and what I wanted.

I realized I couldn't take it. I only have one child. I want to be a good mother to her. Though my relationship is sometimes difficult with Darcey, it is more sane than mine was with my mother. And to have it continue that way, I have to be there at least as much as I have been. I am worried about adolescence. When I was in boarding school, the biggest drama was that one girl became pregnant. Now we are looking at drugs and the tremendous peer pressure to experiment with everything. Her father is the major support for her now, but if, for whatever reason, she feels she needs to have me there, I would give up my career. I'm far from being a real mother type, but there must be some motherly instinct in me because I want to feel that I've completed some cycle with her.

Spring is the busiest season at my work. By the end of June, both Darcey and Howard have had it. If I had taken that job, I would have lost my child, and I know I would have lost my husband. Men who have the primary responsibilities at home are just like women in that position. They feel lonely and tied down with a child. Howard feels he has been up to his neck dealing with the kid, the homework, the plumber, and the damned dog.

Yet, I did pursue that job. It was almost like being a prostitute. I lured them on for months. I made it to seeing the president. I did it because I wanted to know that I am just as competent as a man. And—I'll tell you something—I am. It was very important to me to be offered that job. But I would say to anyone that a woman cannot make it to the top without sacrificing something, and it usually turns out to be the family.

Friends would have dropped by the wayside, too. I would have had a few people who would have continued to seek me out because they knew me before; but it would always be a rushed dinner at a restaurant. In five years those people would be gone, too, and I wouldn't have had a friend in the world except for the people I work with.

Some of them I really do like, but I could never get really close to them, because their wives are threatened by me. I'm pretty, and I dress well, and I come on strong. However, I am not after anybody else's body. I'd almost say that except for my husband, I'm asexual.

A lot of women right here in my town also act pretty peculiar around me. They see me at the PTA meetings all dressed up, and they say, "Boy, she's overwhelming!" Well, I'm coming from work! I don't mean to be overpowering, and I don't flaunt my career or tell them how much money I make, but I'm very assertive. I'm a salesman. I'm on. I resent that they can't treat me well. Sometimes I feel like saying to them, "I'm a woman." I was a woman before I went out and got this big job.

I do understand where they are coming from. I was home with somebody for five years. A lot of these women admit, "These kids are driving me crazy. I want to do something for me, but I don't know what to do." They are afraid to take the next step. It's a big thing to take a step, and I took that step. Everybody has to take a risk in order to succeed.

I did not like staying home with a child. I don't say that negatively. I tell the men I work with, "Staying at home with a child for one week is far more difficult than working for a year; being a mother is a hundred times more demanding and difficult than it is to be the chairman of the board."

And more important, I work for an organization that employs 28,000 people. If I died tomorrow, they would say, "She was great. Boy, was she dynamic!" A month later they would hire somebody else. Well, I can never be replaced as a mother. I could probably be replaced as a wife. Howard could always remarry and say, "Well, she was nice, but I've got a new one now." There's no replacing a mother, though. I really only have eighteen years with this child, and I want to do the best I can.

A lot of women who are younger than I am in top management jobs may view me as provincial. But I think that women who seek career opportunities to the neglect of the family are going to be miserable when they are sixty. When they retire, they will have nothing but a fucking pin from the company. The word isn't in on them or their children yet.

I will never regret that I didn't take that job. You only get one chance to be a mother.

Taking It One Day
at a Time

KATE WALLEN

I've had it with our family problems! Nothing changes! Oh, I say
I've had it, but I say that with a sigh, rather than a scream. Sometimes, though, there just doesn't seem to be any real solution. At
fifteen, my stepdaughter Mickey is still very defensive and erratic
in her behavior and generally quite unpleasant and difficult to deal
with.

This morning was typical. I had a very hard time getting her up
for school. She hates going. She was devastated when she didn't get
into Performing Arts High School with all of her friends, and she's
failing at the Catholic girls' school she goes to. Lately, she's sick
every morning with something or other. But I finally got her up,
and she slammed a door closed on a cabinet that is not too well
glued together to begin with, and the door fell off. She went into
a temper tantrum—curses, screams, pounding her fist on the wall.
She threw a shoe at the door.

Then Salvadore yells at her, "Why do I have to put up with this
shit?" Then he screams at me. "This child of mine is so unpleasant
to be around! I don't want her around anymore!" Joseph, who is
only three, starts whimpering, "Mommy, what's going on? Why is

Daddy so mad at Mickey?'' I want to bury my head under the covers. I'm always the buffer because I don't have that kind of explosive personality. I guess I also don't have the same emotional investment because Mickey is not my daughter.

On top of being a difficult kid, Mickey is trying to grow up and pull away. I keep telling Salvadore not to take it so personally, but he doesn't understand that. Mickey used to be very close to him, and now he feels her withdrawal. When he's around now, she's either on the phone, or she's asking him for money. Salvadore doesn't know what to make of her. It's as if he's almost offended by her womanliness. She's very pretty, with her mother's full mouth and slanted eyes. She's stocky and dark, like Salvadore, though, and very sensual looking, bordering on the exotic.

Sometimes Salvadore gets very emotional remembering her as a little child, almost as if she is somebody who has died. ''What has happened to my little girl? Here I had a wonderful, sweet child who adored me. Now all of a sudden I've got this other woman living in my house who tortures me, who shrieks at me day and night like another wife!'' And he doesn't have the freedom to walk out the way he would with a wife.

I can understand Salvadore's point of view. He feels he has finally made a positive move in his life by marrying me and having Joseph. He just wants to get rid of the past, and Mickey is a reminder of his past mistakes, a reminder of his ex-wife, Carol. Our family therapist has helped Salvadore see that Mickey is indeed a difficult child, and Salvadore is now able to say, ''Yeah, it's not just me. She is a hard kid to deal with.''

You try to do something nice for her and so often it backfires. It's almost as if she can't allow nice things to happen. Last week when we were walking home, she admired a scarf in a boutique window. I thought it would be really nice to give her a present for no reason at all. I bought it for her the next day. When I gave it to her, she said, ''What did you give me this piece of shit for?''

Yet I know that Mickey really cares about me. Well, I should say, she has paradoxical feelings. She really loves me, and she really hates me at the same time for not being worse to her because she is used to that. I think that's one thing that Salvadore has learned from me, that Mickey tries to provoke behavior that is not mature behavior, so that she can turn around and shout to him, ''Look, you're as bad as I am or worse." I really try not to do that. But sometimes I feel like I am the only adult in the house, and it's very lonely.

I have a very hard time with Mickey's relationship with Joseph. She loves him very much and has no idea of the negative impact she has on him. He won't go into her room without me because he wants to know who is in there, the nice Mickey or the screaming Mickey. I don't do anything much to try to promote their relationship, and to a large extent I can't protect him from what's a very big part of his life. He's confused. He's very sensitive. If I look at him the wrong way, he gets upset. I just give him a lot of love and attention.

Mickey absolutely hates Carol, her real mother, and describes her as "the bad mother." I can see why. Once I heard Carol tell our therapist in a perfectly calm voice, "I'd rather put Mickey in the care of the state than *ever ever* have her live in my house again." Can you imagine a mother saying that? There is absolutely no bond. Poor Mickey! To be so totally disconnected from her mother . . . When I heard Carol say that, I just cried and cried.

I never knew anything like that in my life. My mother is a very gentle person, and innate in her are others of the qualities that we associate with motherhood. She has a nurturing, warm, and understanding approachableness, which as a child I needed to balance my father. He is a very strong, almost overbearing person and rather scary.

My mother was truly empathic with my sisters and me. When I think about her as she was to me when I was a teenager, that helps me a lot with Mickey. One of the things that sort of kept me in rein then was the fact that she trusted me and believed in me.

I wanted very much to be the perfect stepmother to Mickey. When Salvadore and I first started seeing each other, I was in my mid-twenties and Mickey was nine. She was very jealous of me. She always used negative behavior to get attention, and even refused to speak to me for quite a long time. Instead, she would beckon to Salvadore to lean down, so that she could whisper in his ear. I could see right away how much she depended on her father and how close they were. I couldn't expect her to give him up like that.

I did not try to be extra wonderful to her. I was just who I was, and I think that was one of the best things I did. Mickey and I got to know each other over a very long period of time. If you meet somebody at a party who is nasty to you, you naturally don't strike up a friendship. But if you were trapped in an elevator with them for a long time, gradually you would get to know them and appreciate certain parts of them and not like other parts. That was the way it was with Mickey and me. She is a difficult person to live with, but she can be tenderhearted and generous. She is also extremely bright and perceptive.

I feel strongly that if I am a good mother, much of it is due to having my mother as a role model. She rarely gives me advice, but she's a good listener, a sympathetic ear. She has a lot of sympathy for Mickey. And the only time she'll ever offer anything that even approximates criticism is when she feels I'm complaining too much. But she won't even say, "You're complaining about Mickey." She'll start introducing possible points of view, Mickey's point of view. Then I know what she's saying.

She feels very strongly that it's part of a mother's and wife's role to do the best you can for your husband and children and to accept them for who they are without trying to change them so that they're more to your liking. As the mother of teenagers, she probably suffered, but our interests were put ahead of her own. We have trouble with that in our house. Salvadore wants his way, and Mickey wants her way. He can't put his interests aside. I do try to, though. You can't expect to bring children into the world and just go on thinking only of yourself. We are, so many of us, children parenting children.

I think, too, that children are no longer clear about what's children's behavior and what is grown-up behavior. Part of it is due to early maturity. The kids are so smart and so articulate that at thirteen they can pass for eighteen. I really bemoan it, but I don't think you can protect them from it. Once you know something, you can't unknow it. When Mickey says to me, "I want to be more like you, Kate," I try to explain that part of the way I am has to do with the fact that I was a real child for a very long time. When I exploded into teenagehood, it was at fifteen, not at nine like Mickey did.

Mickey is already deeply involved with her boyfriend, and fortunately he is really nice. When Mickey is lucid, she's really on the ball. She said to me the other day, "You know, Edward is a lot like

Daddy, but I can deal with it in Edward." Edward is rather jealous and protective, and has very definite ideas about what he likes. He's a little bit overbearing like Salvadore, but they are both very soft underneath.

She wasn't even fourteen when she started going out with him, I mean *sleeping* with him. I found out by accident. I was standing next to her when she emptied out her suitcase, and there was her diaphragm. I wasn't ready for that: Should I say anything or not? But she brought it up that night. We stayed up until four in the morning talking, and I ended up feeling I couldn't have wished anything better for her, really.

These kids are going to have sex if they want to, and there is really nothing you can do about it other than provide sex education and birth control. Beyond that I believe it's private and should be left that way.

These kids are very romantic. They get this whole monogamous situation set up, and it becomes like a mini-marriage, almost, but without any of the responsibility. Mickey has been miserable on and off, in agony over Edward. They have some of the worst fights. She's told me she is afraid she's starting to act like her mother— taking everything so hard, plunging ahead in a wild and haphazard way. She's very perceptive. It's one of her strengths, but it's been kind of a burden too, not to see things simply. "Why can't I be more like you?" she asks. She sees I take things easily and let them go easily too. She'll ruminate ceaselessly over something.

She knows she is self-indulgent, and she hates to disappoint me. In fact, her behavior will even accelerate in a bad direction in order to cover up something she thinks will disappoint me. She'll do something worse to cover. She'll cause a terrible situation instead of saying, "I can't deal with what's going on. Help me." And then, I have to say, I do withdraw my affection from her.

I try to be as patient as possible. I believe that she will go through all this and be a wonderful person. I try to catch the kid at a receptive moment and help her understand some things from a mature point of view, try to reinforce that we do care about her, try to just fill some of that space between the negative with a little bit that is positive.

I have learned so much. It's made me grow up having Mickey here. Having my own child has contributed to this, too. But having

197

a baby is such a positive and loving experience, it doesn't force you to examine yourself in the same way that an older child does. I've really had to *think,* think about myself, my attitudes toward my own teenagehood and much more, and I've had to deal with some very unpleasant thoughts.

I tell Mickey that I've learned from her. Her defenses are so high. She says, "Yeah. I make you miserable." She knows inside, though, that I'm telling the truth. The best part of our relationship is largely unspoken.

I have stopped looking for answers, for the magic solution. Sometimes I think: only three more years until Mickey goes to college. But there are times when these years seem like an eternity. But if you start living in fear of the future, instead of happily anticipating it, you have to come back to the present. So that is what I have been working on. I try to take it one day at a time.

He Said, "Part of Your Job as a Parent Is Over"

JANE BINGLEY

We were all aware that this was our last summer as a family the way we'd always been, the four of us, doing things, always together. We were each preparing ourselves for September when Allen would be going off to college. I think we'd purposely not planned a vacation, so that we could be home every day at five-thirty when Allen came home from his summer job. We'd all be hanging around. Brian, who is five years younger, might be shooting baskets in the driveway. He was feeling most distressed because he knew it was going to be lonely without his brother. So, he was really grabbing all the time he could get to be with Allen. We were each doing that in our own way. When Allen would arrive home, I might be reading on the porch, and maybe Mike would be trimming the hedge or just puttering.

The ritual of eating dinner has always been very important to us. A lot of families have separate meals for their children, but because Mike and I both teach, we are home together at a civilized hour. We all pitch in. Brian sets the table and makes it very lovely with china and silver and candles. We have wine, and we sit down and really talk to each other about ourselves, our work, school, politics.

Around eight-thirty or so Allen would be off again for the rest of the evening with his cronies. But this summer we all especially looked forward to those meals together.

The trip to the college was quite jolly, with Mike being very funny to keep me from being weepy. Everyone kept on a light touch, so that I wouldn't collapse. We went out to some awful restaurant and laughed about that, and then we spent the night in a motel and giggled. We were all in one room with various cots. We're always all in one room because we couldn't ever afford two. It's fun.

Then we got up very early the next morning and Allen hustled us all out because he wasn't going to wait another minute. It was in the car on the way over to the campus that I started realizing that this is it! Allen is leaving. I had a feeling I had better get a grip on things rather quickly. I was just staring out the window trying to think of other things, but I could think only of Allen.

When a child leaves home, you take stock. It was important to me to feel that we had really raised a fine, sensitive, and manly person. I don't know if he will be a super success or not, but I think he'll certainly have a very happy life. He knows what his values are, and he seems very firm about them. I know he's going off to school with lots of rich people, but I don't think he'll be swayed at all. He loves the outdoors, and he loves books, and I don't know, he's not involved with anything destructive or dangerous. I don't think he believes in God, but he does have ethics and values, and he's very loving. He loves his brother. Well, he's been a very easy child to raise.

As we got closer and closer to the campus, I kept thinking of how much I was going to miss him. He was always very easy for me to talk to, and he always told me a lot about his friends and worries. He'd wander into my study late at night when he should have been doing his schoolwork. He'd sit down, and I'd have to say, "Now go away. You have to work, and I have papers to grade." But he loved this chitter-chatter. We enjoyed each other's company.

By the time we got to the campus, I was in quite a state. There he was, seventeen already, a young man. And it seemed that five years would pass so quickly and Brian would be gone, too. I was frightened that my life was over. The child-rearing part was suddenly much shorter than I had expected it to be. I saw emptiness and loneliness ahead.

I feel that I have to be quite productive from the moment I wake up until the moment I go to bed, either writing, doing things to the house, caring for the children, being with people, but never just being with myself. I realized that a day would come when I would have to learn just to be.

We parked the car and found Allen's dormitory. The room was tiny for a triple. The other mothers had taken up the entire closet. There were only two sides. I was getting out my frustrations by *hating* them. I said, "Ah-um, there doesn't seem to be any room left for my son's clothes." And Allen kept saying, "Oh, Mom, it's okay. We'll work it out later." He was embarrassed. There we all were, six parents clinging to our children in this minute room. We were watching every movement of our respective sons and feeling schmaltzy and wishing the other parents would go away, so that we could have some moments of privacy with our child. No one went away. We all stayed there and folded socks.

Then we went to hear a lecture from the administration in the chapel. The president, one of the deans, and a faculty member each spoke. They were all very bright and impressive, but they certainly hit the wrong buttons for me. All three of them were around our age, in their forties, and each of them spoke about their own children recently going off to college. They said things like, "This is the end of an era in your life," and "Part of your job as a parent is over," and "We know how traumatic this is for you." What really set me off, though, was when the president said, "You each must trust that we will take good care of your child because we know how precious he is to you." It was the word "precious." *Precious* is the word that made me cry. I was the only person in the entire chapel who was crying, and I was so ashamed of myself! It was precious, because our children are *precious!*

After that we wandered around for a bit. We were about to leave when Allen said, "Let's go up to the room again." I think he wanted to give me a hug where no one could see us. We opened the door, and there was another family member sitting there. It was something like a date when you want to be alone and everywhere you look there's another couple. So we stood in the hall and hugged

Allen goodbye. I was crying, and I could see that he was about to cry, and so we left.

Mike and Brian and I all got into the car. All three of us were sobbing as we drove off the campus. What a forlorn group! We didn't talk. Brian brooded for a long time in the back seat, and then he finally fell asleep. After about an hour, he woke up. He said, "I've made some resolutions. I am going to work really hard in school, and I'm going to get really good grades, and I'm going to try to be on the high honor roll. I'm going to keep my locker neat and my room neat, and I'm going to be very organized." I don't know what it was. It was sort of a redoing of his life, not being the baby brother anymore.

We moped about for a few evenings. Meals were very hard to sustain without Allen. He didn't call, and he didn't write. Finally, Mike got in touch with him. Oh, he was having a blast! Mike said, "Well, don't you think you could have written home?" He said, "I'm getting around to it."

It's been three weeks, and now we don't feel that forlorn. Brian is much more talkative than he had been before. We fixed up his room so he feels very grown up. We took the Snoopy wastebasket out, and gave him a huge leather chair.

Now Allen calls quite a bit. He's suddenly swamped with work, and it's tough. He's weathering it out, though. He'll be home to visit in three weeks, and it may turn out that he's not such a man when he returns. Maybe he'll be in some way needing care. His room has been somewhat stripped. I borrowed his mirror for the bathroom, and his bulletin board is in the kitchen, so we'll have to run around before he comes back and replace his things. So, life does go on in a somewhat ruthless way.

What Role Will I Take with Virginia?

DIANE CHURCHILL

Until the late sixties, premarital sex was "bad." I didn't even know anything about sex. I shouldn't have become pregnant. It was almost freakish because the intercourse that took place wasn't complete. At the time it was just incomprehensible that this had happened. It was almost as if things had started falling up, instead of down.

I had to be secretive. I didn't feel it was right at the time. At first I had this crazy idea that I was going to tell the college. I was an outstanding student. I had been asked to counsel freshmen at Wellesley. I was this. I was that. I was terrified. The doctor I went to advised me. He said, "Don't be crazy. You can't tell them. They'll kick you out." And, of course, they would have. I was so naive, and so young emotionally.

I was able to finish, however, without being discovered. I completed all my finals, and I graduated with honors. But, there was a war inside me at an intense pitch, every minute. What had I done? What was I going to do? I felt it was the end. There was no relief from the agony.

I went to a home. For the first time in my life, having been rather sheltered, I was exposed to all kinds of girls who had been through all kinds of terribly difficult experiences, sad things, pathetic things. I looked into different places before I chose, so where I went was good. Other places had a very punishing attitude. What bothered me then was that there was no help psychologically. They took very good care of us physically because they wanted the child, because *good* people wanted the child. I was treated kindly, but clearly the interest in us was to provide healthy babies. Most of the girls were people who could live good lives, but who were really in trouble and needed some help, and there was no help whatsoever.

There were no activities. It was boredom and anxiety day after day, waiting there with your problems. Here you are about to provide a child to a family, and for that reason alone, you should be given something more than just a few vitamins. I remember fearing that my child could not be adopted. I think I believed I was so bad that somehow I was going to have a flawed child.

At the home I was given the chance to help select her family. Apparently this isn't the way it's done every place. Because my world had totally fallen apart, I chose a very stable, "traditional" family for her. Each couple they told me about was suitable, but I had to feel—know—this was the *true family* for *her.* There was something about the letter from one woman. I don't remember what it was, but I just knew. Bells went off. Her voice called something in me, and I felt a great sense of peace about my choice.

I had an enormous amount of labor. I think some part of me didn't want to give up the child, so that every time I got to a certain stage, I'd slip back again. I think I also wanted to suffer physically. I never held her. I left, and then my milk came in after a couple of days. I was lost. I felt like I was getting out of jail, and that I had to start living all over.

At the time I felt I couldn't ever consider myself a regular person again. I sought out the most fringe kind of people because I felt inferior to everybody else. They were very destructive and harmful, so I went through a series of really bad experiences. I avoided people who could be my friends, or who could give me positive experiences.

It took me years and years to work it out with the help of a therapist. I always considered myself so bad, and it never occurred to me that, given the circumstances, I did anything right. What was pointed out to me was that I had acted as responsibly as could be expected. That knocked me over. It had never occurred to me. And then when I realized that I had been responsible toward the child, but I hadn't been responsible to myself, it took me many years to start thinking that I was worth being responsible to. Finally, I was able to accept the obvious thing, which was that it wasn't going to help her for me to ruin my life because I felt so badly about her.

I had to work through my problems before I could marry and have another baby. I was thirty-two when I had Tasha, and five years later I had another daughter, Karina.

Over the years I always tried to believe my first child was okay, and that someday the matter would resolve itself. I had been reading about adoptees searching for their birth parents. When she was sixteen, I first began to consider writing to the home where she was born to let them know where I was if she wanted to get in touch. I felt that it was her birthright. I couldn't bear the idea that she would be searching fruitlessly. But whenever I actually tried to write the letter, it was too threatening. I had made peace with it. There was ambivalence. I wanted to be there for her if she wanted it, yet I was afraid. I kept postponing it.

I was afraid that she might come in a destructive way. What if she came with tremendous hate? What if she made demands I couldn't fulfill, or wanted revenge?

And what about my other daughters? Karina was only a toddler, but to me it would be incomprehensible for Tasha, who was then seven, to understand how I, her mother, could give away that child. My marriage was difficult, too, and I felt that we were just too vulnerable as a family to take another blow.

By the time she was eighteen, I realized my feelings were different. At one point I had to stop and think about what *I* wanted. It came as a shock to me that I hadn't thought about what my needs were. I finally realized that I wanted to know her for myself.

I had always tried to believe she was okay, but there was also the nagging worry that she wasn't, that she'd had a tragic life, or that she was sick. I tried not to feed those negative thoughts, but still I needed the reassurance. I wanted to *know* that she was okay.

But the biggest thing, I realized, and this is very important to me, was that I needed to give love. Would she be angry? Would there be a question of forgiveness? Those questions were very minor in my thoughts once I came to terms with what I wanted. I needed to love. It was almost like giving birth and having breasts full of milk and needing to nurse. I felt that this need to love was almost as biological as the act of giving birth.

I began to make a concrete effort to get in touch with her. I tried to contact the minister at the home, whom I had become friendly with. I had been trying to call what I believed was his number. I reached a busy signal or no answer. Each time I would call, it took me a long time to work up to it. Finally, I wrote to the home where I had her and said, "Please facilitate her search."

That Easter I was very low. I knew my marriage was going to end after many years of painful effort to make it work. I had just come in from a long ride in the car. I sat down with all my packages and this big clump of junk mail at my feet. I'd kind of forgotten the letter on the edge of the pile. Then I noticed it. I looked at it, and I thought, who is sending me a letter with a purple heart sticker on the back? I guessed it was a young person, perhaps a student writing me about my work.

I opened it up. The letter was sprinkled with silver and gold glitter. I started reading. When I got to "All my life, every day that I can remember, I have wondered about you, what you were doing, and what you look like," it took my breath away. Before I finished reading the letter, I ran to call her. She was so anxious to hear from me. . . .

I dialed the number. She wasn't home, so I finished the letter. It was a wonderful, sensitive letter. It also told me who she was, where she was, and that her parents had assisted her in finding me. From the letter I loved her immediately. I felt such gratitude and relief. Her family had given her a life that was all I had hoped for and more. It's a moment I'll relive all my life, coming when I was so low, yet trying so hard to be hopeful about my life.

A few hours later, I reached her. It was funny. I said, "Hi, this is Diane." She said, "Hi, this is Virginia!" We both laughed. I said, "I loved the purple heart sticker on your letter." That somehow got to me more than anything else, that she would have put that on. I said, "Purple's my favorite color." "Oh," she said, "I've always been so drawn to purple. I wear purple all the time, and I love purple."

* * *

We have known each other almost a year now. I do remember wondering what role am I going to take with Virginia? A friend said, "Won't it be nice to be Virginia's good friend?" But that isn't quite right because I think there is a primitive—primitive is the best word—a primitive sense that she is from me. She is my daughter, she issued from me. It comes as a surprise that just the physical act of giving birth when you haven't known a person at all for twenty years would be so important. What's the physical act of giving birth? But there really is something very strong there.

The connection, though, is deeper. I think it is more as we shared things and got to know each other that we sensed this. I think this is what is crucial: She has always been in my heart and in my mind, and I have always been in hers. We have not known each other in the conventional sense. But there is a sense that we weren't strangers. It is a mystical connection.

She has told me that as she was growing up she had moments when she experienced an intense awareness of who she was, almost as if there was someone right there, a kind of presence who filled her with a sense of harmony. Her feeling was that it was a sense of me. If you believe that thought has energy, then maybe all my thinking and wondering and loving over the years gave Virginia that certain energy.

I don't want to be emotional, but when you are in the situation I was in, when you give up a child, you can't protect them. You simply have to let go. You have to let go to some higher power, to God, to whatever you might call that higher force, and that is a powerful thing.

I *never ever* wished that I hadn't had her, and despite her resentment, she still cared for me. I feel that's why we've been lucky.

It was also very different from the relationship I have with Tasha and Karina, where I make decisions about their lives. All the ordinary difficulties of mothering my children are taken off my shoulders with Virginia. Her parents have that responsibility.

Whatever I give her is because it just happens. Not because I have to or because she has to have it from me. It is what happens in the flow of our being together.

In this last year she has gone through her good times and her bad times, big crises and little crises, and I have found when we talk I feel I'm really giving her something, that whatever it has cost living forty-three years to gain and learn, I am really able to convey to her. And she is able to take from me, accept it from me or bring it out in me, because I've not been her mother.

I think it's difficult for all adoptees, but I do not feel sorry for her, and I do not reinforce any feelings she has of being a victim of circumstance—because she's not. A few years ago I wouldn't have believed that myself. I would have felt bad.

I find it thrilling, really. I feel I have three daughters in three distinct stages of life. One is still a teddy bear. One is a preteen and just on the threshold of adolescence, and one is a young woman. And I am moving into another stage. I am in my mid-forties and am moving rather early into menopause, as my mother did at this age. It is a passage, and it is one I've been looking forward to. In some ways, it's been very liberating, because since I had a child at a young age, fear of pregnancy has been an active, destructive force in my life, and even though I have worked through it, it's never completely left me. The feeling that my body's not going to play any more tricks on me is a wonderfully liberating feeling.

I know I didn't want any more children, so I am not giving up anything, yet there is also a sadness to letting go of a part of my life. When you have babies and little children, you do feel like you're absolutely in the prime. And I do see certain things happening to my face and body that make me feel kind of sad, sad that I'm not as pretty as I was. But I think all this is easier for me because I have Virginia. If I didn't have her, and I was moving into this stage, I think whatever pain I felt about her absence would have added to this. I never felt complete, and now I do feel complete in my mothering, and I can move on.

My kids make me feel marvelous. Look what I've done! I am excited by their beauty. How thrilling to be close to that and to see them unfolding, and to feel that I've had something to do with it.

Knowing Virginia was not a matter of survival. My life had been good without her, and full. My children have done a good part of the healing. But it is an experience of love, and whenever you have an experience of love, it empowers you so much. I feel that I can harness more of myself in life now than I ever could have before.

At first I was concerned about how I was going to tell my other children about Virginia. One friend said, "Oh boy, how is Tasha, being the older child, going to feel?" But another friend was more helpful. She talked about bringing the children into the joy. That phrase meant a lot to me. Telling them was made easier for me because, as these accidents happen, we had been watching a program called "The Facts of Life," about a girl who is adopted and finds her birth mother. It was handled beautifully, and that provided the context for my telling them.

It was a lot for the children to take in, and when I showed Tasha Virginia's first letter, I could see that it was a shock. She was very quiet. I tried to emphasize that Virginia wouldn't live with us, but she would be like a good friend, a big sister who came to visit. And in fact, it's worked out fine. For all my fretting and worrying and agonizing, it was so very natural to the children.

Margaret, Virginia's mother, and I also have a very special relationship. It felt natural to be together as two women who have had different roles in Virginia's life. I have never been so aware of anyone as being as sympathetic about my feelings. She asked me if I had held Virginia when she was born. I said, "No." Her response was, "I'm so glad you can hold her now."

The feeling between the two of us is natural. Maybe in other societies when there are extended families, other women, other wives, this is also true. She is old enough to be my mother. In fact she mothers me, and I love her.

On the other hand, there have been difficulties for Virginia having two mothers. There's no question about it. Virginia is becoming more independent from her mother, which is what we all have to do as we enter adulthood. I think the feelings this raises are hardest for her when we are all together. I've decided not to go to her college graduation for that reason. They've invited me, but I really feel intuitively that it's best not to go.

I do crave her a great deal. I remember one time she was going to come up and stay with me, but she had friends to see. I told her, "You know that's great. That's fine, but I do have this clutching yearning to be with you, and if you feel it, just forgive me." I still yearn to see her. I have to learn to let go because I can never get enough of her.

Sometimes it worries me that so much of our time together is so intense. We still stay up until all hours of the night talking. I'm hoping that I won't always feel the need to do that, that we can lighten up, go to the movies. We still go back over those first sensations of the first weekend together and all that we shared. We always end up talking about it again, our coming together, rather than politics or art or music.

I've always wondered what the people in Penn Station thought of us when we first met. Virginia came up on the train from Washington. It was one of those huge spring downpours of rain, and I was driving from work, an hour from Summit, New Jersey, in order to get to Weehawken in time to get the bus into New York. I was terrified of getting there late: terrified she'd come out of that train and I wouldn't be there. I was *beside* myself to get there on time. I did, and ran down the stairs to her track. But what I didn't realize was there were several places that she could come out. There was no Virginia! No Virginia! It was awful. I had to go back upstairs to page her.

I told her what I would be wearing, a Mexican dress with colorful embroidery, because one of the first things we discussed was that we had actually been in Mexico at the same time. I thought the dress would set me off in a crowd. I had a bouquet of flowers in my hand. I was staring at the crowd—looking and looking and looking for her. I couldn't bear it! She was nowhere! Waiting all those days and hours, and then not seeing her.

She saw me first. She keeps saying that I looked so calm, which is amazing to me. Then I saw her! Oh, what I saw! I saw such grief and sadness. The trip on the train was hard, to be sitting alone, waiting to see this person you have been wondering about all your life. I saw the pain, not only of the moment, but of all those years.

And the next thing I saw was her biological father. She looked like him, and that was a big shock. I didn't want to see that. I wanted her to look like me.

She was wearing lavender shoes with pale turquoise socks turned down, and lavender stockings with flowers on them, and a turquoise mini-skirt and sweat shirt, and lavender jewelry. The colors of her clothes were incredible, and I loved it because I used to wear wild colors and clothes. It was such an expression of herself. Here was this very dramatic statement of who she was and that she wasn't afraid. And to see that boldness next to the fear in her face told me a lot.

We hugged. I said, "Maybe we should have a cup of coffee or tea before we try to get on the bus and go home." I said, "Don't you want to sit down?" I saw that her eyes were starting to fill with tears, and she said, "I don't think I can," and her voice started breaking, and we hugged again, and this is hard to explain, but we looked into each other's eyes, and I saw her *whole* life. I saw everything, everything. And then we sort of broke down. And that's when we came together, at that moment. So we just sort of held on tight to each other, and we went into the bus together and somehow or other we got to Weehawken. At that point, we were really in another world.

The thing I wonder about is at the end of the weekend back in Penn Station. I think of it often. The entire weekend, we were always arm in arm. I know there was an aura. Try to think about a time in your life when you're on top of the world, and it's vibrating out of you. *Nobody* can fail to sense it. I wondered, do people think we're mother and daughter? Mothers and daughters our age don't do that. Do they think we're lovers? Well, we were in love. What did people think of us?

I took her down to the train. It was *hard* to have her leave. It was such a perfect weekend. She got on the train, and sat by the window. I was standing on the platform. It was all grimy and dirty. The window was so dirty I could hardly see through it. I could see only a blur of Virginia. She looked up, and she smiled. I put my hand on the window, and she put her hand up on the other side. For a long time our hands just moved a little bit together on either side of the glass. We kept our hands on the window together until the train finally started to move. Then I let go. I went out, and thank God my friend Sarah had offered to give me a ride, because when I got back in the car, I broke down. It was just the effort of trying to contain myself in that crowd of people.

But it was so glorious! You know, I felt so grateful that I could be given such a glorious gift. And I felt it *absolutely* wiped out every bit of the unhappiness, the suffering and the damage, the *stupid, stupid* damage I did to myself. I thought it really compensated for absolutely every bit of it.

211

Supporting the Discoveries

FLORENCE SCHNEIDER

My daughter, Nell, and I have always done a lot of talking. I never really had that with my mother. I didn't know what it was like to have a mother with whom you could continually have a relationship into adulthood. When Nell calls me from college, I am surprised that she even wants to talk, but she says, "Nobody knows me the way you do, Mom."

I had to learn. I constantly had to work, and still do, on the fact that she is not me. Through our talking we clearly delineate who she is and who I am. We try to define what we feel differently, about how we see things differently, that we *are* different.

I had a mother who didn't do that. My mother wanted me to be like her, and all she ever did was point out how I was like her. She didn't truly let me separate from her.

Separation is a constant process. It's difficult, but at the same time it's exciting. I often feel great relief when Nell says, "Yeah, but I'm not like you! That's not the way I feel," and then I think, oh God! I've helped her to do that! Sometimes she'll come at me and really tell me that I'm doing something that is totally harmful to her, and she'll be right. I'm open to that. I'm not defensive because I so want her to be herself.

One of the biggest issues that we've done a great deal of talking about since her early adolescence is drugs. I remember when Nell was first exposed to drugs. I said to her, "Look, I know I can't stop you." Her attitude was, "Well, I'm going to do it no matter what you say. I can do anything I want! I'm thirteen." I was upset. I was watching and trying to keep alert. Warren and I would talk. He would say, "Oh, she's not doing anything. Leave her alone." I had to find my own way.

I always said, "Hey, what are you on? What are you doing? Come on." Later, when drugs were more prevalent in high school, I said, "How often are you doing it?" I could always tell she'd had something because she would get these incredible rings under her eyes the next day. I would say, "Gee, Nell, I can tell when you've had grass at a party because you look like hell the next day." I never said, "Don't smoke grass," but I did keep up a conversation about it.

Finally she said to me, "I really want to know what you think about drugs." She wasn't seeing me as an example because I don't smoke grass. I said to her, "I am totally opposed to drugs. I think they are harmful to your body and habit-forming. I think they are a crutch, a way of avoiding problems. People who take a lot of drugs have some kind of problem that is making them do it, and drugs are a way of running away."

After I stated my case, what we started to do was talk about the kids who were stoned all the time. I'd say, "Nell, what do you think that kid's problem is? Why do you think Raphael is stoned every day?" "Well, Mom, he's very unhappy. He doesn't do his school work. His parents are getting separated, and he's very upset about that." We'd talk about his family situation and why it was so painful for him, and maybe what he could do as an alternative to drugs.

I really feel that this was the absolute right thing to do. It doesn't mean that she hasn't had bad times. She has. She once called from college. She'd had cocaine, and she said she was beginning to find that the drug was making her paranoid and frightened. She was upset. She said, "I'm not going to do it anymore." You can't tape their mouths closed. You can't control them. All I could do was try to build some kind of recognition on her part about why people take drugs.

Then there was sex. That was a tough one, too. First of all I had to observe that she was a very sexual person. Sex interested her. She's a sexy little girl. I never avoided the subject the way my mother did. When she was fifteen, she and her friend decided they were going to go to Planned Parenthood to get diaphragms.

I said, "Look, I hear you. I hear you think you're ready for all this." I said, "I wish you wouldn't do this. I think you're too young, but if you have to, please don't go to Planned Parenthood. I want to get you a gynecologist. Let's have you examined. I'm going to find somebody good, who specializes in adolescents." She agreed to that, and she went to a person I found who was terrific, who was young and very straight with her.

Well, he discovered she had a cyst on her breast. She was terrified. I was terrified. We pretty much knew it wasn't cancer, but there is always some doubt. She went to a specialist who told her, "You just go in the hospital. It's nothing. There'll be no scar."

None of that was true. She didn't come out of the anesthetic in the time they said she would. The doctor was a jerk. He forgot to use the right kind of stitching material, the kind that would dissolve, and she had a huge scar on her breast.

So, in other words, the minute she goes to do something about sex to legitimize it, what do they discover but something wrong. We got through it, and thank goodness it put a damper on sex— for a while, at least!

The next year she got involved with a young man at her high school. I could see that she was very attracted to him and that she was also unhappy about the relationship. I've always made it clear to her that sex was something private in her life, but that we could talk about attitudes. I said, "Hey look, you're attracted to somebody who is not nice to you. Who is this guy? How come he won't come over to the house?"

Finally, when he did come, I could see that he had some problems. He was extremely shy. He was kind of defensive and arrogant. I knew that his parents were divorced, that he wasn't doing well in school, and that there were probably too many drugs in his life. I could also see that Nell was being his psychologist. She was wanting more from him than he could give. It was a lot for a fifteen-year-old to be handling, so we talked about what kinds of things you want from a relationship, what kinds of things you can give in return, and whether or not it's realistic to feel you can change another person.

Then the summer before Nell was going to college, the most traumatic event I can think of occurred. My stepson, Ben, committed suicide. The issues that surround drugs and sex do not compare to death by suicide, which is uniquely terrible. I had to get professional help myself, because I felt very desperate.

I was particularly concerned because Nell had had a very close relationship with Ben. He was a very sensitive, rather poetic person, but this was a side he showed to only a few people. Nell was one of them. She felt he really opened up his soul to her, but she didn't feel she could tell anybody about that. Given their closeness, I was just so afraid she might want to join him. I think what happened to me was I became hyperalert for any clues. I was very watchful and had my ears very open all the time. I went through hell.

For the first year she didn't talk about it, then in her sophomore year she wrote a short story about the death of Ben. That's when it all started. She was having a rough year, anyway. She'd been involved with a young man who decided the relationship was becoming too intense for him. It was very painful for her to have to withdraw. She's a very intense person. She feels everything. She'd call home and say, "I feel so alone!" It didn't help that she was taking a course in existentialism. She was asking, "Why do I need people? Why can't I be alone?" Her boyfriend was a philosophy major, and all they did was talk about this stuff. She was also under a lot of academic pressure, and unsure about dropping a particularly difficult course. "Oh, I don't know what I'm going to do about this exam." She started saying things like, "Maybe life isn't worth living!" All this was coming over the telephone, and I was getting more and more upset.

I confronted her directly. On at least four occasions I had to say to her, "Look, you want to kill yourself? Do you *really* want to kill yourself? Is it too painful for you to live? Is that what you are saying?" She kept hinting that "Life is so hard. I feel so alone!" I'd come back with, "Are you saying that you can't resolve this problem enough to want to live?"

Then I did something else. I said, "Okay, make me one promise, and that is if you *ever, ever* feel you are near," and this gives me chills to even think of it, "to killing yourself and you *really* want to do it, you call me first. You absolutely call me first." And she did make that promise. I do trust her, but oh God, if someone really wants to kill himself, he doesn't call you first. He just goes and does it. But I did feel a little better that she was willing to promise a call. That's what I trusted most, her willingness to stay in touch in bad moments.

She continued to call me up when she was very upset about something, but she would qualify her feelings. "Mom, I don't feel like I'm going to commit suicide, but . . ." or "This is not a life-and-death issue, but I'm very upset about it." So we kind of integrated it into the conversation and would talk about her problems in terms of their relative importance. Perhaps she needed to hear how much I cared, and that I was going to protect her from her own despair.

She will be a senior in college this year. She's an adult now and can reflect on her own life and think about what's important to her. I am less identified with her and see her more as a separate person who needs to get her life going herself. You let go in a way. You realize, my God, that is her life. My life is my life. Let her go do what she wants to do in hers.

She's trying to work out a relationship with someone she cares very much for, but not lose herself, not give up what's important to her and start following him. She's really doing all the things of young womanhood. He's delightful, charming, and appealing, and she loves him. He loves her, but never admits it. It's the same old story.

I think being a parent is allowing for your children's discoveries and then supporting those decisions. That's what it is. And as you do that, you keep making discoveries about yourself. And it can be a struggle. I never knew that's what motherhood was. I thought you were terrific all the way through.

When the Nest Doesn't Empty Soon Enough

BETTY McLAUGHLIN

I went to a Catholic girls' college. In ethics class I learned that the end and aim of marriage is first and foremost the procreation of the human race, and secondly conjugal love. Well, for us they were synonymous. We practiced rhythm. Bob and I joke. We say, "Maybe rhythm would have worked if we had worked at rhythm!" We thought we'd have four kids. I was resentful when I was pregnant with the fifth and sixth, but by the time the seventh came along, I thought, oh hell, what's the difference! The last three were born less than three years apart, and I had my gall bladder taken out somewhere in between.

We've learned to accept a great deal. Four of the seven live at home. They are in their early twenties, which is really quite old to be home. My sister and I stayed at home until we were married— I was almost twenty-five—but things were different then. Partly, they can't afford to live someplace else. Susie, who is twenty-three, has graduated from college with a degree in communications. She is well equipped to go into life, but she can't find a job. Now she is bartending at a nice restaurant, but I wouldn't say she is very happy. Michael has a degree in economics and is taking graduate courses in business administration. He works as a waiter. They both had expectations that they would walk into jobs that would pay good money. John is just graduating from St. Louis University. He'll be twenty-two this summer, and will probably go on to law school. The youngest, Jimmy, who is twenty, has just started college. He's sort of at the tail end of everything. We've had more concern about him.

The trouble is that they would like life to be the way it was five, six, or seven years ago when they received services from both their dad and me, like caring for their rooms, washing their clothing, mending, shopping, cooking, everything a child needs and depends upon. I would have to say they are still very self-centered, and I blame ourselves. We have spoiled them.

They are not aware of our needs at this hour of our lives. Bob and I are both fifty-eight. Bob says, "We should be able to be putting away a good bit of money for our future. We should be able to have a great deal more privacy. It interferes with our sexual life." There is no doubt about it. I'm looking forward to getting reacquainted with Bob—he feels they are an intrusion, and that they are not grateful, which is very true. He feels like he's being put upon, and I guess I do too. We have spent a tremendous amount of energy for thirty-one years. Now we want to divert that energy into other things.

The disorder is the hardest thing for me. I've been a person of routine. I've had to be, as a woman with seven kids. That routine is completely disrupted. I go to law school four nights a week, but Bob and I still do all the food shopping. I guess I still feel that's part of being a mother, that you are responsible still, that they get sufficient food and good food. But the kids don't give a damn. It's like a hotel. The door's like a swinging door. They sleep here. They do their laundry, and maybe take a couple of meals. Oh, the boys will cut the grass, and do other odd jobs once in a while *if* you ask them. But I'll come home and find the kitchen a shambles. Susie's room is like a cyclone. Bob says, "Close the door." It took me a couple of years to do that, but there are other irritating things. Maybe her twelve blouses are all dirty, so she'll go out and buy another one instead of doing her laundry. What a waste! She's a beautiful child, and she walks out of the house looking great. So you live with it.

Being an Irish Catholic mother, I am also concerned about the fact that they don't go to church. "Sorry, Mom, but . . ." Their idea is that they have a God, and they stay close to God in many ways, and most of that is in service to their friends.

No matter how old they get, their concerns are still our concerns. Our middle daughter, Kathleen, is living with a young man in the city. This is a very sensitive child, with whom I had to stay very close all of her life. We've never seen her happier. She'll be married in June. It's hard for us, though. You go with someone, and *then* you marry, and that's when you live together.

Maryanne, our oldest daughter, is getting a divorce. We accepted her marriage to a black man. We didn't accept it grudgingly at all, God love her. We thought that he was a bit of a con man, but not to the extent that we found out later. But she feels so foolish that she's been had, and that she's probably never been loved, that she was used. We never said, "We told you so." We said, "Tell us how we can help." You're supportive, and you love her. It's her life, and she is the one who has the pain. It's been a hard two years for her, but she's still only twenty-seven. I can see happiness in the future for her.

We've had problems with Jimmy, our youngest. He has some friends we don't care for. He has been in jail overnight twice here in town, where Bob is a councilman and a volunteer probation officer. The policeman who picked him up practically apologized. "This is happening to everybody. Your kid just happened to have marijuana in his pocket when we picked him up." But Bob said, "It was wrong. Don't apologize." We know the judge. Bob said, "Tim, throw the book at him!" Jimmy was put on probation, and that scared him.

This is a very rebellious kid, but I think I'm learning how to handle him. My heart was hurting, but I had learned to say, "Jimmy, this is harder on you than it is on us. It is your life." I give him lots of strokes for the things he does well, and try to play down the negatives. He's the type of kid who can take a car apart, and then put it back together, and it actually works. I teach communications at Parks Aeronautical College. I thought this might be the right place for him, pilots, mechanics, aeronautical engineers, this and that, but instead of saying anything, I left the brochures around. He said, "Gee, Mom, do you have this stuff over at your school?"

221

A couple of days later he said, "Do you think I could go there?" I said, "I don't see why we can't arrange something."

Six years ago Bob had a heart attack. He lost a lot of confidence in himself, so we joined a group of other heart attack victims and their families. This changed my life a great deal, and it also brought out in me hostile feelings and resentments I had never allowed myself to express. I had been raised to give service to everyone, but particularly to men and children. My mother was that way, too. This attitude extended to everything. Say there would be the good pieces of the chicken. Bob got the best first, and the kids after. I took the worst piece for myself. As a wife you had a place, and that was your place. I used to spend time getting the kids ready for when Dad got home from work. Oh, I used to dress the three little girls up alike in their smocked dresses. It was always to please. However, I had this resentment in my gut. That, coupled with the urgency of taking care of seven children, and I became a less happy person.

We have a little saying that Bob gave me—"Walk by my side, not in front of me or behind me." It's on our bedroom door. Well, as far as the kids go, I have walked both in front of them and behind them. When they were little, I walked ahead. As they got bigger, say in high school, I walked behind everybody, even the youngest kid. Looking back, I can see now that I wasn't as important a person as Bob was. Dad knew the answers to everything. In fact, it was "Mom said that, so it's kind of dumb."

All along I have worked part-time outside of the house. I started twenty years ago as a social worker in foster care at Catholic Charities. As the kids got older, I went back to college and got my masters in communications. Today, I teach that, as well as do a public affairs TV program once a month. It didn't dawn on me until we met with the other families in our group that it was too bad that I had to get my real satisfaction and identity as a person outside of the home. I was "just Mom" here.

Now I think, how did I survive it when five of them were teenagers at the same time? When a thirteen-year-old turns around and says, "I hate you, Mom," and a second one says it with the eyes. Another one would turn around and walk away, and the next one would make a couple of cool remarks that really packed a wallop. And the words that were coming out of their mouths! Words they never learned in our house. It was "shit" this, and "fuck" that, and "Jesus." I thought that was terrible, a desecration. Of course, what they were doing was becoming themselves, feeling their own way, but when you've got a batch of them doing it all at once, not just one or two, it kind of hits you hard.

I was becoming a fishwife. And I guess I was thinking, too, that I knew best. I was never wrong. After all, I was the adult, and they were the kids. I gave out the advice, and I was the disciplinarian. I did an awful lot of hollering. But then if there was a hateful look or remark, I really hurt. Sometimes I would cry. At the end of the evening, I'd feel like there had been a roller coaster going over me.

Bob and I discovered in this group—after twenty-five years of marriage—that we had different ideas about raising kids. Bob's view was, "Let the kids do what they want to do." My view was, "If you are raised in a structured manner, then you will be good, and you will learn what you are supposed to do and take care of yourself and still be able to do other things for other people." He was saying, "Let Michael work at fifteen if he wants to." I was saying, "But he won't get as good grades." He didn't get good grades, and when we finally talked to the priest at school, he said, "But he's learning many other things." But then Michael would go out with his friends after work. I kept saying, "He shouldn't be doing that. He's getting C's when he could be getting B's and A's." Bob insisted, "Let him go." Michael was the fourth child. We also had some dissension because I hadn't let the others do that. I guess I kind of had a formula in raising these kids.

During that time I began to realize that you can't control them. It makes for less harmony if you try. Instead you learn to try to let them fall on their faces if that is what they have to do. But then you want to cushion that fall. No matter how old they get, you want to cushion that fall. Oh yes, you do. I guess, though, all you can really do is extend your love.

Since I've moved up in the pecking order in the family, I also have a different view of the money I earn. Before, it would go right into the household budget. Now I've gotten to the point of thinking the money I earn is mine, and I can make my own decisions about how it's to be spent. I decided, for example, that I wouldn't get into a discussion with Bob about paying Jimmy's tuition at the aeronautical college—"Can we afford it?" or "Should we do it when we haven't done it with the others?'' I was so delighted that he finally wanted to go to school that I said, "I can manage. I can arrange it.'' I'm also doing that with Patrick, our oldest boy. He's thirty-one. For a long time he dropped out of college, and now he is studying to be a doctor. He had to take a loan out just to live on. I cosigned for it. I'm sending him the money because I know he really needs it. I've got it coming in, and I don't need to ask permission anymore.

We are learning to communicate far better than we used to. And we do have fun with the kids. The greatest satisfaction in the world is to fix a big meal for the whole family. Last Christmas we had a delightful time. I said, "Your dad and I have to have one day with all of us together!" Maryanne was going to fly in, but Patrick couldn't be there on Christmas day because he was on duty at the hospital. Susie had to bartend on Christmas Eve. They couldn't get the hour together. I said, "You've got to. If it isn't a whole day, it's got to be seven or eight hours where we can be together." Well, they worked it out. We had a standing rib roast two days before Christmas.

After grace Bob said, "Let us thank God that we are here together, that we are each strong in our own way, and that our problems are small." Then I said, "Please let us go around the table and each talk about ourselves." It's amazing what came out—the hopes and dreams, the resentments and disappointments too. There was a lot of reminiscing.

"Do you remember the night of the big storm when Mom and Dad were out? There we all were, kneeling in our pajamas in front of the picture window with the candles, saying the rosary?" There were things that surprised us. Michael said, "The only reason, Jimmy, that you got caught with beer and marijuana was bad luck. We all did it. We just didn't get caught!" That was good for Jim. He idolizes his older brothers.

And the girls . . . I've got three women's libbers. Susie has felt the discrimination in her job hunt. Maryanne told her, "I know. You go in, and they ask, 'How many words a minute do you type?' Well, you tell them you don't know how! Mom doesn't type." I think they're kind of proud that I started law school at fifty-six. Kathleen said, "You know, you really are a hard act to follow." I told them what my parents said to me, which was, "You are as good as anyone. Anything you want to do, you can do." I believe that about them, too.

When it was my turn, I said, "There are a lot of things I've done as a mother that I'm really sorry about." Oh, there was plenty of agreement! "Your expectations were too high," and "You wanted us to be too good!" But then there was, "Without those expectations, we wouldn't be doing what we're doing." Patrick, the oldest, said, "Mom, you did what you thought was best."

And around and around the table we went. We didn't get up for five hours. When we did, Michael hugged me and kissed me. He said, "Mom, I thought you were really off the wall, but this has been the best thing." This coming together carries over. It renews us. It sustains us all.

Healing the Split

ELEANOR MAGID

I feel a lot of my life began when I started to talk to Gabriell and discovered things I wanted to develop in her. And as a consequence, they began to develop in me. When Gabriell was very young, and we lived in Colorado, I was doing a series of drawings to illustrate a book on insects. We used to take long walks in the fields. Little field animals and insects run away, so we'd look at the plants because they stand still. My thought at the time was I was teaching her something about growth and change, but actually I was formulating ideas for myself just as much.

Then we came back to the city, I had a job teaching art to minority students in the city university, and instead of looking at plants together, Gabriell and I made drawings and prints—etchings, block prints, woodcuts, and silkscreens. When she was eight I started a community printmaking workshop in our loft, and that had a kind of plantlike growth. Then ten years later, she was becoming a botanist. I moved from printmaking back into painting, and began using weeds as my basic subject matter. I began to study botany too. But it all started with Gabriell. I shouldn't say it started with her, but it was a communication with her that started the process in me.

Now Gabriell is married and has almost completed a master's

degree. She and her husband are involved in environmental horti-culture. She has started a community gardening project in some vacant lots in her city. She also gives seminars to children in the public schools. We've become friends who share interests and skills. I've taught her photography because I think she needs that to document her work, and she in turn is teaching me to garden. I am still working with weeds as my primary subject matter.

Nineteen sixty-eight was a year of crisis in the schools from the elementary grades up through college. It was the year of nonnegoti-able demands. Gabriell was in the third grade, and there was a public school strike in our district. The mothers were meeting because it was very difficult for them. We lived in a poor area and many of them worked. We had no access to day care. It was like a war-torn area. There were children wandering around by them-selves because the mothers couldn't stay home. The strike went on for six weeks. We petitioned the school board to let us use the empty school, but to no avail. So the mothers who had enough space and had something to offer opened their homes for the chil-dren in a community effort.

I offered the studio where Gabriell and I lived. I had an etching press, bookbinding facilities, printmaking supplies, woodcut tools, inks, rollers, and so on. I requested that a couple of mothers join me to manage this great group of children with sharp knives and tools. The children were from first grade to third grade, so there was quite a range of experience. We marbleized paper. We bound books and numbered the pages. We all made pictures and wrote stories that included almost the entire school curriculum. It was very exciting.

As this was going on, the college where I was teaching became embroiled in its own version of nonnegotiable demands. The cam-pus was closed down, so I said to my students, "If you would like to, you can come to my studio. You're not required to, but come if you want." They all came, and it was during the time when I had the little children. There would be ten to fifteen little kids and as many college kids, plus three or four mothers. Other people would drop by. The English teacher came and taught the little kids and the big kids. Lois, a painter, and Louise, a sculptor who lived upstairs, joined the group. A friend from Paris came with new etching techniques. It was a very interesting mix. We used rather sophisticated printmaking techniques. A five-year-old, for example, could teach someone else how to do color etching. It was quite a crowd, but we all fit. We used doors and sawhorses for extra tables.

The diversity of mothers in our neighborhood was very great. We had people who were teaching college mathematics and people on welfare. Some of the mothers didn't have very constructive feelings about themselves, either because they were on welfare or had dead-end jobs, or were struggling alone to raise their children. Certainly, they had never made a print before. But the college students and the little kids pulled them in. The college crowd would say, "Come on!" and then the daughter or the son would say, "Yeah, come on, Mom!" I would have to say that the most striking look of wonder and pleasure came from those mothers. It was very nurturing. But then, the making of art is very nurturing in itself. It's like having a good meal. When I set my palette up, I look at this flower garden of color, and then I just dive into it. It's a wonderful, enriching experience. When you go to make a print from your etching plate, you cover the plate with lush veils of color. The cloud of paper goes over that, and then you run it through the press. The paper is raised, and there is your print. It is a magical experience.

After six weeks the public school went back to business as usual. There was a policeman stationed inside to make sure that none of the mothers would go in with their children. We had been labeled "outside agitators." We were very upset by that, and we felt we really had to keep this good spirit going in the community. We kept our printmaking workshop going on the weekends, and we called it "The Printshop."

The college kids, the children, and the mothers kept coming on Saturdays. Some fathers began to come, too. Everyone would be hungry after a session, so somebody would bring onions, and someone else the potatoes, carrots, and meat, and we would make stews. They would be bubbling away, and the good smells would emanate from the pot all day. In the evening, we would have the meal. It was startling to me: There were no hierarchies, no stars or kings. It was like the best kind of family.

There was a negative side, though. The truth is that Gabriell did suffer during all of this. She often took second place: She, by the accident of being my daughter, and I, by choice, were living in the middle of a public institution. If somebody wanted to come over to my studio to make prints, and I was reading a story to her, somehow I wasn't able to say no. She was in competition with my students, and those other neighborhood children and their mothers.

I was educated at a Quaker high school. The Friends have a very direct statement, which is, "If the world hasn't gone well, you haven't done your part." I have always felt, am I doing my part? If you are an artist, you can become very isolated. In my era, doing something entirely for yourself was somehow considered unhealthy. It was just not a good thing. I always felt happier, as a consequence, when there was some sense of sharing.

After two winters Gabriell and I began to feel pushed to the very edges of our living space. However, at that point somebody said, "This is a community facility, and you ought to have a community space." We were given a large loft by the local urban development office. I thought that was great because then Gabriell and I had our loft back.

I thought the program would move easily into a community space, but it didn't. All kinds of squabbling started over money and responsibilities. Everything became bureaucratic. I became the official coordinator, and had to write fund-raising proposals and arrange for community art shows. I was still teaching full-time, and it was all very time-consuming.

Gabriell grew more and more resentful. She felt she had to share me during these seven important years of her life. I feel now that the same things that I didn't do for her, I didn't do for myself, either. I didn't mother me any more than I mothered her, in the sense that I put my own work aside. At the time it seemed what I was doing was more important than my own work. The Printshop was bringing people of all ages and backgrounds together in a poor community and sharing my skills. In a broader sense, it was also an expansion of a possible audience for the arts, which is healthy. But somehow an institution isn't a work of art, just as it isn't a child. Looking back, it now seems that anyone could have started an art program, but not anybody could have been Gabriell's mother.

The more problems there were with The Printshop, the more preoccupied I became. I have a photograph of Gabriell drawing when she was about fourteen. That brings back to me how petulant

230

she was. I think the drawing was useful to her because she sort of drew out her problems. Her resentment came out in different ways. I've always drawn looking at things, but Gabriell draws from her imagination. She used to say, "I don't draw at all like my mother!" It was as if she was saying, "Even though we both draw, it doesn't mean we are doing the same thing!"

Then she became very involved with the Integral Yoga Institute. There she isolated herself in a cocoon of yogic purity. She learned about herbal medicines, and how to sprout all the different beans. She never smoked or went through marijuana experiments. She never even drank coffee.

Everyone kept telling me I ought to be concerned, but I thought the Yoga Institute was a fine place. She was finding a certain warmth, tranquillity, and security in a family type of situation that she didn't find with me. It was a relief to me because I was so busy. It was almost as though I said, "All right. There is another kind of mothering situation for Gabriell."

I did shortchange her, and she told me that I did. I went up to visit her one weekend the year that she went off to college. We were taking a nice walk over a red covered bridge in a beautiful little woodland area. All of a sudden she began to tell me what she didn't like about me. It was very scary because you know you cannot go back, and you can hear truth in what is being said. You have to come to grips with that truth, and it is horribly painful.

She felt that my divorce disrupted her life and that she missed out on a family. Her attitude was, "When I get married, I'm getting married for good." She is interested in the absolute stability of family. At first I tried to defend myself, by arguing that The Print-shop was a social experiment in its own way, that she had certain things that she wouldn't have had in a nuclear family. She had an extended family. The students loved her as if they were her brothers and sisters. She was willing to acknowledge that, but it wasn't what *she* had wanted.

Then she went on to say, "You were so involved with your black students that you made me feel like I was white, and I was the oppressor, and I was no good." I know I didn't say those things, but I guess my attention was on those students to such an extent that that's what she felt about it. What did Pete Seeger say? "Be glad for your enemies because they show you your faults." Your kids tell you your faults in a way that practically nobody else would dare. Perhaps it is because of that closeness, and the assumption that you will not abandon them. But you don't get away with anything when you are a parent. If I ever thought I was going to play a role of the absolute perfect being, it was knocked out of me that day.

The other side of this, however, is that I'm not sure in the long run that this experience did do her harm. She is a terrific person. Compared to what I was at her age, she is a very independent, self-sufficient person. I had a mother who wanted to control me because she never had any other feeling of control over the world except through me. Never has she been able to become my friend because she is still being my mother.

Gabriell and I have made that move. We are friends now. One friend said, "You know Gabriell would never admit it, but she really is a lot like you. Your direction has been her direction." She is a skilled gardener, and spent a great deal of time setting up a community ethnic gardening project, bringing black, Korean, Japanese, Trinidadian, Indian, and other ethnic groups together.

They garden side by side and find it fascinating. Each ethnic group has its own beans. There are black-eyed peas from the South, pigeon peas from Trinidad, navy beans from New England. An Indian woman had beans that no one had ever seen before. Everyone planted their own beans, and then exchanged beans with one another. Each group had a different way of stringing up their beans, different little architectures, strings and poles and different ways of scaring away predators. One garden belonged to a Greek woman and had egg shells on top of the posts. We thought at first that might be for nourishing the plants, but she said it was for good luck.

The differences in gardening were tremendous, but all those people were working together, talking to one another, discussing various ways of fertilizing, and so on. They were doing the most basic thing there is, planting a garden. It's not an analogy. It's a real thing. It's a little like The Printshop, except it's healthier. I would never say that to her, though. It's still very important to her to be who she is, and to not be like me. Maybe in ten or twenty years she might be able to talk about it.

* * *

Right now I'm photographing the milkweed as part of my work. It's just about human height, so I climb a stepladder and hang precariously over the top of the plant. What I'm most interested in is that smallest, most simply formed area at the tip of the flower. That is called the meristem. When you photograph that and blow it up, people say, "That looks like an explosion." I say, "It is. It is a life explosion." It's the central bud, and it keeps growing throughout the life of the plant, moving upward as it explodes out to the sides. Though our bodies stop growing after a point, our minds, like plants, keep growing as long as we live. So I see the meristem as a kind of analogy to the continuing growth in human beings.

Sometimes Gabriell says to me, "You are an artist, and I am just a humble gardener." I let her go on, but I feel that there is something afloat that is attempting to heal that split. I was being as much of an artist talking to her as a little girl, when we used to walk in the field together and look at plants, as I am when I start to work on a drawing. And that there is such a thing as art, and such a thing as manual labor, and such a thing as teaching, and such a thing as mothering is true, but they are all of a piece, all part of a process that supports that meristem, or that forward movement of life. Motherhood is the meristem, the moving tip, the thing that keeps going forward.

Sometimes if you look at the whole earth, and the problems we face, it is very depressing. But I feel it can still be turned by human effort and energy. We have to take ourselves more seriously as women and as mothers because that experience of being a mother transfers itself to everything else we do. It is the taking care of, the taking care of yourself, the taking care of what is yours, whatever your territory is, with all your might.

Children Need Love, Care, Wholesome Food, But They Also Need Adventure

JEAN ROMANO

The divorce didn't come until Alica was six, Daniel was seventeen, and Noel was twenty-four. But when I think about it, almost from the very beginning I was afraid my husband was going to leave me. I was so terrified of it, and lived in so much anxiety, that when the actual event occurred after twenty-four years of marriage I discovered it wasn't as bad as my fear had been. Finally when I had to face the worst, I could get through it.

I tried very hard to let the children know that I was all right, that I was not suffering for that. You want your children to be proud of you and to think your life is happy, and you do things to make it so. You want to be your best self. I remember writing a letter to Daniel saying, "There's just one man in this world who doesn't love me as much as I'd like to be loved, and I'm not going to let that spoil my life." And I added, "Don't let that spoil your life either, because nobody has that kind of power over us, and there are lots of other people we'll enjoy being with and who will enjoy being with us."

It took me some time to come to that verbal statement that there was just one man in the world who didn't love me enough, but once I did, it put the burden on him, and then it was rather small. It sort of turned the telescope around.

Of my three children I would say that my oldest daughter, Noel, even though she was twenty-four, was affected the most by the divorce. When she was three, her father and I had separated for a year, and I think she remembered all of her own suffering from that age, and I think she worried about Alica, who was only six at the time, feeling the way she had. Actually, she imagined all of us suffering. She was marvelous, though. She poured tons of energy into calling me and writing me letters and sending special things to Alica. One of the things she did was to make a book called *Considering the Move to a New Place,* which was all about Alica moving to a new house. She illustrated it beautifully and wrote a charming little story about how Alica discovered a new house and everybody went in and fell in love with the house and painted the walls. Later she said she had done that as a form of therapy for herself. In making it seem like an adventure to Alica, she ended up cheering herself up. She looked on the other side of the experience as an adventure.

I think that attitude had its roots in the separation that Noel lived through when she was three. For a year we lived alone in Greenwich Village and became very, very close. It was almost as if we grew up together—I had never lived on my own before. I listened to the radio a lot, and one day I heard a public interest message saying, "Children need love and care and wholesome food, but they also need adventure." I thought, wow! How wise to be telling all parents to get out and provide some adventures for their children, and since that really was my natural bent anyway, I loved it.

We just got out and walked. She'd go up every flight of stairs, up and down. She learned all the names of all the streets: Cornelia, Jane, Bank, Leroy, Grove, Macdougal, and all the names of the trucks. Then every afternoon we'd go out to the park to climb and swing. Noel was the kind of child who was alert to whatever happened and curious about it. Every day really did seem like kind of an adventure.

* * *

My second child, Daniel, was also very upset by the divorce. He was a person who loved staying home. You could hardly ever get him out of the house, but the house was sold as part of the divorce settlement. Even though he was only seventeen and a bit young to start college, he did. I think he wanted to get away too, because he couldn't face my pain. I think it was more than he could handle on top of his own, and he had to absent himself.

He started the school year off well, and then he just stopped working. Eventually he dropped out. He went up to the town near the college where his father taught for a couple of years and he got a job. My feeling was that he needed to be with his father. His father had always suffered from migraine headaches, and had given less time to him than I had. In high school Daniel became a kayaker. Driving gave his father headaches, so I would take him white-water kayaking in Maine and Vermont. I was doing a lot with him that most fathers would do, and so we had our adventures.

I felt at the time of the divorce that he knew he had his mother, he understood me, and knew that I adored him. I think he didn't know why the marriage had come to an end, and why his father hadn't ever really been there for him. I felt he had unfinished business with his father that they had to work out.

He is twenty-five now, and the kind of young man that a mother would like, very kind and very gentle.

Then there is Alica, who is now fifteen. Some people have asked me, "Isn't it difficult to deal with a teenager now that you're fifty-six and divorced?" I don't feel that way. I think if I didn't live with my children, I would get tired of my own thoughts. I get very tired of always having to turn myself on, so it's just necessary to live with other people and other people's goals and to keep their needs in mind. I also see Alica as a kind of anchor. If I hadn't had her home when I divorced, I probably would have done some nutty things. Because of Alica I maintained a home, which suits me because essentially I am a home builder. My children were so widely spaced, and I've been doing this for such a long time, that I could go on and on, and sort of tuck a new little child under my wing. It's a habit of living in the world that I find very pleasant.

A friend who has been a kind of observer of our family for a number of years said, "Alica is the most stable of your children," and it was a help to hear that because when you're first divorced, you wonder if you'll do a good job as a single parent.

Last week Alica went to visit Daniel and Noel during her school vacation. It was fun for me thinking about the three of them being together, being close and having fun, despite their age differences. I went to the airport to meet her. I was standing at the bottom of a flight of stairs at the end of a long corridor. I saw her feet first. I could just tell by the way they were kind of swaggering along that it was Alica. And it was. She came down the aisle with this self-confident swagger, with her curls bouncing, and she just looked so competent and independent and happy. It was nice. She knew just where to go for her baggage. She came right up to me and said, "Do I look tan?" She hadn't had time to sit still in the sun, and she thought she couldn't come home without a tan, so her brother and sister had taken her to one of those wacky tanning parlors.

I know that I will be ready for Alica to leave when it is time for her to go. I don't need to have her with me, but I know I'll need to be located someplace where the children will have some sense of home, and can come for holidays if they want to. I'm also looking forward to being able to do more art work. I enjoy the short times when she's away and I don't have to make supper. Sometimes I skip a meal or work late.

I get a tremendous amount of pleasure though, at this point, thinking about my children's lives. I don't actually have to have them in the house with me. There's a real sense of completeness there in that I'm always their mother and they are always my adored children, but I'm not clamorous about demanding that they show up for holidays.

This Christmas none of them were home. At first I thought, oh, what am I going to do? I've never had Christmas without my children. But I had a marvelous time with close friends, and then I had New Year's Eve with the children.

I felt pleased about being a mother whose children didn't feel that she would collapse if they didn't get home for Christmas. You know that feeling you get when you think your mother feels you don't love her if you aren't there on her birthday, or if you forget Valentine's day? I remember failing at some of those duties, and my mother used to make me feel bad.

* * *

Noel really has had some hard times over her father since the divorce. As a child she thought he was the most wonderful person in the world, and at the time of the divorce she still felt the same way. Since then she has had her own bad experience with him, but she is very attached to her childhood memory of him as just this magnificent person. She's always trying to turn him back into what he was.

I told her at one point, "You know, Noel, it's going to be so wonderful when you have that child of your own because then you'll be focusing on life ahead of you, and some of this unhappiness over trying to straighten out the past with your father just won't seem so important."

Every child is entitled to have the best relationship he can have with a parent on his own grounds. We all have our own needs. Then a child grows up, gets married, and starts a new family, and that family becomes the priority. I said to my daughter, "When that happens, it will be liberating. You will let go of the past and become part of that forward life."

Joining the
Grand Generation

PAT MAIN

Katherine was visiting us. It was the first time she and her new baby had visited us without her husband. So it was just the daughter coming home with her child to a house with her parents in it, a brother and a sister and a grandmother. We were all assembled, almost like a committee waiting for her. The anticipation was tremendous.

This was the first Christmas we'd not had all the children at home, and we all felt the loss. Sophie, our youngest, kept saying, "It's so quiet here without Katherine." Kate was the sort of *locomotif*. She got things moving. She would not buy the Christmas tree before Christmas Eve. It had to be a Scotch pine, and it had to be big enough to fill the bay overlooking the garden. She orchestrated the great decorating ritual and made sure the stockings were filled.

Earlier in the month she had called me from Louisville. "Mummy, what is your recipe for your marmalade? I want to give it this year." She added, "We can't afford anything else!" This was their first Christmas as a family, and she and her husband, Steve, were talking about establishing their own traditions. She was put-

241

ting all of her energies into *her* home this year. That is as it should be.

When she arrived two days after Christmas, I brought out the old *Mother Goose* for my grandson, and Katherine read it to him. She said to me, "Mummy, I don't *know* these things by *heart*." I said to her, "I can't think why not because I read them to you over and over again." When I see the way she is devoted to caring for young Thomas, it is just like reliving that time in my life.

I enjoyed my own pregnancies, and followed Katherine's with great interest. Before she gave birth, I had said to her, "I really want to know when the baby is being born." She said, "Of course, we'll call when it's over." I said, "No. Call me *when* you go to the hospital. I don't want to be doing anything important. I want to be aware." Jeremy said, "Well, it doesn't make any difference." I said, "It's going to make a difference to me. I want to be thinking about her when this is happening."

The baby was perhaps a week late, and I was at the office that I manage when the call came. When I got off the phone, everybody in the room knew that Kate was on her way to the hospital, and that I would soon be a grandmother. I rang the other kids at college and alerted them. I got Jeremy at his office, and I called my mother-in-law. If I had thought, I would probably have called my own mother in England, but I didn't get that far.

They say that one of the things you do after childbirth is forget the sensations, the way you're going to get hold of that contraction that is going to peak and really be tough to deal with, but I remember them all. I really remember them, so that when Kate had said over the phone, "They are coming every fifteen minutes, and I'm managing well," I thought, very soon it's going to be much tougher than this, and you're going to have more trouble, and then there will be transition. That will be very difficult. I had said to Kate, "You're going to be very nasty and bad-tempered with Stephen then." I knew, if nobody else knew, that there was a lot of hard work going on that evening.

I think I remember childbirth so clearly because these were very, very special events in my life. As a young girl I don't ever remember looking forward to childbirth. I'm sure that my attitude came from my mother's experience, which was totally negative. She had always said, "Johnny's birth was torture, and you, Pat, were an accident." With Johnny she had gone to some drunken midwife. He was a very large child, and she had twenty-four hours of hard, hard labor. It was a nightmare. My father gave no thought to her pregnancies. Apparently she used to become pregnant very easily and consequently she had aborted a number of pregnancies herself. She would do it with a knitting needle or something equally as terrible. I had heard about these things.

I had a different attitude. I was pleased to be pregnant. Jeremy was a journalist, and we were assigned to Berlin. I made contact there with a number of women who had experienced natural childbirth, who did not look upon it as a ghastly event. Because of some difficulties with nationality, I decided not to give birth in Germany. Two weeks before Katherine was born, I went to England and stayed with my parents. I arranged to have the baby at a small maternity home nearby.

The experience is etched indelibly in my memory. I had been across town to tea with friends, and it was while I was having my tea that I became aware that the waters had broken. I did not want to tell anybody this was happening, so instead I said, "Thank you very much for the lovely tea," and went on my way. I took the bus halfway across London, but then realized that there just wasn't enough time to take a second one. So I got off very close to the BBC in Central London. My parents lived just beyond the taxi limit, but I finally found a taxi to take me the whole way. I guess the driver took pity on me because I was so large. He didn't know I was in labor until we reached the house. I paid him and said, "You've been very kind. The baby is on the way!"

I walked into the house. My father was sitting with the newspaper. He always had a habit of reading with his elbows on the table and his head in his hands. My mother was sitting in the chair by the fire. I said, "The baby is coming!" My father said, "Oh dear." He did not move his hands. My mother said, "Are you sure?" I said, "Yes, now I'm just going upstairs to be quiet for a little while, to time my contractions, and then I will call the maternity home and tell them I am coming." There was utter silence. There was no excitement. They were just *panic-*stricken.

When I came down, my mother said, "I'm coming with you." I said, "All right." We got to the home. I put on my nightie and was put into a high bed with a railing around it. My mother was standing beside me. Her face was composed, but she was wringing her hands. I can see those hands to this day, the tension. They were in knots, the knuckles white and the fingers twisted. I said to her, "You know, Mummy, you don't have to stay. Why don't you go home. We will call you. It's going to be all right." And so she joyously started out the door. "Go home," I said. "Call Jeremy and let him know." She did that very well. It was difficult for her to track him down because he had gone to East Berlin.

Once she had gone I was fine. The midwives were comforting and guiding and terribly supportive of the Grantly Dick Reed childbirth method, which is somewhat like Lamaze. They did not say, "Don't you think you should have something for the pain?" A Sister Rose Stockman helped me to breathe. I've never forgotten her name. She kept saying in between these sizable contractions, "Sure it hurts, but we'll handle it." The baby's face was the wrong way around, so she said, "It's going to take a bit more hard work." It *was* hard work, but I was in the swing of things, and I was in control. I could indeed do what Sister Stockman told me.

When the baby, Kate, was born, she was wrapped in a blanket and put beside me. The first thing she did was to yawn. I was overwhelmed, overwhelmed that she should do such a real thing. Sister Stockman then said, "Now what you need is a good strong cup of tea!" I can even remember that the tea was marvelous. It came in one of those great big canteen cups. It was so strong you could have stood a spoon up in it, and it was very sweet. It was delicious, delicious! It was just what I needed at that time.

Then I dispatched somebody to tell my mother that all was well. She then had to call Berlin again. It's amazing how clearly I can remember. I think it will be just as clear in twenty-five more years.

But my mind was on Kate and her labor that evening. It's funny I can't remember, but we must have eaten dinner. Jeremy was conducting a phone interview at some point. I said, "If anybody beeps in, just get off. Leave them hanging! I don't want to hear about it!" We did have a lot of phone calls that night, and every time it rang, I would gasp. Jeremy was getting quite impatient with me: "If you do that once more, Patsey . . ." My mother-in-law kept popping in from her end of the house. "Have you heard yet? Have you heard yet?'' There was a tremendous amount of excitement. Finally, at ten that evening the call came. We had a grandson! Oh, I was terribly thrilled!

I flew down to Katherine's the next day. At the hospital they let grandparents in to see the babies. I washed my hands, and put on a white jacket. I went to pick him up, feeling my emotional connection is still with Katherine, for she is my child. But once I held on to that baby, I felt a real connection to him, too. I thought this child is a little bit of me and all those people that made me and went into making Katherine and the same thing from the other side of the family. I was really quite bowled over by it, this sense of connectedness. I had an awareness that this is as close to immortality that I was ever going to get.

The other thing that struck me was that I had not held a newborn for years. I looked at this totally new person who was a piece of all these other people, but who was also definitely himself. Suddenly there was another person in the world who was not there two days before, and he came with this great package of messages that was him and only him and no one else. I looked at him, at his eyes and at his head and at his nails. The nails are very clear in a newborn, the shape of the nails. They are very specific. I can remember with my own son, Thomas. I looked at his hands and I said, "My God, they are his father's hands." He's twenty-two and I can look at his hands now, and they are still his father's hands.

The baby had a bit of jaundice, and Katherine had to stay in the hospital two days longer. Stephen had to work, and she wanted the company, so I spent an enormous amount of time sitting there. I would go in the morning and do my knitting and chatter. I would return in the afternoon for more chatter. It was an extraordinary time because being there was something that probably only I could do for her.

I was also there to help her get used to nursing. I had nursed my babies with no problems. Fortunately, Kate had inherited the good genes of the Hitchcock women. She had masses of milk. She had some difficulty positioning the baby at first. "Mummy, what do I do now?" I must say watching her nurse was a special sensation because she was physically attached then to a child. It's rather like when you think of your children having sex. You wonder, is that really proper? There was some of that feeling, maybe a little jealousy or envy also, because that is something only *she* can do for the child—though I don't feel any of that now.

Perhaps one of the most memorable moments was the first night Thomas was home. Katherine had set up the nursery, but, of course, she'd no experience of a baby being there. Everything was in the wrong place. We couldn't find anything. Then it seemed that every time the baby nursed, he had a bowel movement. We had not put the diapers on properly, so everything went everywhere. By four o'clock in the morning, we had walked him and patted him and he was still *wide* awake, just *wide* awake.

We looked at each other. We had a pile of laundry in the corner of the room that comprised almost every stitch of clothing the lad owned. We looked at it, and I said to her, "How are we going to manage if he's going to make this much dirty laundry? I don't think we're doing this right!" She said, "You know, I'm sure we're not, Mother." We laughed and we laughed. I said to her, "Kate, you're going to bed. I will rock him. You go to sleep because you will have to be up for many nights to come." And then Thomas, the baby, was fine and quiet.

I do feel like a grandmother now. Oh, there was a slight sense of horror when Kate first called and said, "Mother, are you sitting down?" I said, "Yes," but of course as soon as she said that, I *knew* what she was going to say. I knew she was pregnant. I knew.

At first there was a sort of denial that this was happening, because how could I possibly be old enough to join that grand generation? Having a grandchild made me look realistically in the mirror and say, "Gee, I'm not as young as I picture myself." I'm inclined to see myself as I was at thirty-five—less heavy and less gray than I am. I can see that, indeed, I am very gray. There is no changing it. You can't deny it. It's going to be there. You are enchanted with it, so that you can't be enchanted on the one hand and denying that you're growing old on the other.

There's no way you can have a baby like this one though and not be proud that you're associated with it. This helps to compensate. But again, you are two generations removed from that baby. While you acknowledge a sense of immortality when you look at him, you also are impressed with a sense of mortality.

But it's all very satisfying. It's different from motherhood. I'm much more associated with Katherine than the baby. He's wonderful, but my tie is definitely to Kate. When I do things for him, I'm really doing them for her. I also don't feel possessive about him. I don't feel I have to do everything for him. I'm very willing to pitch in. We had a party at the house, and young Thomas started to fuss as I held him. I said, "Here, Katherine." The delightful thing about being a grandparent is you can give them back when they are a problem. I don't have to get tied in knots.

Then, of course, there is this tremendous to-do about what the child is going to call us. Nobody wants to be called Grandma anymore. You want something special, distinctive, not quite plain or ordinary. My mother-in-law wanted to be called "Grand Mary." Very pretentious! Well, Katherine managed to turn that the first time she said it into "Dumbody." Well, she's been "Dumbody" ever since. It's been a remarkable name!

I vacillate between wanting to be called Grandmother Main and Grandmère, but it really doesn't matter. I have a friend, Gloria, who has been a grandmother for a long time, and she told me, "I didn't want to be called Grandma either, but you know, Pat, in the end you'll fall in line. It's very easy." She said, "The first time I saw that child I threw my arms open to that darling baby and cried, 'Come to your Grandma Glory!' " She's been Grandma Glory ever since!

When My Children Need Me, I'm Available Still

BARBARA HEINRICH

I wonder how people without children stand life, because you do live vicariously through your children. Ours are all grown up and away now. None live nearby. I don't need to be with them all the time, though I love to see them. Just knowing they're happy, or positive, or doing something they like is the greatest thing!

I had an active life. I didn't do a thing for the first seventeen years I had children—oh very little—maybe collect money for the United Way on the block. But the day the youngest went off to nursery school, I had two and a half hours free and began to get things done. As the children got older, I very gradually expanded my activities to fill the entire day, but because they are volunteer, when one of the children needs me, I'm available still.

All of them from time to time have needed me. I think it's wonderful to be available, and wonderful that they still need or want me, not most of the time, but that they can turn to me. Jenny, our youngest, for instance, is still getting away from the feeling that something hasn't happened unless she tells us about it. She just likes to communicate what's going on. If she's depressed, letting off the

249

steam makes her feel better. As she says, "You're not going to like this phone call. Everything's wrong! Everything's terrible! I hate myself!" And she's feeling much better by the end of the call. She knows she will. That's why she calls.

But the child who needed me the most was Ann, who had been very, very independent, and had not shared much with us. Oh, from time to time she would confide various problems, but not frequently. Until she became what turned out to be very, very ill with Hodgkin's disease. Then she shared, not just with us, but with everyone. She was very open and honest about it, not in a maudlin or "pity me" way that made anyone feel sorry for her. When she needed help, she asked for it very directly. "I need help. I'm alone."

I saw a great deal more of her then, partly because her husband, Bill, worked different hours. She shared the good things, and she shared the bad. After her chemotherapy treatments, which made her so very sick, she would come over here to rest. I'd often shop for her, provide meals, run errands, or just listen. Oh, she and Bill were so much in love! She said to me, "Mom, no matter what happens, and despite the cancer, these three years have been the happiest in my life."

I remember when she first came to tell us that she was moving in with Bill. I pointed out all the things that were against it, not morally, but socially. She said, "Mom, if you only knew what this man has done for me. If I ever lose my job, I can get another one because I know I'm worthwhile. If he quits loving me, I know somebody will because I know I'm lovable now." I said, "If he's done that for you, Ann, you go right ahead and live with him. It doesn't matter what anybody thinks." I'd been afraid of what my mother, her grandmother, would think if she found out!

The very last week of her life she had a great deal of me. I wouldn't have been there if I hadn't felt she wanted me to be with her the entire time. I was her nurse, and her protector. I tried to make her as comfortable as possible. It was devastating to see the life just drain out of her. I remember running out of the hospital, when I realized that things were very, very bad, screaming, "My daughter is dying! How, how can this be?" But the whole experience was not altogether a bad experience. It was very beautiful to share totally in an important period in a person's life, even though it was a suffering, sad period.

Lucy, our fourth child, also needed us very much. She is a very sensitive, rather shy person. When she was in fourth grade, she was ill for a long time. Finally the doctor said, "It's psychosomatic. She doesn't want to go to school. She wants to stay home with you." I had to *force* myself to *force* her to go. It was hard helping her grow up because she had been a sickly little baby who probably suffered some real psychological damage at the time.

We don't know what was wrong with her. It was a very strange thing. They gave me too much anesthetic when she was born. She was sensitive then, but she seemed to be growing up normally, not strong, but with no problems. Then we went on a vacation, and left the kids with a housekeeper. When we came back (she had been old enough to almost sit up), she was just limp. She didn't cry. She made no responses to sound. She wouldn't eat anything, but she did drink milk. The only signal she could still give you was a feeble, little smile—catch your eye and give a feeble little smile.

I didn't know anything about autism at the time, but now I'm beginning to think that she was almost becoming autistic. We took her to our family doctor, and he said, "Something has happened, something serious." He sent us to a specialist, a neurologist, and he tested her and said, "Well, she's abnormal. She'll never be normal. She's probably been severely retarded from birth, and you are just now recognizing it, or else she's had some totally damaging brain disease. Since there is no hope for her, I would institutionalize her now."

We just couldn't accept that. We went back to our family doctor and he said, "I don't honestly know what is wrong, but I do know that love never hurt anybody. You love her twenty-four hours a day." And we did. Joe, who was an early riser, would literally pick her up before she was awake in the morning. He'd carry her around and talk and play with her until he left for work. I would then carry her around on my hip all day as I worked around the house. She was part of me. I talked to her whenever I could. When Joe came home, he would play with her again until her bedtime.

Well, she began to respond to sound on one side, and then the other. By the time we took her to the doctor again, she'd begun

251

to whimper occasionally. Then she finally got back to full crying. She didn't eat anything except milk, loaded with vitamins. Her teeth were terrible. It was another six months before she ate any solid food, but gradually everything came back.

She was very shy as a child and demanded a great amount of attention. She still has a psychosomatic pain from time to time, but now she is a successful, happy, practicing lawyer. She's going with a young man I think she's in love with. We just had him for the weekend. Lucy said, "We have to take a float trip in the Ozarks together, so that you and Dad can get to know him." So we're planning one for June. They'll probably get married this year.

Of all our children, Eliza has needed the least of us. She was one of those children who seem to have been born with a star. She was always a relaxed, happy, popular child with both the boys and the girls. Fundamentally, she loved fun. Even when she got married, she was still climbing trees and playing games. She didn't have the personal problems that most children have growing up. I think she rarely had a feeling of being left out, and perhaps grew up needing us in a way less because of that.

She got married at nineteen. It was hard at the time, to suddenly be in a grown-up world with an older man and his friends, but she was away from us and learned how to handle it.

But six years later, she needed us. She knew there was something wrong with him, but he would not let her tell anyone. I have felt guilty about each one of my children at some point, and I feel guilty that I wasn't there when she needed someone. Mark finally told his own family four days before he killed himself. He said, "I'd been suffering from depression, but I'm better now." Imagine the guilt Eliza felt! She was only twenty-five, and I don't think we were able to help much. We all went up to be with her, but I felt like I was living under water.

Since then she's been very unhappy. She knows nice people, and has an exciting job, so she can stand it. She fell in love again, and she lived with a guy for a couple of years. Finally, she felt that they ought to decide whether or not to get married. She decided she wanted to, and he decided he didn't. She said to me, "Mom, now the two men I love have both walked away from me." It has been very hard on her. We're not able to help Eliza much, and she doesn't ask us for help. She does share, but I don't know whether for our sake or for her own.

Next to Eliza, John, our oldest, has shared with us the least, even though he got a great deal of attention. As a child, he had polio and required a great deal. He was three and a half. Ann was not yet two, and the others were not born. Ann probably had it, too. She'd been sick with what seemed like the flu. His began something like flu, too, but then he suddenly became extremely ill. He was lying in my bed one morning. All of a sudden he started screaming, "Pain, pain, pain!" and then he got sick and passed out. This happened three or four times before we got the doctor there. He was just suddenly very acutely ill.

Once we knew he was going to live, I became terrified that he would have to spend his life in an iron lung. When we first brought him home from the hospital, he was a bed patient for a long time. He was a twenty-four-hour-a-day job. It took two hours to get him fed because he couldn't swallow very well. He couldn't sleep very well at night. He was in a lot of pain and helpless always.

For four months Ann had to be shuffled back and forth between the two grandmothers and finally, when John could get up a little bit, we brought her home. This is part of what made Ann so shy, I'm sure. I think she realized he had to have the first attention. She knew that even as a two-year-old.

The hardest time was when, because of muscle loss, his back started to curve. The doctors here were very discouraging. They wanted to do these dangerous spinal operations that they couldn't predict success from. We finally got him to Warm Springs, where Franklin Roosevelt had been. They put him in traction. The doctors and we would meet and discuss what should be done. Joe suggested something that made the traction brace more comfortable, a ball bearing in the back, so that he could turn in any direction.

He was there for four months. We stayed with him the first few days and then left him screaming. "Daddy, you may leave me, but Mommy won't leave me. She loves me too much!" It was very hard. He was only four. After he came home, we still had to go back every six months to get his brace refitted. They had to make a new corset each time and adjust the brace as he grew.

He had tremendous difficulty. He kept hurting himself badly. I remember a couple of years after he had polio I took him to the doctor, and I said, "How can I keep him from hurting himself?" The doctor said, "Well, you can either keep him from hurting himself, or you can raise a normal boy." So we chose to raise a normal boy and relegated only the necessary attention to him beyond what we gave all our children.

He seldom complained about anything, though. I remember he did tell me once that a boy at school kept tripping him, knocking him over, tearing up his art work, and hurting him. I wanted to report it immediately to the school. He said, "No, Mom, I'm just beginning to be accepted at school. If I tell on somebody, I won't be!" He would not let me complain. He said, "It's something I have to work out myself." He would not accept defeat. He had to conquer. In the end he and this boy became good friends.

He grew up a normal and independent person. He's been home very little since he went to college. He's happily married with three children, and I think this is specifically due to that doctor's advice to "raise him as a normal boy."

When I think about it, those early years were frazzling, absolutely frazzling. We also had a baby, Geoffrey, who died, who had colic every night for nine months. I thought all grown-ups were tired all the time. We had a good time, we were happy, but I was tired *most* of the time. But as I said, that was part of being a grown-up in my mind. It amazed me when the children all got in school, and I found out that I wasn't tired anymore.

I had to be short with them. I couldn't give them each too much time. I had to put them on their own. I think it's good for children. I don't think I was ever mean with them, or at least not very often. We didn't punish them particularly. We expected the best. But to grow up realizing the world is not your oyster, and that other people have requirements, is important. Not everybody's always going to be pitching for you. That's being realistic.

I think I would have enjoyed those early years more, been less tired and a better mother, if I'd been more patient. Oh, they were darling babies, but as soon as their problems became less physical and more intellectual, they began to fascinate me more and more and still do. But at the time, it never occurred to me that I should be leading any other life than what I was living. It was what life was all about. I think it's harder for young mothers today than it was for us because that was the role I was going to play. It never occurred to me to agonize over, "Should I give up my new job now?" or "Should I work full- or part-time?" or "I could be doing something else."

I wouldn't have had six children if I had planned. But I'm glad I had them. So I'm glad the problem of making the decisions about having them didn't come up. I made the decision not to have eight or ten, though, which apparently I would have had if I hadn't done anything about it.

It must be hard for full-time working mothers to come home and have the patience after working eight or nine hours. Some of them do it beautifully, and I admire them. But I wouldn't have had the strength. I didn't do anything in the daytime for myself. I did enjoy my husband thoroughly, though, and we had a pretty active social life at night. We got baby-sitters and went out. But I missed the intellectual stimulation during the day. When Jenny was four, I served on a grand jury. I had a ball. It was the first time I'd been able to get my teeth into anything in ages, and I cried when it was over.

It's funny, if there were problems I tend mostly to remember the happy times. All of our kids are people who interest me, and we prefer a good conversation to chitchat. Three of the kids have become lawyers, and before she died, Ann covered the courts for the newspaper. I'm very involved in reforming the court system now and do a lot of work with prisons. Jenny's thinking of going on to law school, too. We're all also interested in history. While John is the one who is scrupulously moral, and has a doctorate in ethics, we all like to discuss the rights and wrongs of things. We're interested in analyzing. I remember we sometimes used to tape dinner table conversations. We would all be talking at once. We used to play them back and roar because everyone was interrupting everyone else.

I think children teach you a lot. When I look at it, having had many children and having them right away kept Joe and me from being alone together. I wonder how we could have stayed in love and had so much fun all that time. But the fact is that we were able to, and I think we both became better people than before we got married largely because we had children to think about, to put ahead of ourselves.

255

Letting your children grow up and go one by one is not so hard. When Jenny finally went off to college, everybody felt sorry for Joe and me. The kids worried, "Oh, Mom and Dad will be alone. What will they do?" They worried because they realized we love them. We had a second honeymoon. It was absolutely thrilling! There was the time to be alone. I have so many projects I'm involved with, I'm out of the house before eight in the morning.

I think mother love is one of the two great loves in the world. The other love is love for your spouse, and there is a difference between the two. In spouse love you are going on forever. In mother love, you are letting go, raising a person to live without you. It's a love that has to be able to let go, yet be there, available always. You don't stop loving your children. Their happiness is always your happiness. Their sorrow is your sorrow.

But then, that is true of a spouse, too, so what is the difference? Mother love is more protective, and yet it's more letting go. You can't ask that they live with you forever the way you do with a happy spouse. It's both more·possessive and more letting go at the same time. It grows in the way any living thing grows. Its nature changes. It's an older plant rather than a young plant.

I miss Ann a lot more than I missed our nine-month-old baby, Geoffrey, when he died. He was an adorable, lovely baby. It was hard, but yes, I loved Ann much more. She'd become a full human being in every sense. She was a magnificent person. And I love her husband almost as much as if he were one of my own children.

I love my grandchildren, too. I spoil them. I also found I've gotten used to the house being neat and quiet, and it bothers me if things aren't that way.

But oh, that John! He knows I'm not the most patient grandmother. He called up and said, "Mom, you know this trip I'm going to take to India for a year? It means everything to my career!" I said, "Yes, John." He said, "Well, we've just talked to one doctor after another. They all say we shouldn't bring three children to India. Do you think you and Dad could keep them for a year?"

I couldn't even be polite. I said, "John, there is no point. There is no way I would do it, much as I love you and your children."

Then he said, "April Fool!"

I could have shot him!

256

I'm on My Soapbox

JANE HOPPER

I've had a happy life these ninety-two years. Oh, in between there's been a little sadness, but everybody gets that. I was born at home. We all were in those days. I was the second of six children. There was a seven-year span from the first to the last. At first we lived in the city, but my mother had very bad asthma, so Dad built her a house up here in the country. When we moved to Pearl River, Dad was the one-thousandth person. I remember the young fellow who brought us up them muddy roads with a horse and wagon telling him that.

I think my mother deserves a place in heaven raising all of us. It must have been a struggle in those days. When I think of her leaving a house with modern conveniences like a bathroom and moving up to a new home with a little outhouse and water pump and gas lamps. It was hard work and all by hand. She swept with a broom, boiled our clothes on top of the stove in a kettle, and washed with a board. When you had two boys and four girls to wash for, it was a lot. The girls wore petticoats on top of the long underwear, and it all was starched and ironed, don't forget. My mother done all that work and all our sewing, too. Well, she did have my grandmother to help, and a maiden aunt. Families were that way back then. No one lived off by themselves if they didn't have a husband.

There was kerosene lamps, and it was my job to clean the chimneys and cut off the wicks. We lived across the street from a nice brook where we would swim on hot days. Sometimes I'd forget to clean the lamps. My mother would never say anything mean. She'd just say, "Did I ask you to do something, Jane?" and then she'd always say, "Please." I never remember any violence. I never remember her hitting us. I can't understand these people today, you know? Of course I can see the difference in the world now. I wouldn't want to be bringing up a child now. Kids always seek for the lowest because it's a thrill.

I never remember any discord. The women didn't go out and work or seek pleasure during the day. They might sometimes go out at night. I can remember my mother and Dad going to the theatre, vaudeville then. But it was home life. There's so much going on nowadays, people hardly concentrate on the home. These nine-to-five jobs the women have are hard, with the kids going into an empty house the way the world is today. I think it's frightening. I grant you, I have old ideas. I do admire a woman who goes to work if she needs to because it's hard living today with prices so high. But for the glory of the job, no. I don't admire that.

I don't like this domineering talk of the women's libbers. I never had to liberate myself and neither did my mother. We were all on the one level. When Dad's money came in, it was put there and whoever needed to use it, used it. There was never any of this stuff, you spend this, and I spend that.

It was hard work living and raising a family, but it was also happiness. I think when you're happy, hard work don't mean anything. You just go about it naturally. I find the same thing with myself even today. I'll tackle anything if I know I'm going to be happy with it.

When I was about twenty-seven I married a fellow who was just as good as gold. I wasn't such a young bride, but you see the war come in between, and all the men were away. I was married for three years before I had my girl, Jane. You don't know how many times I'd wish and wish and wish. God heard my prayers. Childbirth didn't mean anything to me because I had to wait a long time for her. I wouldn't have complained anyhow because she's a wonderful gal, even today. She's sixty-one now. We're pals just like my mother was with me, two good pals.

When Jane was three, my mother took sick. This was right before my son was born. I lived on the other side of the railroad tracks at the bottom of the hill. It was a good mile, but I'd put Jane in the baby carriage and push her up. I'd stay there all day until my youngest sister got home from high school, so that my mother was never alone. Then my husband would send one of his men up with a truck, and he'd load the carriage in the back and ride us home. One day I come home, and I knew my son was coming. Well, he was born just like nothing. I guess it was the exercise walking up that long hill every day. We named him Lloyd and call him Bud.

My father was only forty-nine when he died. My mother wouldn't move back to the city. Thank God Dad left her the business that she could sell. But she was a wonderful manager, too. We always said she could make a meal out of nothing.

My mother died shortly after that, and I brought up my sister. She was seven years younger than me. She'll be a great-grandmother too next month. Then when one of my other sisters died and left a boy, twelve, my husband went right down and took him and brought him home. He was the same age as our boy, Bud. He was like a son, and he never forgot. He's married now and has two children. We was all very close. We was brought up that way, and it's good.

It wasn't just the families that was close. It was people. When we were kids, whenever anybody was sick, and the houses weren't so close, you went over and helped them. It's tragic to me that people won't help each other nowadays. It's selfishness. Maybe I've got old-fashioned ideas, but I think it's the almighty dollar that's got ahold of people. It's the darn old charge accounts! I myself wouldn't use one because of the temptation. In my day, you could do without. The mothers have to keep up with the trend now. And the kids have too many things. They don't want to be the bad guy.

I've been a widow now for thirty-three years. No matter how many years you've been one, it's lonesome. When my husband died, my daughter was already married with three kids, but my son was planning to get married that fall. He had all the arrangements made. I made him go through with it. Then they came to live with me because I had the big house, eight nice rooms. Later when he built a house, he built a big studio apartment out back. That's where I live now.

Thank God both my children turned out very good. I never had any trouble with either of them. Oh, I wouldn't say I didn't have my moments. I was supposed to be the boss. I used to get mad at the little fella. I shouldn't call him little. He's over six feet now. He always loved football, and I used to get mad at him when he'd wind up in football and forget he had a home. But I never chastised him for it because he enjoyed it. And he lived clean, and this is all I hope for.

It's very thrilling to have great-grandchildren. Let's see, Jane has seven grandchildren, and I have six on my son's side, so I have thirteen great-grandchildren. Oh, it's grand. It's lovely. The youngest one is eight months now. It's just thrilling to hold that little baby girl. It's different if they're your own and you got all that ahead of you. But with me, it's just the joy because they got a mother and a father to take care of them. I don't have them worries.

I worry, though, about the world they're going to grow up in. I do wonder about the next generation, and what it's going to bring. There's so much cruelty in this world: violence, stabbing, shooting, theft, drugs, drink. I pray for change, but it's taking too long to get better. The mothers got the worries ahead of them. The family's got to stay strong for all of us, the old and the young alike.

Still, I'm content. At my age it don't take much to make me happy. I have my family. I've got my health and my home. I can still do for myself. When I look at my children and my grandchildren and my great-grandchildren, I'm darn proud. I'm darn proud that they are mine.

Providing

AUGUSTA JACKSON

When I was growing up, there were so many things that I wanted to have that my friends had, that my mama wasn't able to get for me. I didn't want my children to go through what I had been through. But you see, you don't know what the Lord has in store for you. I had a big family, and I'm proud today. Even after I lost my husband, I brought all my children up to work. I was able to provide for them, and we made it.

I had an injury when I was a young girl. I was plowing, and the plow hit a root and jumped up and kicked me in the side. The doctor said I wouldn't be able to carry kids. Well, I gave birth to nineteen children. I had two sets of twins. Fifteen of them was born living, and four were stillborn. They were all born at home with a midwife. Today I got twelve of those children, and fifty-four grandchildren, and twenty-seven great-grands. So that doctor, he didn't know nothing, now did he?

I think I had a great farm life. You can make it on a farm, but you got to work for it. It was beautiful country. Around us there was some sand, some red clay and some black clay. We lived in the black clay section. I had my own house on eleven acres. We did what you call sharecropping. I worked my own land as well as somebody else's and then we got half of what was made off of it.

We had to till the soil to raise practically everything we ate. We raised corn and all kinds of beans and greens. We raised potatoes, tomatoes, and peanuts. We raised cotton, and we had our own fruit trees. We raised our own hogs and killed them for our meat. If you wanted to catch some extra money during the year, you raised turkeys and geese and chickens. I'd take four or five chicks to different markets in town, and different homes, too.

My kids helped. They all went to school. Two didn't finish high school, but they'd all help before school and after. They had to be seven or eight before they were able to do anythin' like chop cotton, but even a little one can thin corn, weed in the garden. They can bunch up the turnip greens and wash up the roots. We had two or three crops of vegetables a year. When they got to be twelve or thirteen years old, my husband started them plowing. The children in those days weren't like the children now. We told our children what to do in those days, but now they tell us.

I used to win prizes for my canning. I won a pressure cooker once. They had this program where they'd teach you to can, some kind of government thing in the local schoolhouse. But I already knew from my mama.

Well, I canned and I canned. We didn't waste nothin'! I'm the same way like that today. I don't believe in wastin'. I canned all kinds of green vegetables, tomatoes, beans, peaches, and apples. I used to make barrels of sauerkraut, too.

The kids helped. They still laugh about that today. If I wanted to can lima beans or green peas, you got to shell 'em. And their fingers would get so sore! We'd set up late at night and shell and shell, and then I'd sell some of them fresh by the quart, and put up some. We'd put the rest right with their snaps and strings into a burlap bag and dry them.

Nobody would have an idea of what I had to do, but you look back over the years, think about it, and it was an honest living. I enjoyed it, really. You see it as a challenge. It's the happiest when you work all summer, and then the weather gets cold and somebody looks for food to cook, and I've got it. Just go in the pantry and get out what I need, or go outside in the smokehouse and cut a piece of ham.

There was some people who'd be walkin' around all winter and have nothin' canned. So many of 'em was like that, even some of my friends. And I done worked hard all through the summer. Sometimes I'd give to 'em, and then again sometimes I'd make 'em pay me for my food 'cause they had the same opportunity.

I'll never forget one day a friend of mine sent her daughter down. The little girl said, "Well, Miss Gussie, my mama says would you send her a mess of collard green, and, and, and . . ." She's kind of shufflin' her feet like she don't know what to say. "And, and, and." That's what she kept sayin' because I think she hated to ask me for anythin', but she finally says, "An' a nice piece of your ham?"

I said, "You tell your mama the hams that I got, I'm not cuttin' 'til July or August." I told her, "I got a nice hog jowl she can have if she wants it." So I went on out to the smokehouse, and I pulled down an ol' jowl from the hook. Well, it's got all these big ol' yellow teeth. My daughter, Edwina, just laughed and laughed and laughed. She thought that was the funniest thing, sendin' that ol' jowl back with that little girl. I said to Edwina, "Some people is just too sorry to do anything."

Cookin' for that big family was no problem. My oldest girl, Stella, was the cook. I taught her just as my uncles had taught me when my mother would have a baby.

You made your own dough in them days. We raised our own wheat and made our own flour and our own cornmeal.

I didn't work the farm on Saturdays. That's the day you do your shopping an' washing, and you houseclean, too. We had the washboards and you scrub the clothes, then you put them in a big black pot and boil them, then you take them and rub them again if they need it and rinse and hang 'em. I finally got a washin' machine, the wringer type. It still works. Every time I go south I still use that washin' machine. My mother-in-law has it.

I didn't iron everything, but you still have to fold the clothes and put them away. I used to iron the white shirts that the kids wore to church, and as soon as they got old enough, I told my kids, "Iron your school clothes." Today, I don't have a kid who puts on a pair of dungarees without putting a crease in them.

I learned to sew when I had my first twins. Twins weren't born often in my neighborhood, and the women got together and gave me bolts of diaper material. You see, people didn't use diapers. I made them by hand when it rained, and I couldn't be working outside.

Sunday you went to church. We stayed at church until three o'clock in those days. We used to take the kids to church in a two-horse buggy, but that finally broke with such a big load. So then we put them in the wagon. I always fixed a basket of food. I'd bring fried chicken, cake, and bread. I'd make them a jug of lemonade or tea. I was an usher. My kids and I were choir members, too. In fact, I still have kids singing and ushering right behind me. I brought my kids up in the church. Some of them don't go now, but I did my job.

They often tell me right now how proud they are of the way I brought them up. They don't know what they would have done if I hadn't raised them up the right way. You know, being a mother is not easy.

I never had to whop my kids too bad. I had to once with the oldest twin, Monroe. He loved to throw rocks. I remember one day he had kids betting that he could hit my chickens. He was saying, "Watch him go across that yard. I'll hit him." Well, I got home and he'd knocked the legs out from under the chickens. One was dead, and the others had broken legs and were all bruised up. Oh, I gave him a strapping. He didn't do that no more.

I can't tell you I haven't had problems with some of my kids. I had one son who spent some time in jail, but if he'd listened to me, he never would have went there. I was standing at the window ironing in my living room, and this boy come tootin' his horn. I said, "Whose car is that?" I said to him, "Don't you be ridin' around because you're going to get in trouble." Well, the next morning the telephone rang. It was the police wondering if I have a son by the name of Thomas Jackson. I said, "Yes, I do." "Well, we got him in custody here. He was riding with a friend in a car that's reported stolen." He spent his eighteenth birthday in jail, but he never did that again.

I have one son who had been on drugs, but through my teachin' him and guidin' him it didn't get to be too bad. Twice he was in the hospital with hepatitis, and though I'm a missionary for my church, an' we go in groups to visit in the hospitals, I told him, "I'm not comin' to see you." I was down there, and Sister Turner said to me, "Sister Jackson, who's that way down there at the end of the ward?" I said, "I don't know." I knew who it was. So she goes down and she come back and says, "There's a young man down there, but he says 'Don't come near' because he doesn't have any pajamas on." I still wouldn't tell her that was my son.

I came back later alone and I went in that room, and I told him just how I felt. I said, "The Lord let you live, and you can do what you want, but I don't want anybody to know you are my son if you are on drugs." So he started to cry. He cried and he cried. I left him cryin', but I didn't care.

The next day he called me and said, "Could you bring me a pair of pajamas?" I took him them. I said, "You ready to come home yet?" He said, "I can come home tomorrow, but I've been here all day and night prayin' to God." I went the next day and got him, and he's been okay since.

Now I'm gonna hear from practically all my children practically every week. That makes me feel good. Lemay called me this morning. "I'm just calling, Mama, to see how you feelin'." You see, I got four pins in this ol' leg. I ain't no good for climbing stairs anymore. Now when they call, if they happy, I'm happy. That's just the way I am about them. And if they are having problems, it bothers me just like it did when they was kids. I have one daughter, my youngest daughter, Marcella, and she tries so hard not to let me know if somethin's wrong, but I can tell. I know.

And any time I got my own trouble, my kids are there. When my brother died in Macon, nine of my kids come down to his funeral. Now my sister, she only had three of hers there. When my baby brother died in St. Louis, I had seven kids there. Oh yes, when somethin' happen, they come. It makes me feel good to know I got that support.

You know if you've been good to your kids, they're going to be good to you. When there ain't nobody else, they're gonna be there. They're going to be there loving you right to the end.

As I worked on *Mothers Talking*, I was reminded again and again of the simple truth that by talking openly and listening without judging, we can learn so much from each other. Each person who reads this book will have his or her own story to tell. I would love to hear these stories. If you would like to share them, please write to me care of my editor, Barbara Anderson, at St. Martin's Press, 175 Fifth Avenue, New York, N.Y. 10010.